EXERCISE WORKBOOK

for

Beginning AutoCAD®

2002

by
Cheryl R. Shrock

Chairperson
Drafting Technology
Orange Coast College, Costa Mesa, Ca.

Registered Author/Publisher

Shrock Publishing, Newport Beach, Ca. 92658

Original Edition 2002

Published by:
Shrock Publishing
P.O. Box 9767
Newport Beach, Ca. 92658
support@shrockpublishing.com
714 557-2555

Limits of Liability and disclaimer of Warranty

The author and publisher make no warranty of any kind, expressed or implied, with regard to the documentation contained in this book.

AutoCAD ® 2002 are registered trademarks of Autodesk, Inc.

ISBN 0-9714255-0-7

Visit our website: **www.shrockpublishing.com**

This book is dedicated to my parents, Vern and Armella Shrock. They made my childhood safe, happy, full of love and allowed me to be me. Everything a child could hope for.

Other workbooks written by this author:

Exercise Workbook for Beginning AutoCAD **R12 for DOS**   Isbn 09640934-0-5

Exercise Workbook for Beginning AutoCAD **R13 for DOS**   Isbn 09640934-2-1

Exercise Workbook for Beginning AutoCAD **R13 for Windows**   Isbn 09640934-4-8

Exercise Workbook for Beginning AutoCAD **R14**   Isbn 09640934-5-6

Exercise Workbook for Beginning AutoCAD **2000**   Isbn 09640934-7-2
Exercise Workbook for Advanced AutoCAD **2000**   Isbn 09640934-6-4

Exercise Workbook for Beginning AutoCAD **2000, 2000i & LT**   Isbn 09640934-8-0
Exercise Workbook for Advanced AutoCAD **2000, 2000i & LT**   Isbn 09640934-9-9

Exercise Workbook for Advanced AutoCAD **2002**   Isbn 09714255-1-5

Table of Contents

INTRODUCTION

About this workbook
Exercise Workbook for Beginning AutoCAD® 2002 is designed for classroom instruction or self-study. There are 30 lessons. Each lesson starts with step by step instructions followed by exercises designed for practicing the commands you learned within that lesson.

You may find the order of instruction in this workbook somewhat different from most textbooks. The approach taken is to familiarize you with the drawing commands first. After you are comfortable with the drawing commands, you will be taught to create your own setup drawings. This method is accomplished by supplying you with "templates" (1 Class template. dwt, 9A Template.dwt and Class.ctb). For the first 8 lessons you should not worry about settings, **you just draw.**

I realize that not everyone will agree with this approach and if this is the case, you may want to change the order in which the lessons are learned. I have had success with this method because my students feel less intimidated and more confident. This feeling of confidence increases student retention. Learning should be fun not a headache.

Exercises, in the workbook, that include printing are designed for a Hewlett Packard 4MV printer. These exercises can be amended to match your printer or plotter specifications. To configure your printer, refer to Appendix A, "Add a Printer / Plotter. It is important to note that you can configure a printer / plotter even though your computer is not attached to it.

How to get templates?
Please download the 3 files mentioned above from our website,
www.shrockpublishing.com

About the Author
Cheryl R. Shrock is a Professor and Chairperson of Computer Aided Design at Orange Coast College in Costa Mesa, California. She is also an Autodesk® registered author / publisher. Cheryl began teaching CAD in 1990. Previous to teaching, she owned and operated a commercial product and machine design business where designs were created and documented using CAD. This workbook is a combination of her teaching skills and her industry experience.

"Sharing my industry and CAD knowledge has been the most rewarding experience of my career. Students come to learn CAD in order to find employment or to upgrade their skills. Seeing them actually achieve their goals, and knowing I helped, is a real pleasure. If you read the lessons and do the exercises, I promise, you will not fail."

Configuring your system

AutoCAD ® 2002 allows you to customize it's configuration. While you are using this workbook, it is necessary for you to make some simple changes, to your configuration, so our configurations are the same. This will ensure that the commands and exercises work as expected. The following instructions will walk you through those changes.

A. First start AutoCAD® 2002.
B. The "AutoCAD 2002 Today" dialog box will appear. Select the **"X"** in the upper right corner, of this dialog box. This will <u>close</u> the dialog box.

C. At the bottom of the screen there is a white rectangular area called the command line. Type: **_Options_** then press the <enter> key.

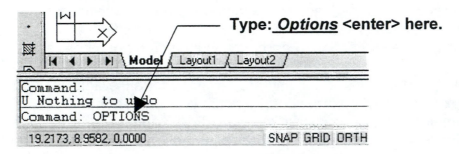

D. Select the **_Display_** tab and change the settings on your screen to match the dialog box below. Pay special attention to the settings with an ellipse around it.

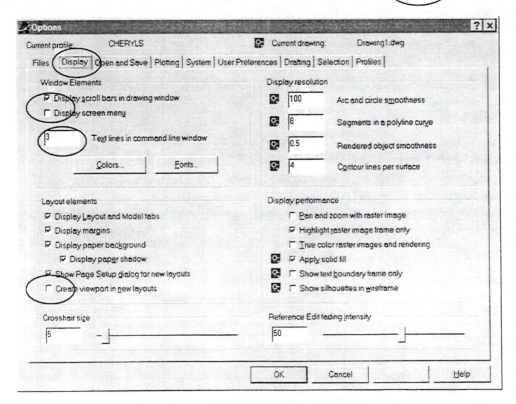

E. Select the **Open and Save** tab and change the settings on your screen to match the dialog box below.

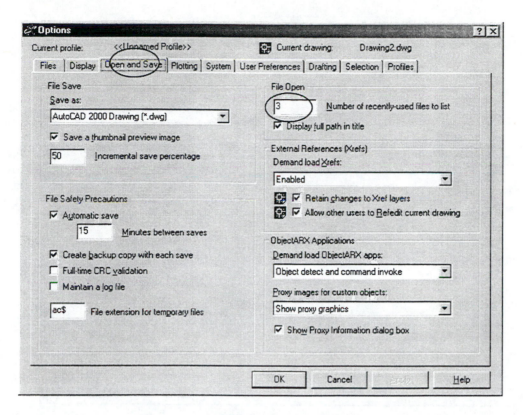

F. Select the **Plotting** tab and change the settings on your screen to match the dialog box below.

IMPORTANT: Add this printer.
See Appendix A for instructions
(Don't worry, it is not difficult)

Download this file
from our website

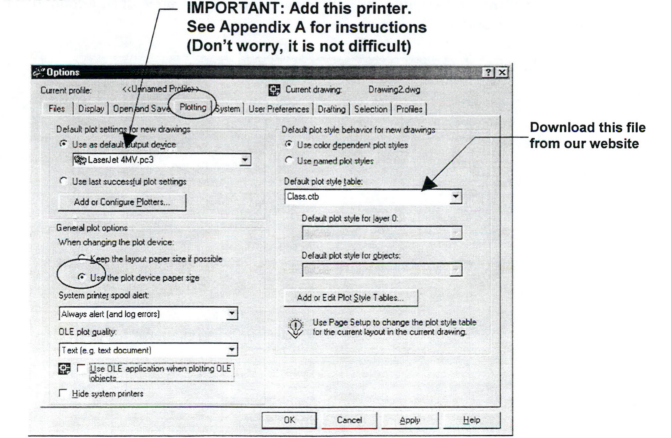

G. Select the **System** tab and change the settings on your screen to match the dialog box below.

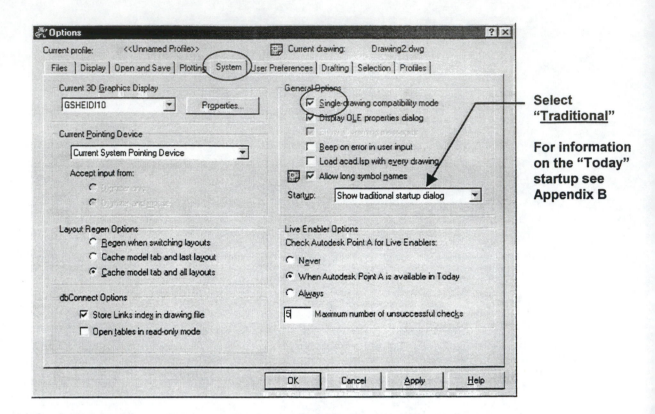

Select "Traditional"

For information on the "Today" startup see Appendix B

H. Select the **User Preferences** tab and change the settings on your screen to match the dialog box below.

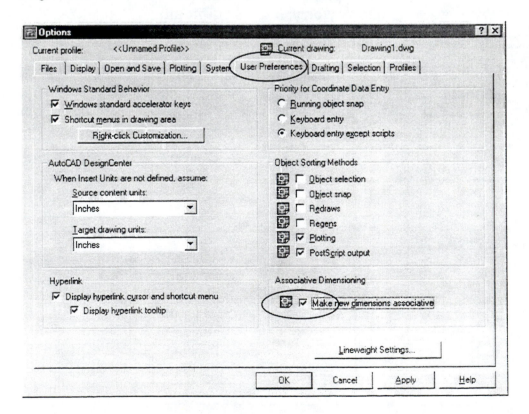

I. Select the ***Right-click Customization..*** box and change the settings on your screen to match the dialog box below.

Select "Right-click customization" button

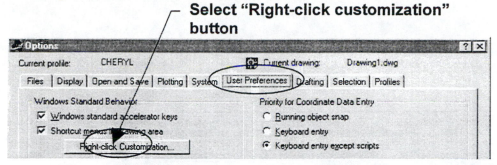

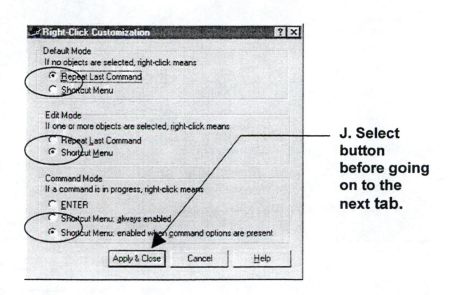

J. Select button before going on to the next tab.

J. Select the ***Apply & Close*** button, shown above, before going on to the next tab.

K. Select the ***Drafting*** tab and change the settings on your screen to match the dialog box below.

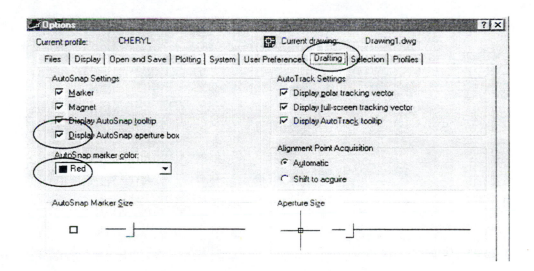

L. Select the *Selection* tab and change the settings on your screen to match the dialog box below.

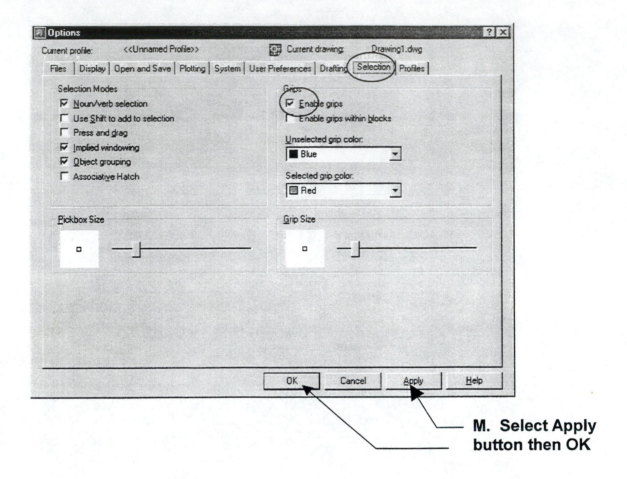

M. Select Apply button then OK

M. Select the *Apply* button then the *OK* button.

Customizing your Wheel Mouse

A Wheel mouse has two or more buttons and a small wheel between the two top side buttons. The default functions for the two top buttons are as follows. The Left Hand button is for **input** and the Right Hand button is for **Enter** or the **shortcut menu**. (You will learn more about this later) But the new item is the wheel.

Using a Wheel Mouse with AutoCAD®

To get the most out of your Wheel Mouse set the **MBUTTONPAN** setting to **"0"** as follows:

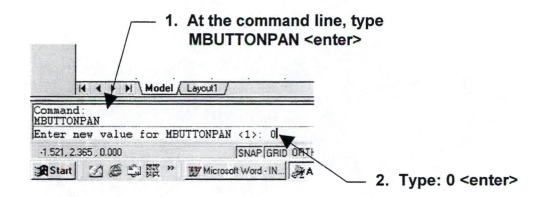

1. **At the command line, type MBUTTONPAN <enter>**

2. **Type: 0 <enter>**

MBUTTONPAN setting 0:

ZOOM   Rotate the wheel forward to zoom in
Rotate the wheel backward to zoom out

OBJECT SNAP   Object Snap menu will appear when you press the wheel

MBUTTONPAN setting 1:

ZOOM   Rotate the wheel forward to zoom in
Rotate the wheel backward to zoom out

ZOOM EXTENTS   Double click the wheel

PAN   Press the wheel and drag

NOTES:

LEARNING OBJECTIVES

After completing this lesson, you will be able to:

1. Understand basic computer terms.
2. Understand what is meant by CAD.
3. Determine what computer to purchase.
4. Know the system requirements for AutoCAD.
5. Start AutoCAD four ways.

LESSON 1

Part 1. UNDERSTANDING COMPUTERS

A BRIEF HISTORY OF COMPUTERS AND SOFTWARE.
The first computers were developed in the 1950s, shortly after the transistor was invented. In the mid 1960s General Motors, Boeing and IBM began developing CAD programs, but the development was slowed by the high cost of computer hardware and programming.

In 1971, Ted Hoff developed the first microprocessor. All circuitry of the central processing unit (CPU) was now on one chip. This started the era of the personal computer (PC). In the 1980s, additional improvements to the microprocessor changed the mainframe computers to powerful desktop models.

Of course, computer software was advancing along with the computer hardware. CAD started as a simple drafting tool and has now evolved into a powerful design tool. CAD has progressed from two-dimensional (2-D) to three-dimensional (3-D), to surface modeling and to solid modeling with animation. Each generation becoming more powerful and more user friendly.

HARDWARE

Microprocessor
The complex procedure that transforms raw input data into useful information for output is called processing. The **processor** is the "brain" of the computer. The processor interprets and carries out instructions. In Personal Computers (PCs) the processor is a single chip plugged into a circuit board.   This chip is called a **microprocessor**.

Central Processing Unit (CPU)
The CPU is the term used for the computer's processor. The CPU contains the intelligence of the machine. It is where the calculations and decisions are made.

Memory (RAM)
Your CPU needs memory to hold pieces of information while it works. While this information remains in memory, the CPU can access it directly. This memory is called **random access memory (RAM)**. RAM holds information only while the power is on. When you turn off or reset the computer, the information disappears.
The more RAM a computer has, the quicker it works and the more it can do.
The most common unit of measurement for computer memory is the **byte**. A **byte** can be described as the amount of memory it takes to store a single character. A **kilobyte (KB)** equals 1,024 bytes. A **Megabyte (MB)** equals 1,024 kilobytes, or 1,048,576 bytes. So a computer with 64 MB of memory actually has (64 X 1,048,576) 67,108,864 bytes. This is equal to approximately 1024 pages of information.

Input / Output devices
Input devices accept data and instructions from the user. The most common input devices are the keyboard, mouse and scanner. Output devices return processed data back to the user. The most common output devices are the monitor, printer and speakers.

Storage

The purpose of storage is to hold data that the computer isn't using. When you need to work with a set of data, the computer retrieves the data from storage and puts it into memory. When it no longer needs the data, it puts it back into storage. There are 2 advantages to storage. First, there is more room in storage and second, storage retains its contents when the computer is turned off. Storage devices include: Hard disks, floppy disks, zip disks, CDR/W, etc.

SOFTWARE

Operating Systems

When you turn on the computer, it goes through several steps to prepare itself for use.

The <u>first step</u> is a self-test. This involves:
   a. Identifying the devices attached to it. (Such as the monitor, mouse and printer)
   b. Counts the amount of memory available.
   c. Checks to see if the memory is functioning properly.

The <u>second step</u> is searching for a special program called the Operating System. When the computer finds the operating system, it loads it into memory. (remember RAM) The operating system enables the computer to:
   a. communicate with you.
   b. use devices such as the disk drives, keyboard and monitor.

The operating system is now ready to accept commands from you. The operating system continues to run until the computer is turned off. Examples of operating systems are: Windows 95, Windows 98, Windows NT, ME, 2000, XP, OS/2, Unix and more.
Note: 1. Apple/Macintosh computers have their own operating system.
2. AutoCAD 2002 will not work with Windows 95 or Apple/Macintosh.

Application software

The operating system is basically for the computer. The Application Software is for the user. Application Software is designed to do a specific task.
There are basically four major categories: Business, Utility, Personal, and Entertainment.

Business application software would be desktop publishing, spreadsheet programs, database software and graphics. *AutoCAD is a "graphics" business application software.*

Utility application software helps you maintain your computer. You would use a utility program to recover an accidentally deleted file, improve the efficiency of your computer and help you move, copy or delete files. *Norton Utilities is an example of a "utility application" software.*

Personal application software is basically what it sounds like. This software is designed for your personal needs, such as: balancing your checkbook, making an address book, creating a calendar and many more tasks.

Entertainment application software are video games, puzzles, flight simulators and even educational programs.

COMPUTER SIZES AND CAPABILITIES

Computers are divided into five catagories:
Supercomputer, Mainframe, Minicomputer, Workstation and Personal Computer.

Supercomputers are the <u>most powerful</u>. These computers process huge amounts of information very quickly. For example, scientists build models of complex processes and simulate the processes on a supercomputer.

Mainframe computers are the <u>largest</u>. These computers are designed to handle tremendous amounts of input, output and storage. For example, the government uses mainframe computers to handle the records for Social Security.

Minicomputers are <u>smaller than mainframe</u> computers but bigger than personal computers. They do not handle as much as the mainframe computers but they are less expensive. A company that needs the features of a mainframe but can't afford such a large computer, may choose a minicomputers.

Workstations <u>resemble a personal computer</u> but are much <u>more powerful</u>. Their internal construction is different than a PC. Workstations use a different CPU design called reduced instruction set computing (RISC), which makes the instructions process faster. Workstations using the UNIX operating system are generally used by scientists and engineers.

Personal computers (PC), originally named microcomputers, are <u>small computers</u> that usually reside on a desktop.

What is a Clone?
In 1981, IBM called its first microcomputer the IBM PC. Many companies copied this design and they functioned just like the original. These copies were called "clones" or "compatibles". The term PC is now used to describe this family of computers.
Note: the Apple/Macintosh computer is neither an IBM or a compatible. It should <u>not</u> be called a PC.

Part 2.   What is CAD?

Computer Aided Design (CAD) is simply, design and drafting with the aid of a computer. Design is creating a real product from an idea. Drafting is the production of the drawings that are used to document a design. CAD can be used to create 2D or 3D computer models. The CAD drawing is stored in a file that consists of numeric data, in binary form, that will be saved on to a disk.

Why should you use CAD?
Traditional drafting is repetitious and can be inaccurate. It may be faster to create a simple "rough" sketch by hand but larger more complex drawings with repetitive operations, are drawn more efficiently using CAD.

Why use AutoCAD?
AutoCAD is a computer aided design software developed by Autodesk Inc.
AutoCAD was first introduced in 1982. By 2000, it is estimated that there are over 4 million AutoCAD users worldwide.
What this means to you is that many employers are in need of AutoCAD operators.
In addition, learning AutoCAD will give you the basics for learning other CAD packages because many commands, terms and concepts are used universally.

Part 3.   Buying your first computer

Buying your first computer is not an easy task. Here are a few tips.

1. Make a list of tasks for which you will use your computer?
    a. Select the software for those tasks.
    b. Select the computer that will run that software.

2. Talk to other computer owners.
    a. Listen to their good and bad experiences.

3. Educate yourself.
    a. Go to your local library and spend an evening reading through the computer magazines. Most are written with the novice in mind.

4. Decide how much you can afford.
    a. Remember, you can always upgrade or add components later.

5. Find the right company to buy from. A great deal can turn into a bad investment if you can't get help when you need it.
    a. Ask about their customer service and support.
    b. How long is the warranty?

Part 4. AutoCAD 2002 system requirements

Operating system:
  Windows 98, NT 4.0, ME, 2000, XP (Windows 95 can not be used)

RAM and Hard Disk Space
  128 MB of RAM minimum, 256 MB recommended
  130MB of hard disk space
  64MB of swap space
  100MB free disk space in system folder

Hardware (required)
  Pentium II based PC with 450 MHz processor or better
  Mouse or other pointing device
  1024 x 768 video display
  CD-ROM drive for initial installation only
  Disk drive (3-1/2 floppy, Zip or CDW)

Hardware (optional)
  Printer or Plotter
  Serial or Parallel port (for peripheral devices)
  Sound card with speakers

STARTING AutoCAD

To Start AutoCAD, select the **START** button / **PROGRAMS** / **AutoCAD 2002** / **AutoCAD 2002**. (Note: If the "**AutoCAD Today**" window appears, you skipped the "**Intro**" that instructs you to configure your system to match this workbook.)

I prefer the "**Traditional Startup Dialog Box**" for students new to AutoCAD. But if you prefer to use the "**AutoCAD Today**" window, refer to Appendix B for instructions.

After you enter AutoCAD, the "**Startup**" dialog box, shown below, will appear. Notice the four buttons located in the upper left corner of this dialog box. Each button provides a different way to start a drawing. A brief description of each is listed below.

Open a Drawing
Allows you to select a drawing from a list of the most recently opened drawings or select the "Browse" button to search for more drawing files. After you select the file desired, select the OK button. The file selected will appear on your screen. (This option is only active when you first enter AutoCAD. Normally you will use **File / Open** refer to page 2-14)

Start from Scratch
Allows you to begin a new drawing from scratch. Starting from scratch means, all settings are preset by AutoCAD. You must select which measurement system on which to base your new drawing, English or Metric.

Use a Template
Allows you to choose a previously created template. You can choose one of the templates supplied with AutoCAD or create your own.
Note:
We will be using the Template "1 class template.dwt" for lessons 2 through 8. (Refer to page 2-2)

Use a Wizard
Allows you to start a new drawing using either the "Quick" or "Advanced" setup wizard. The wizard sets the units, angle, angle measurement, angle direction and area for your new drawing. (Don't worry, you will learn all of these settings in Lesson 9)

NOTES:

LEARNING OBJECTIVES

After completing this lesson, you will be able to:

1. Start AutoCAD using a template.
2. Recognize the areas and function of the AutoCAD Window.
3. Understand the use of the function keys.
4. Select commands using the Pull-down Menu Bar, Toolbars or typing at the Command Line.
5. Recognize a dialog box.
6. Open, Close and Move a toolbar.
7. Draw, Erase and Select Lines.
8. Clear the screen.
9. Save a drawing.
10. Open an existing drawing.
11. Exit AutoCAD.

LESSON 2

STARTING AUTOCAD WITH
"USE A TEMPLATE"

After starting the AutoCAD program, the following dialog box should appear. Follow the instructions 1, 2 and 3 to select the template "1 class template.dwt".

*(If the dialog box shown below does not appear, hold the **CTRL** key down and press the **N** key. If the **"AutoCAD Today"** box appears, please refer to page 1-7)*

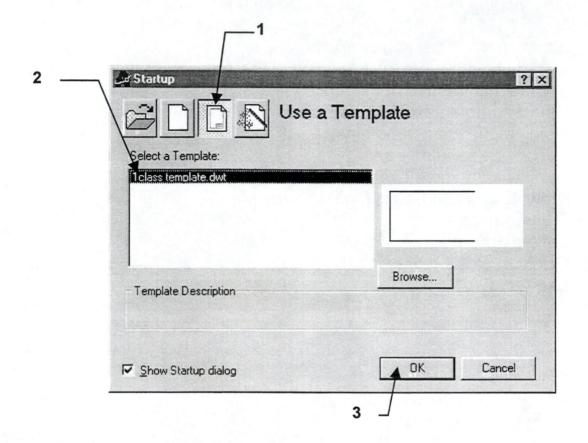

1. Select the **"Use a Template"** box. (Third from the left)
2. Select **"1Class template.dwt"** from the list of templates.
3. Select the **OK** button located in the lower right corner.

Note: If you do not have the file "1Class template.dwt" shown above, download it from our website, **www.shrockpublishing.com**.

AutoCAD WINDOW

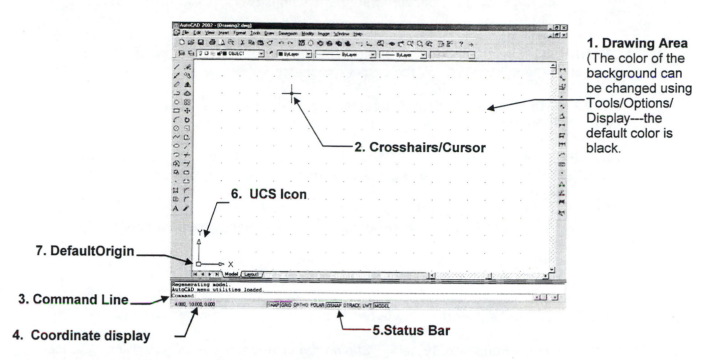

1. Drawing Area
(The color of the background can be changed using Tools/Options/Display---the default color is black.

2. Crosshairs/Cursor

6. UCS Icon

7. DefaultOrigin

3. Command Line

4. Coordinate display

5.Status Bar

1. DRAWING AREA
The large area in the center of the screen. This is where you will draw.
The size of this area can be changed at anytime using "Drawing Limits".

2. CROSSHAIRS / CURSOR
The movement is controlled by the movement of the pointing device (mouse).
Use to locate points, make selections and draw objects. The size can be changed using Tools / Options / Display / Crosshair Size.

3. COMMAND LINE
The three lines at the bottom of the screen. (The number of lines displayed can be changed using: Options / Display / Window Elements. The default is three). This is where you enter commands and Autocad will prompt you to input information.

4. COORDINATE DISPLAY (F6)
In the **Absolute mode (coords = 1)**: displays the location of the crosshairs / cursor in reference to the Origin. The first number represents the horizontal movement (Xaxis), the second number represents the vertical movement (Yaxis) and the third number is the Zaxis which is used for 3D.

In the **Relative Polar mode (coords = 2)**: displays the distance and angle of the cursor from the last point entered. (Distance<Angle)

5. STATUS BAR
Displays your current settings. These settings can be turned on and off by clicking on the word (Snap, Grid, Ortho, etc.) or by pressing the function keys, F1, F2, etc. (See pg. 2-4)

SNAP (F9)
Increment Snap controls the movement of the cursor. If it is off the cursor will move smoothly. If it is ON, the cursor will jump in an incremental movement. The increment spacing can be changed, at any time using **Tools / Drafting Settings / Snap and Grid**.
The default spacing is .250.

GRID (F7) The grid is merely a visual "drawing aid". The default spacing is 1 unit. You may change the grid spacing at any time using: **Tools / Drafting Settings / Snap and Grid.**

ORTHO (F8) When Ortho is ON, cursor movement is restricted to horizontal or vertical. When Ortho is OFF, the cursor moves freely.

POLAR (F10) POLAR TRACKING creates "Alignment Paths" at specified angles. (More detailed information on page 11-2)

OSNAP (F3) RUNNING OBJECT SNAP (More detailed information on page 4-3) Specific Object Snaps can be set to stay active until you turn them off.

OTRACK (F11) OBJECT SNAP TRACKING
Creates "Alignment Paths" at precise positions using object snap locations.

LWT LINEWEIGHT. Displays the width assigned to each object. (Not used in this workbook.)

MODEL Switches your drawing between paperspace and modelspace. (Lesson 26)

6. **UCS ICON (User Coordinate System)** Shows the location of the Origin. (The UCS icon appearance can be changed using: **View / Display / Icon / Properties.**)

7. **ORIGIN** The location where the X, Y and Z axes intersect. 0,0,0 (Page 2-4)

FUNCTION KEYS

F1	Help	Explanations of Commands
F2	Flipscreen	Toggles from Text Screen to Graphics Screen.
F3	Osnap	Toggles Osnap On and Off.
F4	Tablet	Toggles the Tablet On and Off.
F5	Isoplane	Changes the Isoplane from Top to Left to Right.
F6	Coordinate Display	Changes the display from Absolute / Off / Relative Polar.
F7	Grid	Toggles the Grid On or Off.
F8	Ortho	Toggles Ortho On or Off.
F9	Snap	Toggles Increment Snap on or off
F10	Polar	Toggles Polar Tracking On or Off.
F11	Otrack	Toggles Object Snap Tracking On and Off.

SPECIAL KEY FUNCTIONS

Escape Key Cancels the current command, menu or Dialogue Box.

Enter Key Ends a command; or will repeat the previous command if the command line is blank.

Space Bar Same as the Enter Key except when entering text.

PULL-DOWN "MENU BAR"

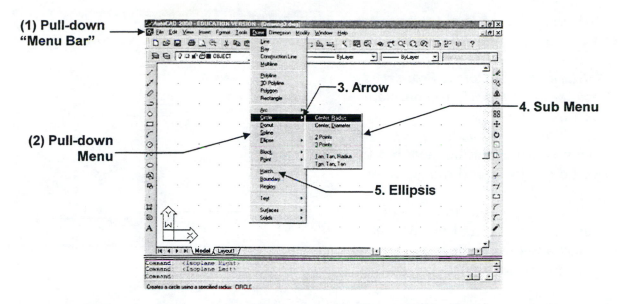

(1) Pull-down "Menu Bar"

(2) Pull-down Menu

3. Arrow

4. Sub Menu

5. Ellipsis

(1) The pull-down "MENU BAR" is located at the top of the screen. By selecting any of the words in the menu bar, a **(2) Pull-down menu** appears. If you select a word from the pull-down menu that has an **(3) Arrow ➤** a **(4) Sub Menu** will appear. (Example : Draw / Circle)

If you select a word with **(5) Ellipsis ...** a dialog box will appear. (Example: Draw / Hatch...)

DIALOG BOX

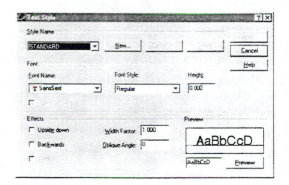

Many commands have **multiple options** and require you to make selections. These commands will display a dialog box. Dialog boxes, such as the *Text Style* dialog box shown above, make selecting and setting options easy.

TOOLBARS

AutoCAD provides several toolbars for access to frequently used commands.

The *(1)Standard*, *(2)Object Properties*, *(3) Draw*, *and (4) Modify* toolbars are displayed by default.
Toolbars contain **icon buttons (5)**.
These icon buttons can be selected to Draw or Edit objects and manage files.

If you place the pointer on any icon and wait a second, a **tool tip (6)** will appear and a **help message (7)** will appear at the bottom of the screen.

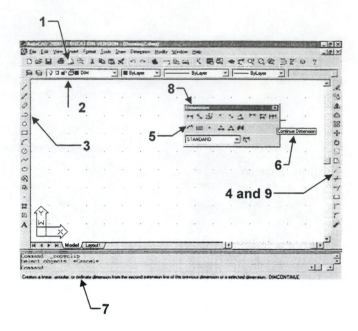

Toolbars can be *"floated"* or *"docked"*.

Floating toolbars (8) move freely in the drawing area and can be resized.
To move; place the pointer on the toolbar title then hold the left mouse button down, drag to the new location and release the mouse button.
To resize; place the pointer on the right or bottom edge of the toolbar. When the pointer changes to a double ended arrow, hold the left mouse button down and drag. When desired size is achieved, release the mouse button.

Docked toolbars (9) locked into place along the top, bottom or sides of the AutoCad Window.
To dock; place the pointer on the toolbar title, hold the left mouse button down and drag to the top, bottom, or either side of the AutoCAD window. When the outline of the toolbar appears, release the mouse button.

OPEN OR CLOSE TOOLBARS
Many other toolbars are available by selecting **View / Toolbars** from the Pull-down menu. Select the "Toolbars" tab. A list of available toolbars will appear.
(A check mark indicates the toolbars that are **"open"**.)

To Open a new toolbar, place the cursor in the box next to the toolbar name and press the left mouse button.
A "check mark" indicates the toolbar is open.

Select Toolbar tab.

To close a toolbar, select Close button

2-6

METHODS OF ENTERING COMMANDS

AutoCAD has 5 different methods of entering commands. All 5 methods will accomplish the same end result. AutoCAD allows you to use the method you prefer. The following are descriptions of all 5 methods and an example of how each one would be used to start the Line command.

1. **Pull down Menu (Select Draw / Line)**
The Pull down menus are activated by: **a**. moving the cursor to the Menu Bar (page 2-5)
b. Highlighting a Menu header **c**. Pressing the left mouse button.

2. **Tool Bars (Select the Line icon from the Draw toolbar)**
Move the cursor to an icon on a toolbar and press the left mouse button.

3. **Keyboard (Type L and <enter>)**
Type the command on the command line.

4. **Screen (side) menu (Select the Draw 1 menu and then the Line command)**
a. Move the cursor to the Screen Menu, **b**. highlight a Menu option **c**. Press the left mouse button. AutoCAD does not normally include this menu. If you want to activate this menu select Tools / Options / Display. In the "Window Elements" area, select the "Display Screen Menu" box. When activated, the Screen menu is located on the right side of the screen.

5. **Tablet Menu (Move pointer to Line command box and press)**
The Tablet Menu can only be used with a Digitizer. Move the mouse on the tablet overlay to the desired box and press the mouse button.

What are SHORTCUT MENUS?
In addition to the methods listed above, AutoCAD has shortcut menus. Shortcut Menus give you quick access to command options. Shortcut Menus are only available when brackets [ ] enclose the options, on the command line. (Example below)
To activate a Shortcut Menu, press the right mouse button.

Example:

Select Draw / Circle / Center, Radius
_circle Specify center point for circle or **[3P/2P/Ttr (tan tan radius)]**:

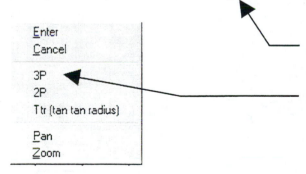

If you press the right mouse button now, the shortcut menu on the left will appear. This allows you to select the options *3P, 2P or Ttr* with the mouse rather than typing your selection.

Selecting the **Shortcut menus** is the AutoCAD's **"Heads Up"** drawing method within AutoCAD. Using this method should improve your efficiency and productivity.

DRAWING LINES

A **<u>LINE</u>** can be one segment or a series of connected segments. Each segment is a separate object.

Lines are drawn by specifying the **"first"** point and then the **"next"** point and the **"next"** point and so on. A point location can be placed by moving the cursor and pressing the left mouse button or X,Y,Z coordinates can be typed on the command line. (Refer to Lesson 9)

Once you have drawn two or more line segments, the endpoint of the last line segment drawn can be connected automatically to the first line's endpoint using the **CLOSE** option. To use this option, draw two or more line segments, then type **C** <enter>.

To draw perfectly **Horizontal** or **Vertical** lines turn **ON** the **ORTHO** command by pressing **F8** or clicking on the **ORTHO button** on the **Status Bar** (at the bottom of the screen).

To **STOP** drawing lines, press the right hand mouse button, then select **"Enter"** from the short-cut menu. (Or press the ENTER key or the SPACE BAR)

To **REPEAT** the LINE command: Select the Line command again or press the right mouse button, or press the ENTER key or the SPACE BAR.

Start the Line command by using one of the following methods:

Type = L <enter>
PULLDOWN MENU = DRAW / LINE
TOOLBAR = DRAW [/]

the following will appear on the Command line:

Command: _line Specify first point: ***place the cursor then press the left mouse button***
Specify next point or [Undo]: ***place the cursor then press the left mouse button***
Specify next point or [Undo]: ***place the cursor then press the left mouse button***
Specify next point or [Close/Undo]: ***to stop press <enter> or right mouse button and select "Enter"***
or "Close".

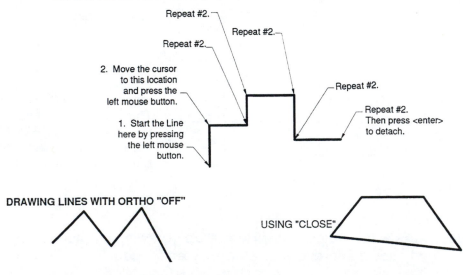

DRAWING LINES WITH ORTHO (F8) "ON"

Repeat #2.
Repeat #2.
Repeat #2.
2. Move the cursor to this location and press the left mouse button.
Repeat #2.
1. Start the Line here by pressing the left mouse button.
Repeat #2. Then press <enter> to detach.

DRAWING LINES WITH ORTHO "OFF"

USING "CLOSE"

ERASE

There are 3 methods to erase (or delete) objects from the drawing. As always, AutoCAD gives you multiple methods. You decide which one you prefer to use. They all work equally well.

Method 1. (Select the Erase command and then the objects.)

1. Start the command by using one of the following:

   TYPING = E
   PULLDOWN = MODIFY / ERASE
   TOOLBAR = MODIFY [✎]

2. Select objects: ***pick one or more objects***
   Select objects: ***press <enter> and the objects will disappear***

Method 2. (Select the Objects and then the Erase command from the shortcut menu.)

1. Select the object(s) to be erased
2. Press the right mouse button.
3. Select **"Erase"** from the short-cut menu.

Method 3. (Select the Objects and then the Delete key)

1. Select the object(s) to be erased
2. Press the Delete key.

NOTE, Very important:
If you want the objects to return, press **U <enter>** or **Ctrl + Z** or the **Undo arrow icon.**
This will **"Undo"** the effects of the last command.

METHODS OF SELECTING OBJECTS

When you want to erase, move, copy, ect. objects, you must first select them. There are 2 methods. **Method 1. Pick**, is very easy and should be used if you have only 1 or 2 objects to select. **Method 2. Windows**, is a little more difficult but once mastered it is extremely helpful and time saving. Practice the examples shown below right.

Method 1. PICK :   place the cursor (pick box) on top of the object and click the left mouse button.

Method 2. WINDOWS: C̲rossing and W̲indow

C̲rossing:
Place your cursor at the upper right corner (P1) location and press the left mouse button. Then move the cursor to the lower left corner (P2) and press the left mouse button again. **Only** objects that this window **crosses or completely encloses** will be selected.

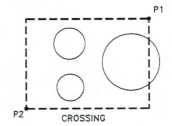

In the example on the right, all 3 circles have been selected. (The 2 small circles are *completely enclosed* and the large circle is *crossed* by the window.)
Note: Crossing windows are identified by a *dashed* linetype.

W̲indow:
Place your cursor at the upper left corner (P1) location and press the left mouse button. Then move the cursor to the lower right corner (P2) and press the left mouse button. **Only** objects that this window **completely encloses** will be selected.

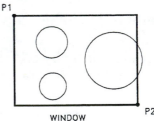

In the example on the right, only 2 circles have been selected. (The large circle is *not* completely enclosed.) This Window is identified by a *continuous (solid)* linetype.

Note: if these windows do not show up on your screen, it means that your "implied windowing" is turned off. Select Tools / Options / Selection tab. In the upper left section "Selection Modes", place a check mark in the "implied windowing" box. Now select "Apply" and "OK" at the bottom of the dialog box.

STARTING A NEW DRAWING
(or CLEARING THE SCREEN)

1. START THE COMMAND BY USING ONE OF THE FOLLOWING METHODS:

TYPING: **NEW or CTRL + N**
PULLDOWN: **FILE / NEW**
TOOLBAR: **STANDARD** ▢

The Dialog box shown below should appear.
(If "AutoCAD Today" menu appears refer to Intro-4G to change the startup setting or refer to Appendix-B to use "AutoCAD Today")

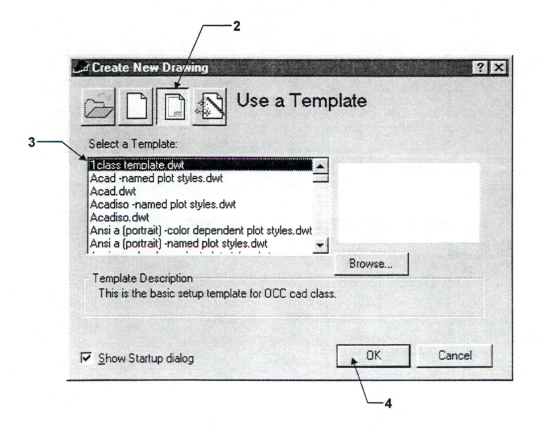

2. Select the **Use a Template** box. (third from the left)
3. Select **1Class template.dwt** from the list of templates.
    (NOTE: If you do not have this template, refer to page 2-2)
4. Select the **OK** button (bottom right).

NOTE: It is important that you have configured your AutoCAD software to only allow one drawing open. It will be less confusing for now. When you progress to the Advanced workbook, you will configure AutoCAD for multiple open drawings. Refer to Intro-4 for "Single drawing compatibility mode" setting.

SAVING A DRAWING

After you have completed a drawing, it is very important to save it. Learning how to save a drawing correctly is more important than making the drawing. If you can't save correctly, you will lose the drawing and hours of work.

There are 2 commands for saving a drawing: **Save** and **Save As**. I prefer to use **Save As**. The **Save As** command always pauses to allow you to choose where you want to store the file and what name to assign to the file. This may seem like a small thing, but it has saved me many times from saving a drawing on top of another drawing by mistake. The **Save** command will automatically save the file either back to where you retrieved it or where you last saved a previous drawing. Neither may be the correct destination. So play it safe, use **Save As** for now.

1.   Start the command by using one of the following methods:

TYPING: SAVEAS
PULLDOWN: FILE / SAVEAS
TOOLBAR: No icon for <u>Save As</u>, only for <u>Save</u>

This Dialog box should appear:

Descriptions on page 2-13

Note: your directories may appear different

2.   Select the appropriate drive and directory from the **"SAVE IN"** box.
     (This is where your drawing will be saved)
3.   Type the new drawing file name in the **"FILE NAME"** box.
4.   Select the **"SAVE"** box.

BACK UP FILES

When you save a drawing file, Autocad creates a file with a **.dwg** extension. For example, if you save a drawing as **House**, Autocad saves it as **House.dwg**. The next time you save that same drawing, Autocad replaces the old with the new but renames the old version to **House.bak**. The old version is now a back up file.

How to open a back up file.
You can not open a **.bak** file. It must first be renamed to a **.dwg** file extension.

How to view back up files.
Only .dwg extension files are displayed in the "Open" or "Save As" dialog boxes. To View .bak extension files you must use "Microsoft Explorer".

The following is information only. We will not be using these in this workbook.

History: Displays shortcuts to the files most recently accessed from the dialog box. Note: The shortcuts remain until you remove them. This list can get very long. To delete the shortcuts go to: Windows / Application Data / Autodesk / AutoCAD / Recent / Save Drawing As.

Desktop: Displays the contents of your desktop.

Personal / My Documents:
Displays the contents of the Personal or My Documents folder for the current user profile. The name of this location depends on your operating system version.

Favorites: Displays the contents of the Favorites folder for the current user profile.

Buzzsaw: Provides access to projects hosted by Buzzsaw.com—a business-to-business marketplace for the building design and construction industry.

RedSpark: Provides access to projects hosted by RedSpark—a business-to-business marketplace for the manufacturing industry.

FTP: Displays the FTP sites that are available for browsing in the standard file selection dialog box.

OPENING AN EXISTING DRAWING FILE

1. Start the command by using one of the following methods.

TYPING: **OPEN or CTRL + O**
PULLDOWN: **FILE / OPEN**
TOOLBAR: **STANDARD** 📂

This Dialog box should appear.

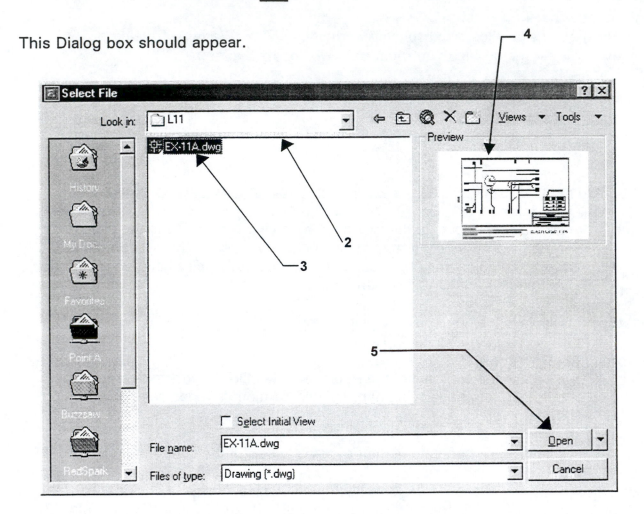

2. Select the **Drive and Directory** from the **"LOOK IN"** Box.
3. Select the drawing file from the list. (You may double click on the file name to automatically open the drawing)
4. Displays a "Thumbnail Preview Image" of the selected file.
5. Select the **OPEN** button.

NOTE: It is important that you have configured your AutoCAD software to only allow one drawing open. It will be less confusing for now. When you progress to the Advanced workbook, you will configure AutoCAD for multiple open drawings. Refer to Intro-4 for "Single drawing compatibility mode" setting.

EXITING AUTOCAD

1. Start the command by using one of the following methods:

TYPING: **EXIT OR QUIT**
PULLDOWN: **FILE / EXIT**
TOOLBAR: **NONE**

This Pull-down menu should appear when you select "File / Exit:

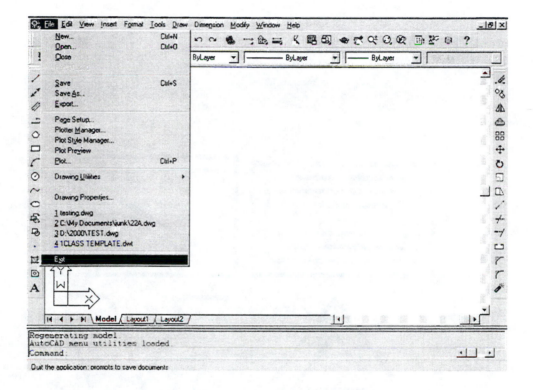

If any changes have been made to the drawing since the last save, the dialog box below will appear asking if you want to **SAVE THE CHANGES**?

You will have to select **YES, NO or CANCEL**.

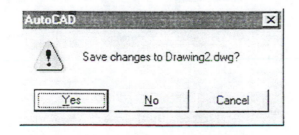

EXERCISE 2A

INSTRUCTIONS:

1. Start a **New** file (refer to 2-11) and select **1class template.dwt**.
2. **Draw** the objects below using:
   LINE command
   Ortho (f8) **ON** for **Horizontal** and **Vertical** lines
   Ortho (f8) **OFF** for lines drawn on an **Angle**.
   Increment Snap (f9) **ON**
   Osnap (f3) **OFF**
3. **Save** this drawing using:
   File / Save as / **EX2A**

EXERCISE 2B

INSTRUCTIONS:

1.   Using drawing **EX2A**, **ERASE** the missing lines.
2.   **Save** this drawing using:
        File / Save as / **EX2B**

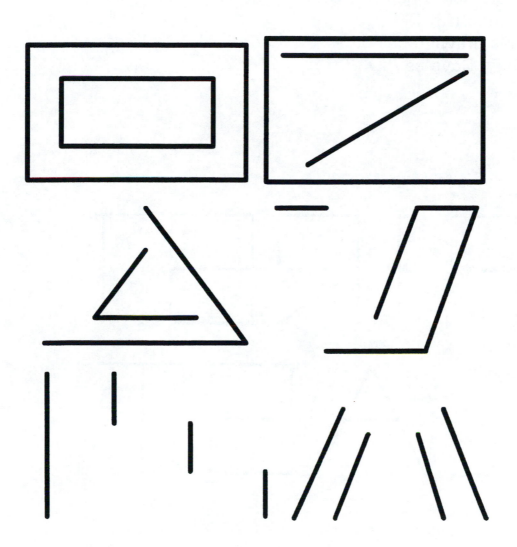

EXERCISE 2C

INSTRUCTIONS:

1. Start a **New** file and select **1class template.dwt**.
2. **Draw** the objects below using:
    Draw / Line
    Ortho (f8) **ON** for **Horizontal** and **Vertical** lines
    Ortho (f8) **OFF** for lines drawn on an **Angle**.
    Increment Snap (f9) **ON**
    Osnap (f3) **OFF**
3. **Save** this drawing using:
    File / Save as / **EX2C**

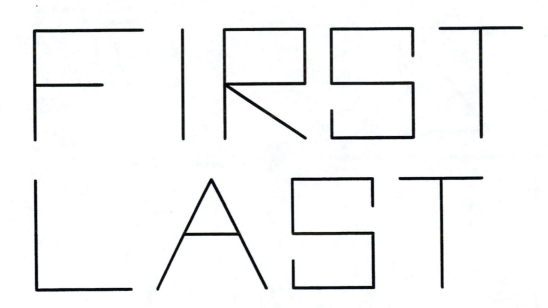

EXERCISE 2D

INSTRUCTIONS:

1. Start a **New** file and select **1class template.dwt**.
2. **Draw** the objects below using:
   Draw / Line
   Ortho (f8) **ON** for **Horizontal** and **Vertical** lines
   Ortho (f8) **OFF** for lines drawn on an **Angle.**
   Increment Snap (f9) **ON**
   Osnap (f3) **OFF**
3. **Save** this drawing using:
   File / Save as / **EX2D**

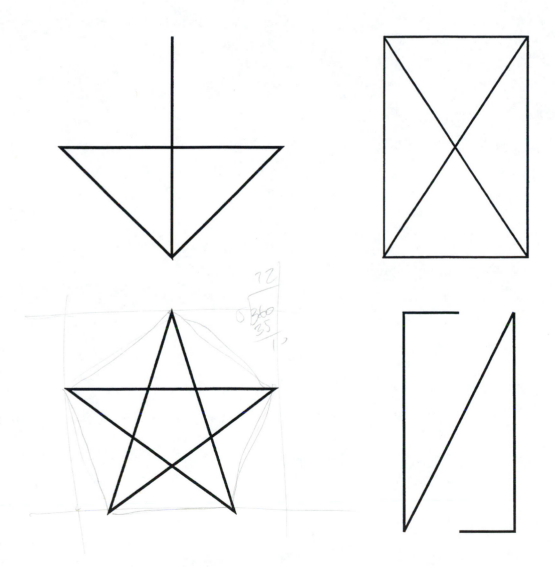

NOTES:

LEARNING OBJECTIVES

After completing this lesson, you will be able to:

1. Create a Circle using 6 different methods.
2. Create a Rectangle with width, chamfers or fillets.
3. Set Grids and Increment Snap using the Drafting Settings option.
4. Change current Layers.

LESSON 3

CIRCLE

There are 6 methods to create a circle. The default option is "Center, radius". (Probably because that is the most common method of creating a circle.) We will try the "Center, radius" option first.

1. Start the **Circle** command by using one of the following:
    TYPING = C
    PULLDOWN = DRAW / CIRCLE
    TOOLBAR = DRAW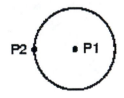

2. The following will appear on the command line:
    Command: _circle Specify center point for circle or [3P/2P/Ttr (tan tan radius)]:

3. Locate the center point, for the circle, by moving the cursor to the desired location and pressing the left mouse button.

4. Now move the cursor away from the center point and you should see a circle forming.

5. When it is approximately the size desired, press the left mouse button, or to be exact, type the radius, then press <enter>.

Note: To use one of the other methods described below, first select the Circle command, then press the right mouse button. A short cut menu will appear. Select the method desired by placing the cursor on the option and pressing the left mouse button.

Center, Radius: Specify the center (P1) then the Radius (P2).

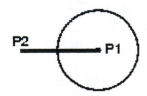

Center, Diameter: Specify the center (P1) then the Diameter(P2).

2 Points: Specify the 2 points (P1 and P2) that will determine the Diameter .

3 Points: Specify the 3 points (P1, P2 and P3) on the circumference. The Circle will pass through all three points.

Tangent, Tangent, Radius: Specify two objects (P1 and P2) for the Circle to be tangent to by placing the cursor on the object and pressing the left mouse button, then specify the radius.

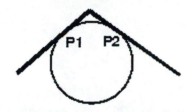

Tangent, Tangent, Tangent: *(You must use the pull down menu for this option)* Specify three objects (P1, P2 and P3) for the Circle to be tangent to by placing the cursor on the object and pressing the left mouse button. (The diameter will be calculated by the computer.)

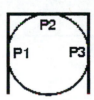

RECTANGLE

To create a rectangle you must specify two diagonal corners. The rectangle can be any size and the sides are always drawn horizontal and vertical. A Rectangle is one object, not four separate lines.

1. Start the **RECTANGLE** command by using one of the following:

    TYPING = REC
    PULLDOWN = DRAW / RECTANGLE
    TOOLBAR = DRAW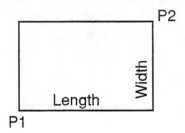

2. The following will appear on the command line:

Command: _rectang
Specify first corner point or [Chamfer/Elevation/Fillet/Thickness/Width]:

(Note: to select an option, press the right mouse button, and a shortcut menu will appear. The options are listed below)

3. Specify the location of the first corner by moving the cursor to a location (P1) and then press the left mouse button.

    The following will appear on the command line:

    Specify other corner point or [Dimension]:

4. Specify the location of the **diagonal** corner by moving the cursor (P2) and pressing the left mouse button.

    --OR—

    Type **D** <enter> (or use the short cut menu)
    Specify length for rectangle <0.000>: ***Type length<enter>***
    Specify width for rectangle <0.000>: ***Type width<enter>***
    Specify other corner point or [Dimension]: ***move the cursor up, down, right or left to specify where you want the second corner relative to the first corner.***

OPTIONS:

CHAMFER	Automatically draws all 4 corners with chamfers. (All the same size)
FILLET	Automatically draws all 4 corners with fillets. (All the same size)
WIDTH	Sets the width of the rectangle line. (The width straddles the line)
ELEVATION	Used in 3D only.
THICKNESS	Used in 3D only.

DRAFTING SETTINGS

The **DRAFTING SETTINGS** dialog box allows you to set the **INCREMENT SNAP** and **GRID SPACING**. You may change the Increment Snap and Grid Spacing at anytime while creating a drawing. The settings are only drawing aids to help you visualize the size of the drawing and control the movement of the cursor.

INCREMENT SNAP controls the movement of the cursor. If it is **OFF** the cursor will move smoothly. If it is **ON**, the cursor will jump in an *incremental* movement. This incremental movement is set by changing the **"Snap X and Y spacing"** .

GRID is the dot matrix in the drawing area. Grid dots will not print. It is only a visual aid. The Grid dot spacing is set by changing the **"Grid X and Y spacing".**

1. Select **DRAFTING SETTINGS** by using one of the following:

    TYPING = RM or DSETTINGS
    PULL-DOWN = TOOLS / DRAFTING SETTINGS
    TOOLBAR = NONE

2. The dialog box below will appear.

3. Select the **"Snap and Grid"** tab.

3

Note: the tabs "Polar Tracking" and "Object Snap" will be discussed in lessons 4 and 11.

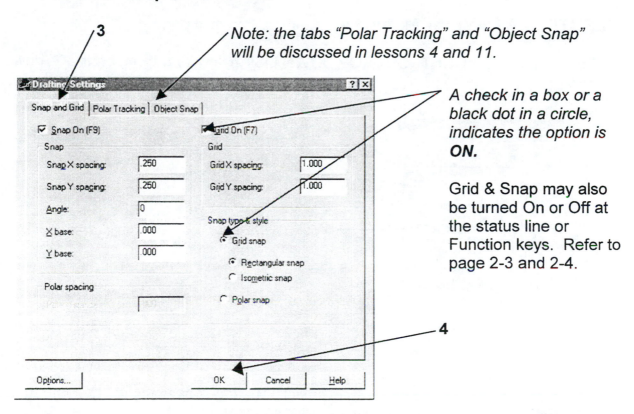

A check in a box or a black dot in a circle, indicates the option is **ON.**

Grid & Snap may also be turned On or Off at the status line or Function keys. Refer to page 2-3 and 2-4.

4

4. Make your changes and select the **OK** button to save them. If you select the **CANCEL** button, your changes will not be saved.

LAYERS

A **LAYER** is like a transparency. Have you ever used an overhead light projector? Remember those transparencies that are laid on top of the light projector? You could stack multiple sheets but the projected image would have the appearance of one document. Layers are basically the same. Multiple layers can be used but it is still only one drawing.

It is good "drawing management" to draw related objects on the same layer. For example, in an architectural drawing, you could have the walls of a floor plan on one layer and the Electrical and Plumbing on two other layers. These layers can then be Thawed (ON) or Frozen (OFF) independently. If a layer is Frozen, it is not visible. When you Thaw the layer it becomes visible again. This will allow you to view or make plots with specific layers visible or invisible. (We will talk more about layers in lesson 26)

Note: Do not use layer "0". Layer "0" has a specific use, described on page 28-3, and
_   should not be used for general drawing._
_   To create new Layers or change their settings and properties, refer to_
_   Lesson 26, page 3._

SELECTING A LAYER - Method 1. (Method 2 on next page)

1. Display the LAYER CONTROL DROP-DOWN LIST below by clicking on the ▼ down arrow.

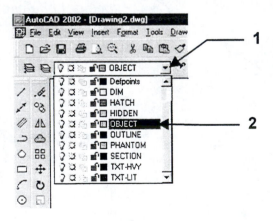

2. Click on the LAYER **NAME** you wish to select. The Layer selected will become the **CURRENT** layer and the drop-down list will disappear.

SELECTING LAYERS - Method 2.

1. Select the Layer command using one of the following:

    TYPE = LA
    PULLDOWN = FORMAT / LAYER
    TOOLBAR = OBJECT PROPERTIES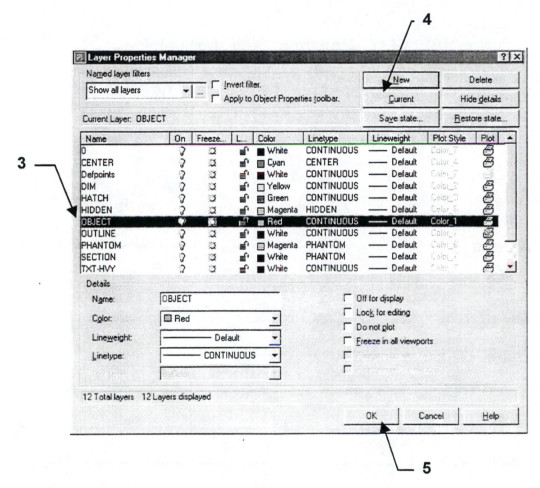

2. The dialogue box below will appear.

3. First select a layer by Clicking on it's name.

4. Select the **CURRENT** button.

5. Then select the **OK** button.

The layer you have just selected is now the **CURRENT** layer. This means that the next object drawn will reside on this layer and will have the same properties as this layer. Properties such as color and linetype.

EXERCISE 3A

INSTRUCTIONS:

1. Select **FILE / NEW** then select **1Class Template.dwt**.
2. **Draw** the **LINES** below using:
   Draw / Line
   Ortho (f8) **ON** for **Horizontal** and **Vertical** lines
   Increment Snap (f9) **ON**
3. **Change** to the appropriate **layer** before drawing each line.
4. **Save** this drawing using:
   File / Save as / **EX3A**

Layer HIDDEN — — — — — — — — — — — — — — —

Layer OBJECT ————————————————

Layer PHANTOM — — — — — — — — — — —

Layer SECTION — — — — — — — — — — —

Layer TXT-HVY ————————————————

Layer TXT-LIT ————————————————

Layer DIM ————————————————

Layer HIDDEN – – – – – – – – – – – – –

Layer CENTER —— — —— — —— — ——

Layer HATCH ————————————————

EXERCISE 3B

INSTRUCTIONS:

1. Select **FILE / NEW** then select **1Class Template.dwt**.
2. Change the **GRID SPACING** to .40 and **SNAP** to .20
    Using: **TOOLS / DRAFTING SETTINGS**
3. Draw the objects below using the **layers** indicated.
4. **Save** this drawing using:
    File / Save as / **EX3B**

LAYER = OBJECT   **LAYER = OBJECT**

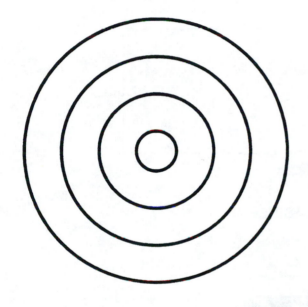
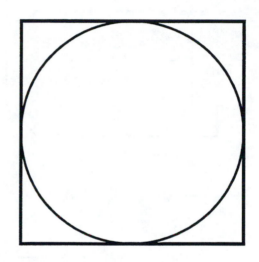

LAYER = HIDDEN

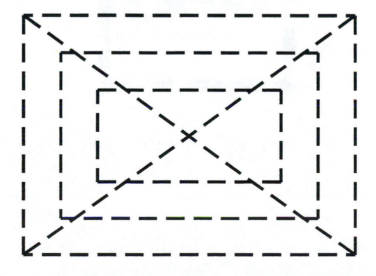

EXERCISE 3C

INSTRUCTIONS:

1. Select **FILE / NEW** then select **1Class Template.dwt**.
2. Draw the **RECTANGLES** below using one of these options:
   CHAMFER, FILLET and **WIDTH**
3. **Save** this drawing as: **EX3C**

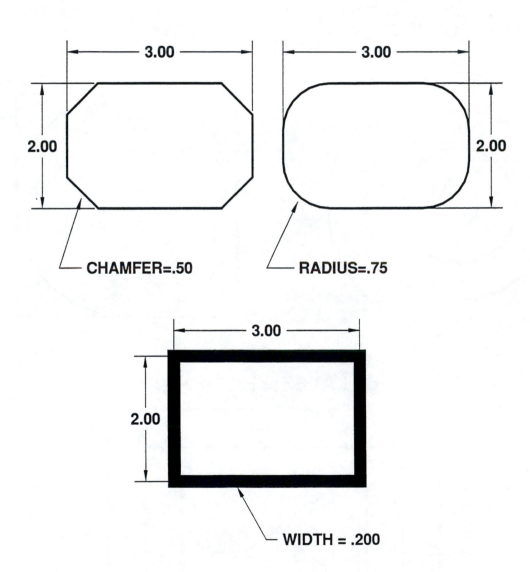

CHAMFER=.50

RADIUS=.75

WIDTH = .200

EXERCISE 3D

INSTRUCTIONS:

1. Select **FILE / NEW** then select **1 Class Template.dwt.**
2. Draw the house below using at least <u>4 layers</u>.
3. You can change the **GRID** and **INCREMENT SNAP** settings to whatever you like.
4. You decide when to turn Ortho and Snap On or Off.

   Have some fun with this one!

5. Save this drawing as: **EX3D**

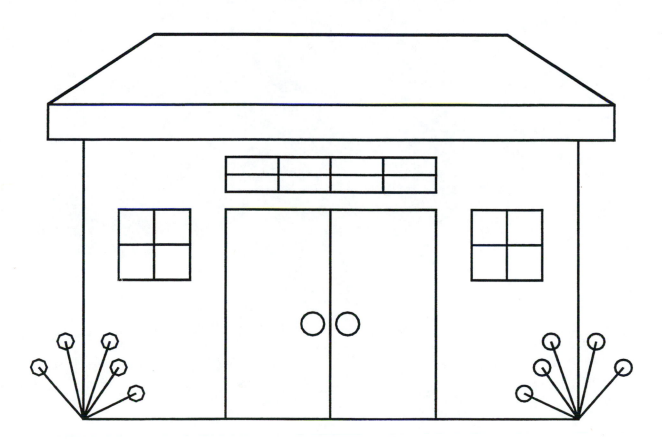

NOTES:

LEARNING OBJECTIVES

After completing this lesson, you will be able to:

1. Understand the function of Object Snap.
2. Use 7 Object Snap modes.
3. Operate the Running Snap function.
4. Toggle the Running Snap function On and Off.
5. Use the Zoom options to view the drawing.
6. Understand the basic concept of Setting up your drawing.
7. Change the drawing paper size.
8. Select the Units of Measurement to draw with.

LESSON 4

OBJECT SNAP

OBJECT SNAP enables you to snap to objects at very precise locations on the object, such as: the endpoint or midpoint of a line. (Step by step instructions are on the next page)

You may select object snap options using the icons on the Object snap toolbar or from the object snap pop up menu.

To open the object snap toolbar: select View / Toolbars. Then select the toolbar tab and then the Object Snap box.

To use the pop up menu:
If you have a Wheel mouse: Press the wheel and the **OBJECT SNAP** menu will appear. *(**Note**: The command **"Mbuttonpan"** must be set to **0**. Refer to Intro-7)*

If you have a 2 button mouse: While holding down the **shift key**, press the **right mouse button** and the **OBJECT SNAP** menu will appear

OBJECT SNAP OPTIONS:

ENDpoint — Snaps to the closest endpoint of a Line, Arc or polygon segment. Place the cursor on the object close to the end.

MIDpoint — Snaps to the middle of a Line, Arc or Polygon segment. Place the cursor anywhere on the object.

INTersection — Snaps to the intersections of any two objects. Place the Pick box directly on top of the intersection or select one object and then the other and Autocad will locate the intersection.

CENter — Snaps to the center of an Arc, Circle or Donut. Place the cursor on the object, or the approximate center location.

QUAdrant — Snaps to a 12:00, 3:00, 6:00 or 9:00 o'clock location on a circle. Place the cursor on the circle near the desired quadrant location.

PERpendicular — Snaps to a point perpendicular to the object selected. Place the cursor anywhere on the object.

TANgent — Calculates the tangent point of an Arc or Circle. Place the cursor on the object as near as possible to the expected tangent point. (Note: nothing happens until you select the next point.)

(Note: Refer to Lesson 5 for more Object Snap selections.)

How to use OBJECT SNAP

In Lesson 2 you learned about <u>Increment Snap.</u> Increment Snap moves the cursor in an incremental movement. So you could say your cursor is "snapping" to increments preset by you. Now you will learn about <u>Object Snap</u>. If Increment Snap, snaps to increments, what do you think Object Snap, snaps too? That's right, object snap allows you to snap to "objects" , in very specific and accurate locations.

You may preset the object snap options, using the Running Object Snap method explained on the next page. Or you can select the object snap option for each location.

The following is an example of attaching line segments to two previously drawn vertical lines. The new line will start from the upper endpoint (P1) to the midpoint (P2) to the lower endpoint (P3). Here is the step by step procedure.

1.   Select the Line command
2.   Draw two vertical lines as shown below.
3.   Select the Line command again.
4.   Select the "Endpoint" object snap option (use one of the methods listed on the previous page.)
5.   Place the cursor close the upper endpoint of the left hand line (P1). *(Notice that a square appears at the end of the line, an "endpoint" tool tip should appear and the cursor snaps to the endpoint like a magnet. This is what "object snap" is all about. You are snapping the cursor to a previously drawn object.)*
6.   Press the left mouse button to attach the endpoint of the new line to the previously drawn line.
7.   Now select the "Midpoint" object snap option.
8.   Move the cursor to approximately the middle of the right hand vertical line (P2). A triangle and a "midpoint" tool tip appear and the cursor should snap to the middle of the line like a magnet.
9.   Press the left mouse button to attach the endpoint of the new line to the previously drawn line.
10. Select the "endpoint" object snap option.
11. Move the cursor close to the lower endpoint of the left hand vertical line (P3).
12. Press the left mouse button to attach the endpoint of the new line to the previously drawn line.
13. Disconnect by pressing <enter>

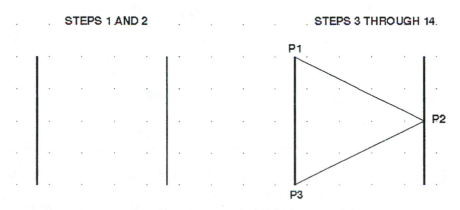

STEPS 1 AND 2   STEPS 3 THROUGH 14.

RUNNING OBJECT SNAP

RUNNING OBJECT SNAP is a method of **presetting** the **object snap options** so specific options, such as center, endpoint or midpoint, stay **active** until you **de-activate** them. When Running Object Snap is active, markers are displayed on the object at the location of the Object Snap selection and the cursor is drawn like a **magnet** to the object snap location.

For example, if you need to snap to the endpoint of 10 lines, you could preset the running object snap **endpoint** option. Then when you place the cursor near the endpoint of one of the lines, a marker will appear at the endpoint of the nearest line and the cursor will automatically snap to the endpoint of the line like a magnet. This method is very efficient because you will not have to invoke the object snap menu for each endpoint.

1. Select the **Running Object Snap** option using one of the following:

   - **TYPE = OSNAP**
   - **PULL DOWN = TOOLS / DRAFTING SETTINGS**
   - **Right Click on the OSNAP tile, on the Status Bar, and select SETTINGS.**

   (The dialog box below will appear.)

2. Select the **OBJECT SNAP** tab.

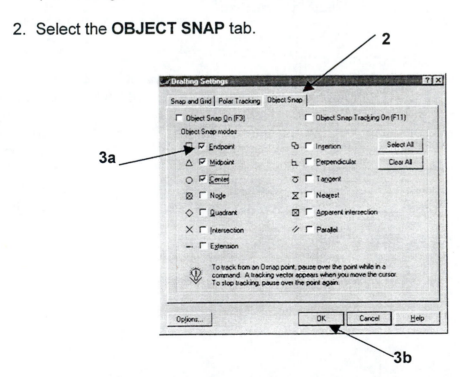

3. Select the Object Snap desired (3a) and then OK. (3b)

RUNNING OBJECT SNAP can be toggled **ON** or **OFF** using the **F3** key or **clicking** on the **OSNAP** button on the status bar.
Note: Do not preset more than 3 object snaps, you will lose control of the cursor.

DRAWING SET UP

When drawing with a Computer, you must "set up your drawing area" just as you would on your drawing board if you were drawing with pencil and paper. You must decide what size your paper will be, what type of scale you will use (feet and inches, decimals, etc) and how precise you need to be. In CAD these decisions are called "Setting the **Drawing Limits, Units** and **Precision**".

DRAWING LIMITS

Consider the drawing limits as the size of the paper you will be drawing on. You will first be asked to define where the lower left corner should be placed, then the upper right corner, similar to drawing a Rectangle. An 11 x 17 piece of paper would have a **lower left corner** of 0,0 and an **upper right corner** of 17, 11. *(17 is the horizontal measurement or X-axis and 11 is the vertical measurement or Y-axis).*

1. Select the **DRAWING LIMITS** command using one of the following:

   > **TYPE = LIMITS**
   > **PULLDOWN = FORMAT / DRAWING LIMITS**
   > **TOOLBARS = NONE**

2. The following will appear on the command line:

   > Command: '_limits
   > Reset Model space limits:
   > Specify lower left corner or [ON/OFF] <0.000,0.000>:

3. Type the X,Y coordinates **0, 0** for the lower left corner location of your piece of paper then press the <enter> key.

4. The command line will now read:

   > Specify upper right corner <16.000,10.000>:

5. Type the X,Y coordinates **17, 11** for the upper right corner of your piece of paper then press the <enter> key.

6. **Important:** Select **VIEW / ZOOM / ALL** to make the screen display the new drawing limits.

A personal note: *I love drawing limits. I can remember when I used to draw with pencil and paper and I would find that I had under estimated the size of the paper needed. With drawing limits you merely type a new size and magically the paper gets bigger or smaller. So you can look forward to beautiful drawings in the future.*

---

continued next page....

DRAWING SET UP continued

UNITS AND PRECISION
You now need to select what unit of measurement you want to work in.
Such as: Decimal (0.000) or Architectural (0'-0").
Next you should select how precise you want the measurements. Meaning, do you
want the measurement rounded off to a 3 place decimal or the nearest 1/8".

1. Select the **UNITS** command using one of the following:

> **TYPE = DDUNITS**
> **PULLDOWN = FORMAT / UNITS**
> **TOOLBAR = NONE**

(the dialogue box below will appear)

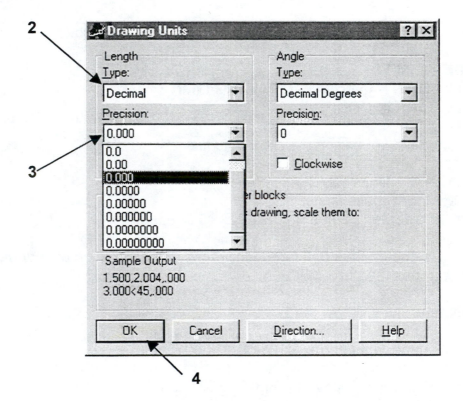

2. Select the appropriate **TYPE** such as: decimals or architectural.

3. Select the appropriate **PRECISION**

4. Select the **OK** button to save your selections.

ZOOM

The **ZOOM** command is used to move closer or farther away.

The following is an example of Zoom / Window to zoom in closer to an object.

1. Select the Zoom command by using one of the following:

   TYPING = Z
   PULLDOWN = VIEW / ZOOM
   TOOLBAR = STANDARD

2. Select the **"Window"** option and draw a window around the area you wish to magnify by moving the cursor to the lower left of the objects and left click. (Do not hold the left mouse button down while moving the cursor) Then move the cursor diagonally to form a rectangular shape around the objects, and left click again.

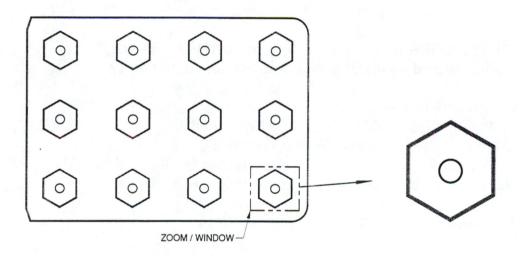

ZOOM / WINDOW

The **ZOOM ICONS** are the most efficient method of selecting zoom.

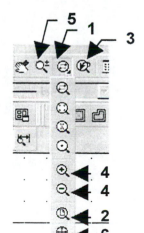

1. WINDOW = zoom in on an area by specifying a window (rectangle) around the area.

2. ALL= Displays the *drawing limits*. If you have objects outside of the drawing limits, ZOOM ALL will display them too.

3. PREVIOUS = returns to previous display. (up to 10 previous displays)

4. IN or OUT = moves in 2 or out 2X

5. REALTIME = Interactive Zoom. You can zoom in or out of the drawing by moving the cursor vertically up or down. To stop, press the Esc key.

6. EXTENTS = Displays all objects in the drawing file, using the smallest window possible.

EXERCISE 4A

INSTRUCTIONS:

1.   Start a **New** file using **1 Class Template.dwt**.

2.   Using **FORMAT / UNITS:**
      set the units to **FRACTIONS**
      set the precision to **1/2"**

3.   Using **FORMAT / DRAWING LIMITS** set the drawing limits to:
      Lower left corner = **0,0**
      Upper right corner = **20, 15**

4.   Use **VIEW / ZOOM / ALL** to make the screen change to the new limits

5.   Turn **OFF** the **GRIDS** (F7)   **SNAP** (F9) and **ORTHO** (F8)
      (Your screen should be blank and your crosshair should move freely)

6.   Draw the objects below using:
      DRAW / CIRCLE (CENTER, RADIUS) and **LINE**
      OBJECT SNAP = CENTER and TANGENT

Very Important: Use the Tangent option at each end of the line. AutoCAD needs to
be told that you want each end of the line to be tangent to a circle.

7.   **Save** this drawing as **EX4A**

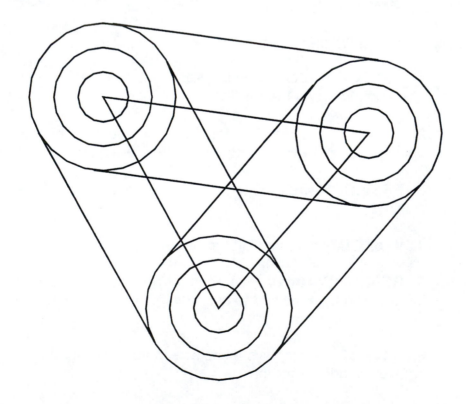

EXERCISE 4B

INSTRUCTIONS:

1.   Start a **New** file using **1 Class Template.dwt**.

2.   Using **FORMAT / UNITS:**
     set the units to **FRACTIONS**
     set the precision to **1/4"**

3.   Using **FORMAT / DRAWING LIMITS** set the drawing limits to:
     Lower left corner = **0,0**
     Upper right corner = **12, 9**

4.   Use **VIEW / ZOOM / ALL** to make the screen change to the new limits

5.   Turn **OFF** the **GRIDS** (F7)   **SNAP** (F9) and **ORTHO** (F8)
     (Your screen should be blank and your crosshair should move freely)

6.   Draw the objects below using:
     DRAW / CIRCLE (CENTER, RADIUS) and **LINE**
     OBJECT SNAP = **QUADRANT**

7.   **Save** this drawing as: **EX4B**

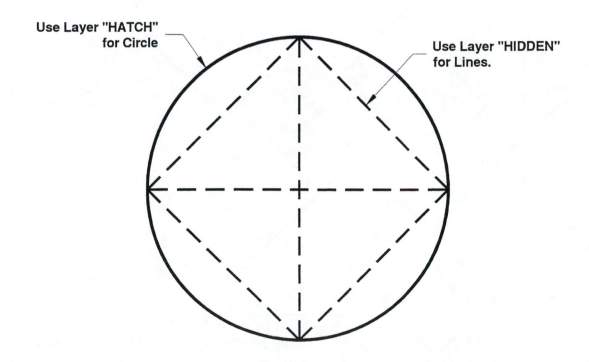

Use Layer "HATCH"
for Circle

Use Layer "HIDDEN"
for Lines.

EXERCISE 4C

INSTRUCTIONS:

1.　Start a **New** file using **1 Class Template.dwt**.

2.　Using **FORMAT / UNITS:**
　　　　set the units to **ARCHITECTURAL**
　　　　set the precision to **1/2"**

3.　Using **FORMAT / DRAWING LIMITS** set the drawing limits to:
　　　　Lower left corner = **0, 0**
　　　　Upper right corner = **25, 20**

4.　Use **VIEW / ZOOM / ALL** to make the screen change to the new limits.

5.　Turn **OFF** the **GRIDS** (F7)　**SNAP** (F9) and **ORTHO** (F8)
　　(Your screen should be blank and your crosshair should move freely)

6.　Draw the objects below using:
　　　　DRAW / LINE
　　　　OBJECT SNAP = **PERPENDICULAR**

7.　**Save** this drawing as:　**EX4C**

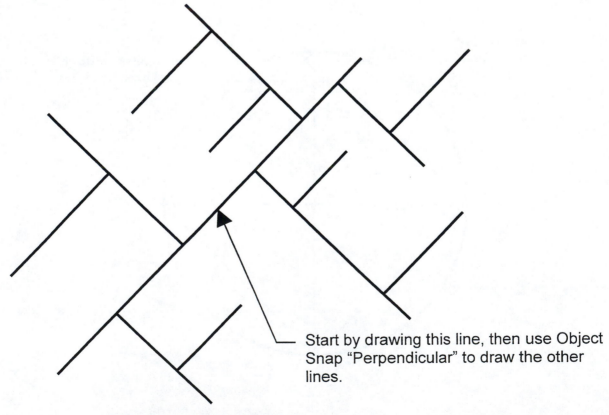

Start by drawing this line, then use Object Snap "Perpendicular" to draw the other lines.

EXERCISE 4D

INSTRUCTIONS:

1.   Start a **New** file using **1 Class Template.dwt**.

2.   Using **FORMAT / UNITS:**
        set the units to **DECIMALS**
        set the precision to **0.00**

3.   Using **FORMAT / DRAWING LIMITS** set the drawing limits to:
        Lower left corner = **0,0**
        Upper right corner = **12, 9**

4.   Use **VIEW / ZOOM / ALL** to make the screen change to the new limits

5.   Turn **OFF** the **GRIDS** (F7)   **SNAP** (F9) and **ORTHO** (F8)
      (Your screen should be blank and your crosshair should move freely)

6.   Draw the Lines below using:
        DRAW / LINE
        OBJECT SNAP = **MIDPOINT**

7.   **Save** this drawing as: **EX4D**

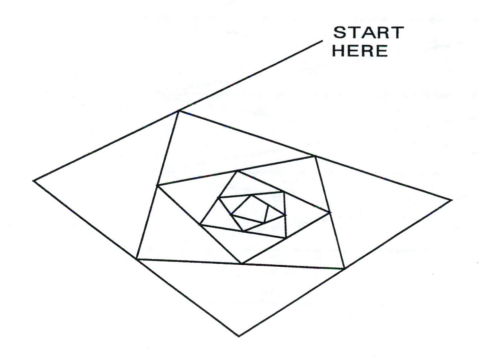

START
HERE

EXERCISE 4E

INSTRUCTIONS:

1.   Start a **New** file using **1 Class Template.dwt**

2.   Draw the objects below using:
     DRAW / LINE
     ORTHO **ON** for Horizontal Lines
     OBJECT SNAP = **ENDPOINT**

3.   **Save** this drawing as: **EX4E**

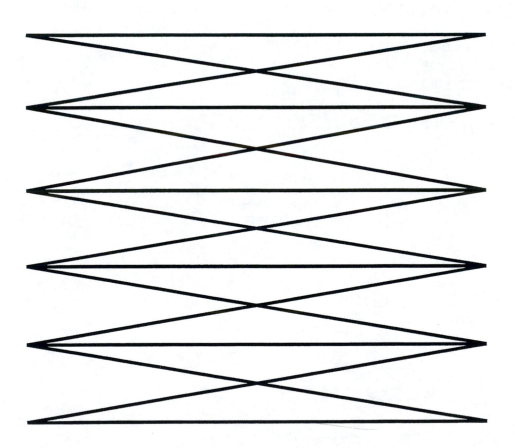

EXERCISE 4F

INSTRUCTIONS:

1. Start a **New** file using **1 Class Template.dwt**

2. Draw the 2 vertical and 4 horizontal lines using:
    DRAW / LINE
    ORTHO **ON**

3. Then draw the diagonal lines using:
    DRAW / LINE
    ORTHO **OFF**
    OBJECT SNAP = **INTERSECTION**

4. **Save** this drawing as: **EX4F**

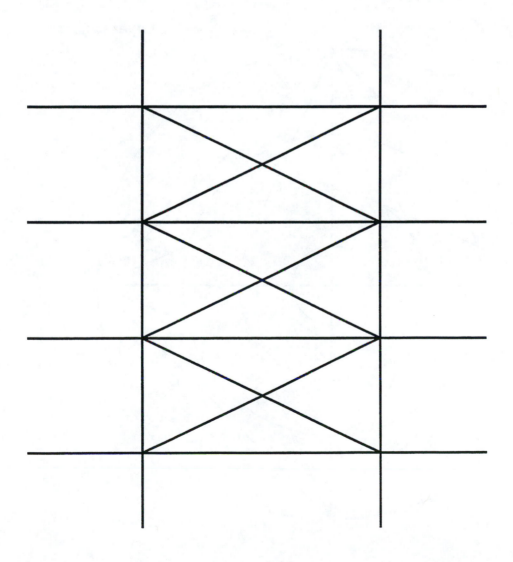

EXERCISE 4G

INSTRUCTIONS:

1. Start a **New** file using **1 class template.dwt**.

2. Draw the 4 circles with the following Radii: 1, 2, 3, & 5
   (Use Object snap "Center" so all Circles have the same center)

3. Draw the LINES using:
   DRAW / LINE
   ORTHO and SNAP = **OFF**
   OBJECT SNAP = **QUADRANT** and **TANGENT**

4. Use Layers: Object and Center

5. **Save** this drawing as **EX4G** using:
   FILE / SAVE AS

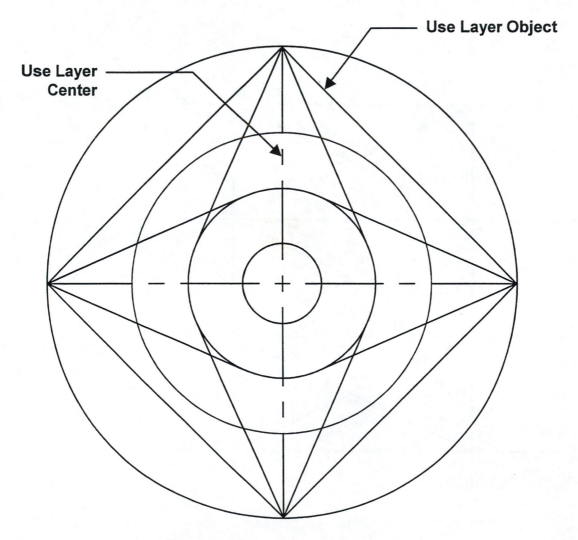

Use Layer Object

Use Layer Center

LEARNING OBJECTIVES

After completing this lesson, you will be able to:

1. Draw an Inscribed and Circumscribed Polygon.
2. Create an Ellipse using two different methods.
3. Draw an object called Donut.
4. Define a Point location.
5. Select various Point Styles.
6. Use 2 new Object Snap modes.

LESSON 5

POLYGON

A polygon is an object with multiple sides of equal length. You may specify from 3 to 1024 sides. A polygon appears to be multiple lines but in fact it is one object. You can specify the edge length or the center and a radius. The radius can be drawn inside (Inscribed) an imaginary circle or outside (circumscribed) an imaginary circle.

CENTER / RADIUS METHOD

1. Select the **Polygon** command using one of the following:

> **TYPING = POL**
> **PULLDOWN = DRAW / POLYGON**
> **TOOLBAR = DRAW**

2. The following prompts will appear on the command line:

> _polygon Enter number of sides <4>: *type number of sides <enter>*
> Specify center of polygon or [Edge]: *specify the center location*
> Enter an option [Inscribed in circle/Circumscribed about circle]<I>: *type I or C <enter>*
> Specify radius of circle: *type radius or locate with cursor.*

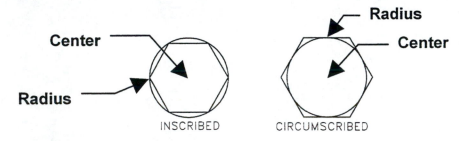

INSCRIBED   CIRCUMSCRIBED

EDGE METHOD

1. Select the **Polygon** command using one of the following:

> **TYPING = POL**
> **PULLDOWN = DRAW / POLYGON**
> **TOOLBAR = DRAW**

2. The following prompts will appear on the command line:

> _polygon Enter number of sides <4>: *type number of sides <enter>*
> Specify center of polygon or [Edge]: *type E <enter>*
> Specify first endpoint of edge: *place first endpoint of edge (P1)*
> Specify second endpoint of edge: *place second endpoint of edge (P2)*

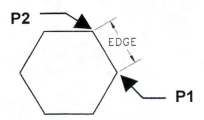

ELLIPSE

An Ellipse may be drawn by specifying the 3 points of the axes or by defining the center point and major / minor axis points.

AXIS END METHOD

1. Select the **ELLIPSE** command using one of the following:

    TYPING = EL
    PULLDOWN = DRAW / ELLIPSE
    TOOLBAR = DRAW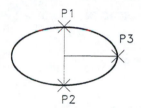

2. The following prompts will appear on the command line:

Command: _ellipse
Specify axis endpoint of ellipse or [Arc/Center]: *place the first point of either the major or minor axis (P1).*
Specify other endpoint of axis: *place the other point of the first axis (P2)*
Specify distance to other axis or [Rotation]: *place the point perpendicular to the first axis (P3).*

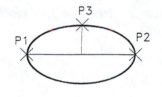

CENTER METHOD

1. Select the **ELLIPSE** command using one of the following:

    TYPING = EL
    PULLDOWN = DRAW / ELLIPSE
    TOOLBAR = DRAW

2. The following prompts will appear on the command line:

Command: _ellipse
Specify axis endpoint of ellipse or [Arc/Center]: *type C <enter>*
Specify center of ellipse: *place center of ellipse (P1*
Specify endpoint of axis: *place first axis endpoint (either axis) (P2)*
Specify distance to other axis or [Rotation]: *place the endpoint perpendicular to the first axis (P3)*

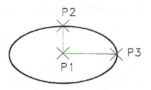

DONUT

A Donut is a circle with *width*. You will define the **Inside** and **Outside** diameters. The appearance is controlled by the **"Fill"** mode. If the **"Fill"** mode is **On**, the donut width will be solid. If the **"Fill"** mode is **Off**, the donut width will appear with lines somewhat like the spokes of a wheel. These lines enable you to visually differentiate between donuts and concentric circles.

1. Select the **DONUT** command using one of the following:

    TYPING =DO
    PULLDOWN = DRAW / DONUT
    TOOLBAR = DRAW (not a default icon)

2. The following prompts will appear on the command line:

    Command: _donut
    Specify inside diameter of donut: *type the inside diameter*
    Specify outside diameter of donut: *type the outside diameter*
    Specify center of donut or <exit>: *place the center of the first donut*
    Specify center of donut or <exit>: *place the center of the second donut or*
    <enter> to stop

Controlling the "FILL MODE"

Command: *type FILL <enter>*
Enter mode [ON/OFF] <OFF>: *type ON or Off   <enter>*

FILL =ON

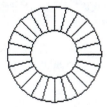

FILL = OFF

Select **VIEW / REGEN** or type *REGEN* <enter> at the command line to update the drawing to the latest changes to the *FILL* mode.

POINT

A Point is an object that has no dimension and only has location. A Point may be represented by selecting one of many Point styles shown below. The default Point Style is a "dot". Points are basically used to locate a point of reference.
You may select the "Single" or "Multiple" point option. The Single option creates one point. The Multiple option continues until you press the ESC key.
The only Object Snap mode that can be used with Point is "**Node**". (See page 5-6)

1. Select the **POINT** command using one of the following:

   TYPING = PO
   PULLDOWN = DRAW / POINT (Single point or Multiple point)
   TOOLBAR = DRAW

2. The following prompts will appear on the command line:

   Command: _point
   Current point modes: PDMODE = 3 PDSIZE = 0.000
   Specify a point: *place the point location*
   (If you selected "multiple point" you must press the "EXC" key to stop.)

TO SET THE "POINT STYLE"

1. Select one of the following:
   TYPE = DDPTYPE
   PULLDOWN = FORMAT / POINT STYLE
   TOOLBAR = NONE

2. This dialog box will appear.

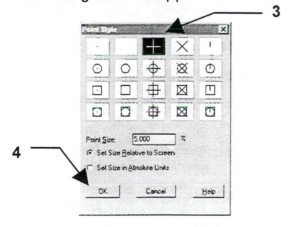

3. Select a tile.
4. Select the OK button.

MORE OBJECT SNAP

OBJECT SNAP OPTIONS:

NODe   This option snaps to a POINT object.
Place the pick box on the POINT object.

NEArest   Snaps to the nearest location on the nearest object.
Select the object anywhere on the object.

EXERCISE 5A

INSTRUCTIONS:

1. Start a **New** file using **1 class template.dwt**

2. Draw the Circle first, Polygon second and Lines last.

3. Draw the objects below using:
   DRAW / CIRCLE (Center, Rad)
   DRAW / POLYGON (Circumscribed)
   Ortho = **ON**
   Snap = **OFF**
   Object Snap = Center, Midpoint, Endpoint and Quadrant

4. **Save** this drawing as: **EX5A**

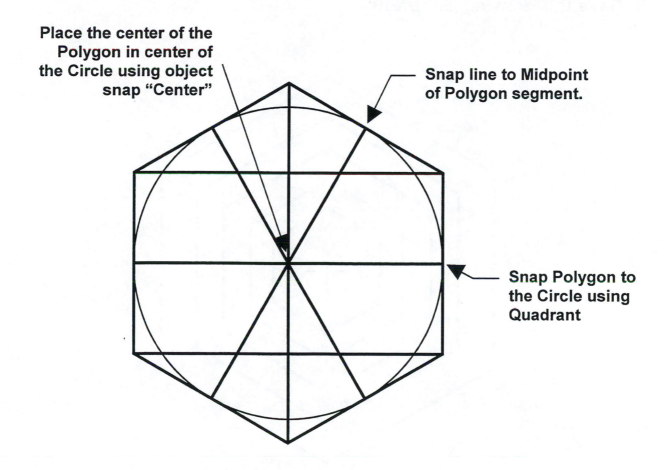

Place the center of the Polygon in center of the Circle using object snap "Center"

Snap line to Midpoint of Polygon segment.

Snap Polygon to the Circle using Quadrant

EXERCISE 5B

INSTRUCTIONS:

1. Start a **New** file using **1 Class Template.dwt**.

2. Draw the Point first, then the Polygons

3. Draw the objects below using:
   DRAW / POINT and **POLYGON** (Inscribed)
   Ortho and Snap **ON**
   Object Snap = Node

4. Locate the center of the Polygon by snapping to the Point using
   Object snap: **Node**

5. **Save** this drawing as: **EX5B**

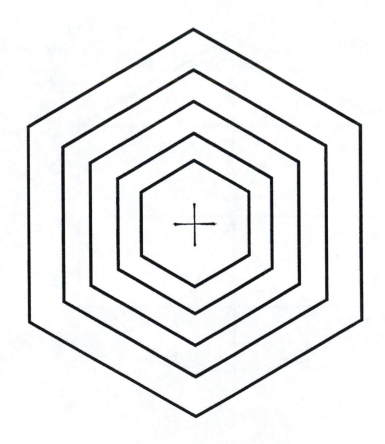

EXERCISE 5C

INSTRUCTIONS:

1. Start a **New** file using **1 Class Template.dwt.**
2. Draw the objects below using:
   DRAW / ELLIPSE (Axis, End) **LINES** and **CIRCLE** (center, rad)
   Ortho **ON** and Snap **OFF**
   Object Snap = Perpendicular and Quadrant
3. Have fun with this one.
4. **Save** this drawing as: **EX5C**

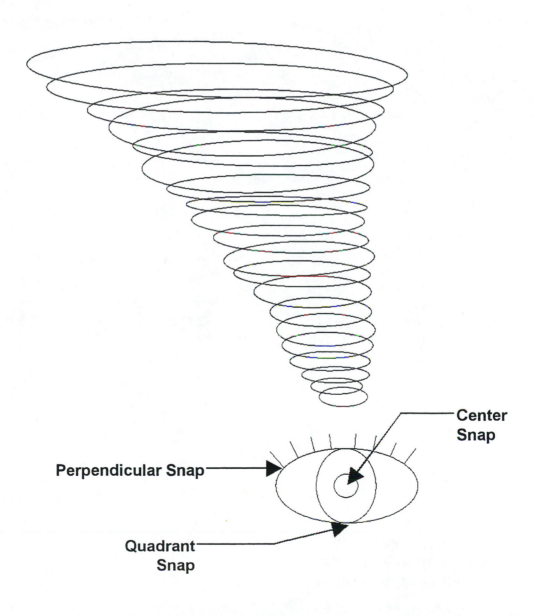

Center Snap

Perpendicular Snap

Quadrant Snap

EXERCISE 5D

INSTRUCTIONS:

1. Start a **New** file using **1 Class Template.dwt**.
2. Draw the Point first, then the Ellipse
3. Draw the objects below using:
   - **DRAW / POINT**
   - **DRAW / ELLIPSE** (Center method)
   - Ortho **ON** and Snap **OFF**
   - Object Snap = Quadrant and Node
4. **Save** this drawing as: **EX5D**

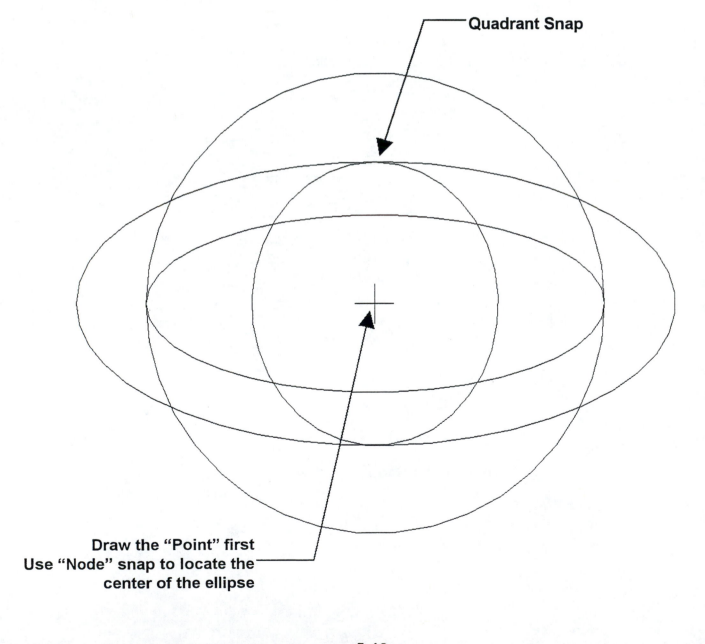

Quadrant Snap

Draw the "Point" first
Use "Node" snap to locate the
center of the ellipse

EXERCISE 5E

INSTRUCTIONS:

STEP 1.
1. Start a **New** file using **1 Class Template.dwt.**
2. Draw the objects below using:
  DRAW / DONUT
  Ortho and Snap **OFF**
  Object Snap = Center

STEP 2.
3. Turn the **FILL** mode **OFF** (Type: Fill < enter >   Off < enter >)
4. Select **View / Regen** or   Type: **REGEN** < enter >

5. **Save** this drawing as **EX5E**

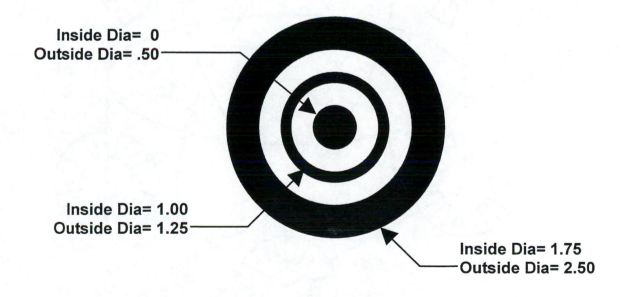

Inside Dia= 0
Outside Dia= .50

Inside Dia= 1.00
Outside Dia= 1.25

Inside Dia= 1.75
Outside Dia= 2.50

EXERCISE 5F

INSTRUCTIONS:

1. Start a **New** file using **1 CLASS TEMPLATE.dwt**.
2. Draw the objects below using:
   DRAW / POINT, POLYGON, ELLIPSE (center) and **DONUT**
   Ortho **ON** and Snap **OFF**
   Object Snap = Node, Endpoint and Midpoint
3. **Save** this drawing as: **EX5F**

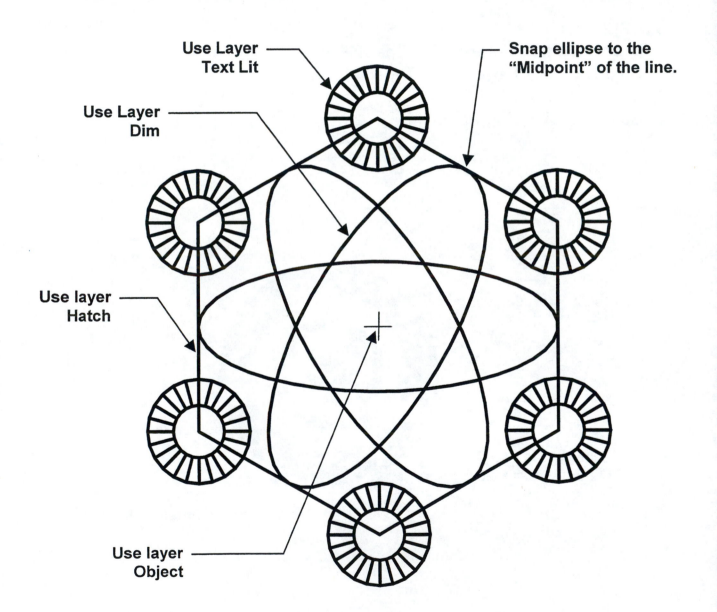

Use Layer
Text Lit

Snap ellipse to the
"Midpoint" of the line.

Use Layer
Dim

Use layer
Hatch

Use layer
Object

LEARNING OBJECTIVES

After completing this lesson, you will be able to:

1. Use the 4 Break command options.
2. Trim an object to a cutting edge.
3. Extend an object to a boundary.
4. Move an object(s) to a new location.
5. Explode objects into their primitive entities.

LESSON 6

BREAK

The *BREAK* command allows you to break a space in an object, break the end off an object or split a line in two. I think of it as taking a bite out of an object. There are 4 break methods described below.

You may select the **BREAK** command by using one of the following:

TYPING = BR
PULLDOWN = MODIFY / BREAK
TOOLBAR = MODIFY

METHOD 1

How to break one object into two separate objects with no visible space in between. (If you are not fussy about where the break point is)

a. Select the **BREAK** command using one of the methods listed above
b. _break Select object: *pick the break location (P1)*
c. Specify second break point or [First point]: *type the @ symbol*

(this will duplicate the last point)

Before Break

After Break

METHOD 2

This method is the same as method one with the exception that you are very specific where you want the break point.

a. Select the **BREAK** command using one of the methods listed above
b. _break Select objects: *select the object to break (P1)*
c. Specify second break point or [First point]: *type F <enter>*
d. Specify first break point: *select break location (P2) accurately*
e. Specify second break point: *type @ <enter>*

Before Break

After Break

Method 2 can also be accomplished easily by selecting the "Break at point" icon. But I wanted you to understand how it works.

BREAK (continued)

METHOD 3
Take a bite out of an object, but you are not fussy where the BREAK lies.
   (This is the Default option)

a. Select the **BREAK** command
b. _break Select object: *pick the first break location (P1)*
c. Specify second break point or [First point]: *pick the second break location (P2)*

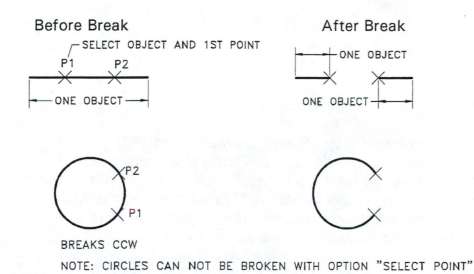

NOTE: CIRCLES CAN NOT BE BROKEN WITH OPTION "SELECT POINT"

METHOD 4
Take a bite out of an object and you are very specific where the gap is located.

a. Select the **BREAK** command
b. _break Select objects: *select the object to break (P1) anywhere on the object*
c. Specify second break point or [First point]: *type F <enter>*
d. Specify first break point: *select the first break location (P2) accurately*
e. Specify second break point: *select the second break location (P3) accurately*

TRIM

The **TRIM** command is used to trim an object to a **cutting edge**. You first select the "Cutting Edge" and then select the part of the object you want to trim. The object to be trimmed must actually intersect the cutting edge or could intersect if the objects were infinite in length.

1. Select the Trim command using one of the following:

    TYPE = TR
    PULLDOWN = MODIFY / TRIM
    TOOLBAR = MODIFY

2. The following will appear on the command line:

Command: _trim
Current settings: Projection = UCS   Edge = Extend
Select cutting edges ...
Select objects: ***select cutting edge(s) by clicking on the object (P1)***
Select objects: ***stop selecting cutting edges by pressing the <enter> key***
Select object to trim or shift-select to extend or [Project/Edge/Undo]: ***select the object***
that you want to trim. (P2) (Select the part of the object that
you want to disappear, not the part you want to remain)
Select object to trim or [Project/Edge/Undo]: ***press <enter> to stop***

> Note: You may toggle between Trim and Extend (page 6-5). Hold down the shift key and the Extend command is activated. Release the shift key and you return to Trim.

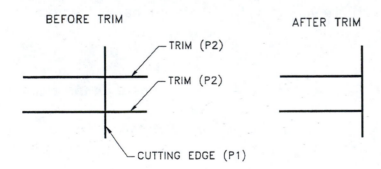

EDGE (Extend or No Extend)
In the **"Extend"** mode, (default mode) the cutting edges and the Objects to be trimmed need only apparently intersect if the objects were infinite in length.
In the **"No Extend"** mode the cutting edges and the objects to be trimmed must visibly intersect.

PROJECTION
Same as Edge except used only in "3D".

EXTEND

The **EXTEND** command is used to extend an object to a **boundary.** The object to be extended must actually or theoretically intersect the boundary.

1. Select the **EXTEND** command using one of the following:

   TYPE = EX
   PULLDOWN = MODIFY / EXTEND
   TOOLBAR = MODIFY

2. The following will appear on the command line:

Command: _extend
Current settings: Projection = UCS   Edge = Extend
Select boundary edges ...
Select objects: *select boundary (P1) by clicking on the object*
Select objects: *stop selecting boundaries by selecting <enter>*
Select object to extend or shift-select to Trim or [Project/Edge/Undo]: *select the object*
    that you want to extend. (P2 and P3) (Select the end of the object that you
    want to extend.)
Select object to extend or [Project/Edge/Undo]: *stop selecting objects*
                                        by selecting <enter>

> You may toggle between Extend and Trim (page 6-4). Hold down the shift key and the Trim command is activated. Release the shift key and you return to Extend.

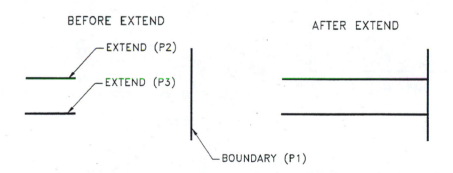

BEFORE EXTEND   — EXTEND (P2)   — EXTEND (P3)   BOUNDARY (P1)   AFTER EXTEND

EDGE (Extend or No Extend)
In the **"Extend"** mode, (default mode) the boundary and the Objects to be extended need only imaginarily intersect if the objects were infinite in length.
In the **"No Extend"** mode the boundary and the objects to be extended must visibly intersect.

PROJECTION   Same as Edge except used only in "3D".

MOVE

The MOVE command is used to move object(s) from their current location (basepoint) to a new location (second displacement point)

1. Select the Move command using one of the following:

    TYPE = M
    PULLDOWN = MODIFY / MOVE
    TOOLBAR = MODIFY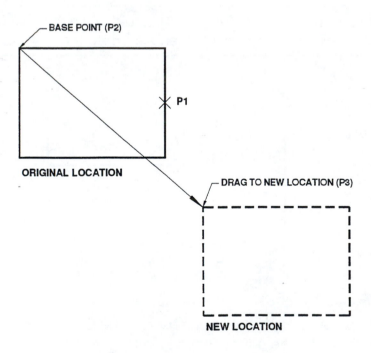

2. The following will appear on the command line:

    Command: _move
    Select objects: *select the object(s) you want to move (P1)*
    Select objects: *stop selecting object(s) by selecting <enter>*
    Specify base point or displacement: *select a location (P2) (usually on the object)*
    Specify second point of displacement or <use first point as displacement>: *move the object to it's new location (P3) and left click.*

    (Note: if you press <enter> instead of actually picking a new location, Autocad will send it into <u>Outer Space</u>. If this happens, press U <enter> and try again.

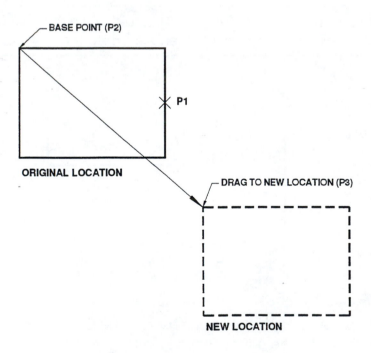

BASE POINT (P2)

P1

ORIGINAL LOCATION

DRAG TO NEW LOCATION (P3)

NEW LOCATION

EXPLODE

The EXPLODE command changes (explodes) an object into its primitive objects. For example, a rectangle is originally one object, if you explode it, it changes into 4 lines. Visually you will not be able to see the change unless you select one of the lines.

For example: Draw a rectangle and then click on it. The entire object highlights. Now explode the rectangle, then click on it again. Only the line you clicked on should be highlighted. Each line that forms the rectangular shape is now an individual object.

1. Select the Explode command by using one of the following:

   TYPE =X
   PULLDOWN = MODIFY / EXPLODE
   TOOLBAR = MODIFY

2. The following will appear on the command line:

Command: _explode
Select objects: *select the object(s) you want to explode*
Select objects: *select <enter>*

```
BEFORE EXPLODE
```

```
ONE OBJECT
(RECTANGLE)
```

```
AFTER EXPLODE
```

```
4 OBJECTS
(4 LINES)
```

EXERCISE 6A

INSTRUCTIONS:

1. Start a **New** file using **1 class template.dwt**.
2. Draw the objects below:
   Locate the center of the circles using object snap = **Nearest**
   Ortho and Snap = **OFF**

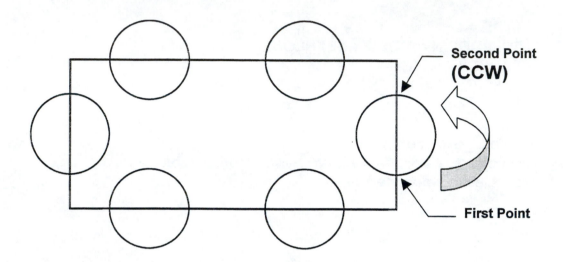

3. Modify the drawing above to look like the drawing below using:
   MODIFY / BREAK (Refer to 6-3, use Method 3)
   OBJECT SNAP = INTERSECTION and ENDPOINT

4. <u>Remember the Circles break **CCW**.</u>

5. **Save** this drawing as **EX6A**.

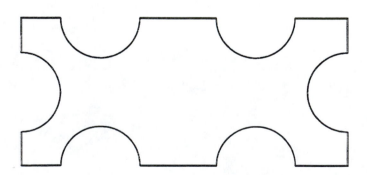

EXERCISE 6B

INSTRUCTIONS:

1.   Start a **New** file using **1 class template.dwt**.
2.   Draw the objects below:
OBJECT SNAP = CENTER
ORTHO and SNAP **OFF**

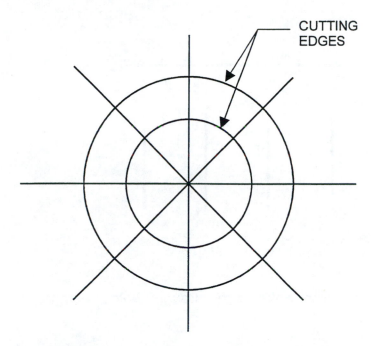

CUTTING
EDGES

3. Modify the drawing above to look like the drawing below using:
MODIFY / TRIM
4. **Save** this drawing as **EX6B.**

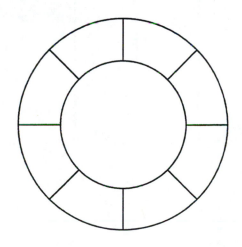

EXERCISE 6C

INSTRUCTIONS:

1. Start a **New** file using **1 class template.dwt**.

2.   Draw the LINES below exactly as shown.
        ORTHO and SNAP **ON**

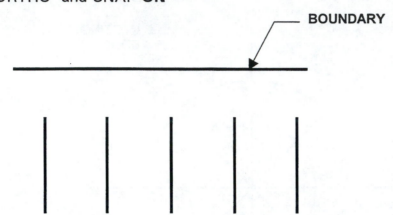

BOUNDARY

3. Modify the drawing above to look like the drawing below using:
        MODIFY / EXTEND

4. **Save** this drawing as **EX6C.**

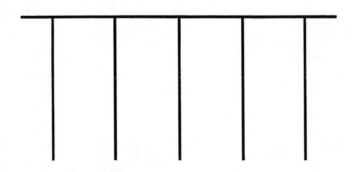

EXERCISE 6D

INSTRUCTIONS:

1. Start a **New** file using **1 class template.dwt**.

2. Draw the drawing below using:
   RECTANGLE, CIRCLES and LINES (FOR THE X'S)

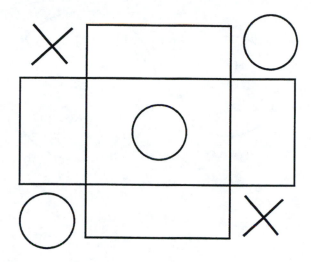

3. Modify the drawing above to look like the drawing below using:
   MODIFY / EXPLODE and ERASE

4. **Save** this drawing as **EX6D**.

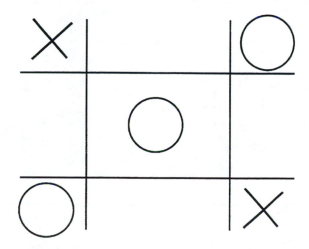

EXERCISE 6E

INSTRUCTIONS:

1. Start a **New** file using **1 class template.dwt**.

2. Draw the drawing below using:
   CIRCLES, POINT and LINES

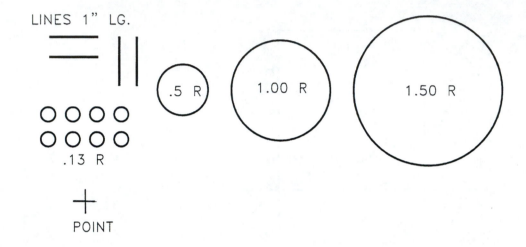

LINES 1" LG.

.5 R

1.00 R

1.50 R

.13 R

+ POINT

3. Assemble the objects as shown below using:
   MODIFY / MOVE
   OBJECT SNAP = CENTER, INTERSECTION, NODE, ENDPT and QUADRANT

4. **Save** this drawing as **EX6E**.

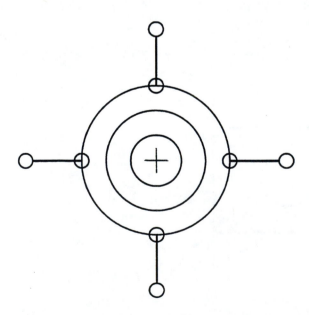

EXERCISE 6F

INSTRUCTIONS:

1. Start a **New** file using **1 class template.dwt**.

2. Draw the drawing below using all the methods you have learned in the past lessons. Use whatever layers you want and set snap and ortho on or off depending on the application.
    Be as creative as you like

3. Save this drawing as **EX6F**

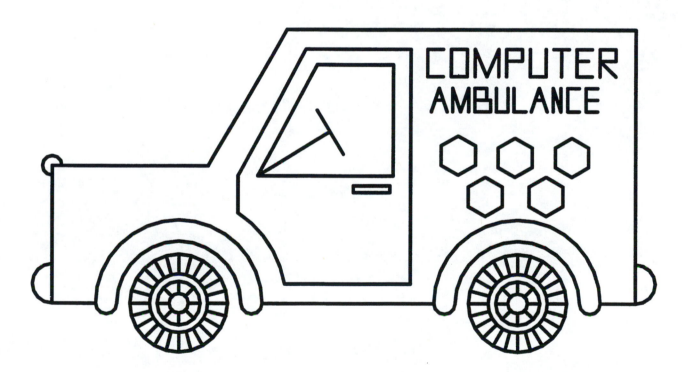

NOTES:

LEARNING OBJECTIVES

After completing this lesson, you will be able to:

1. Copy objects.
2. Make a mirrored image of one of more objects.
3. Add rounded corners to rectangular objects and lines.
4. Add angles to corners.

LESSON 7

COPY

The COPY command creates a duplicate set of the objects selected. The COPY command is similar to the MOVE command. You must select the objects to be copied, select a base point and a new location. The difference is, the Move command merely moves the objects to a new location. The Copy command makes a copy and you select the location for the new copy.

Select the Copy command using one of the following commands:

TYPE = CO
PULLDOWN = MODIFY / COPY
TOOLBAR = MODIFY

TO MAKE ONE COPY:
Command: _copy
Select objects: *select the objects you want to copy*
Select objects: *stop selecting objects by selecting <enter>*
Specify base point or displacement, or [Multiple]: *select a base point (P1) (usually on the object)*
Specify second point of displacement or <use first point as displacement>: *select the new location (P2) for the copy*

TO MAKE MULTIPLE COPIES:
Command: _copy
Select objects: *select the objects you want to copy*
Select objects: *stop selecting objects by selecting <enter>*
Specify base point or displacement, or [Multiple]: *M <enter>*
Specify base point: *select a point (P1) (usually on the object)*
Specify second point of displacement or <use first point as displacement>: *select the new location for the first copy (P2)*
Specify second point of displacement or <use first point as displacement>: *select the new location for the next copy*
Specify second point of displacement or <use first point as displacement>: *select the new location for the next copy*
To Stop select <enter>

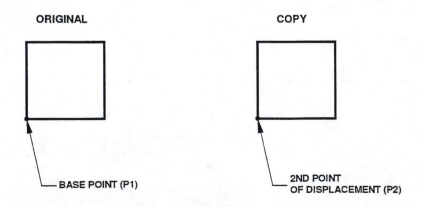

ORIGINAL   COPY

BASE POINT (P1)   2ND POINT
                         OF DISPLACEMENT (P2)

7-2

MIRROR

The MIRROR command allows you to make a mirrored image of any objects you select. You can use this command for creating right / left hand parts. You can draw a symmetrical object more efficiently by only drawing half of it.

Select the **MIRROR** command using one of the following:

> **TYPE = MI**
> **PULLDOWN = MODIFY / MIRROR**
> **TOOLBARS = MODIFY**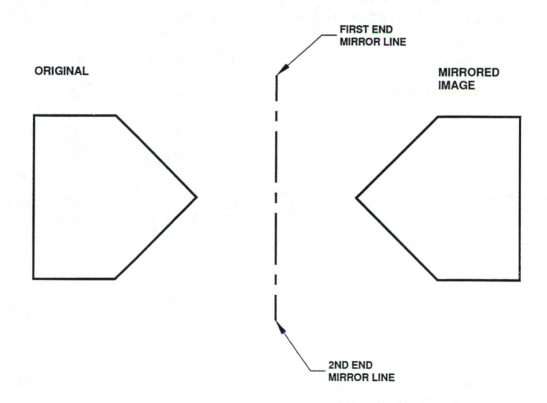

The following will appear on the command line:

Command: _mirror
Select objects: *select the objects to be mirrored*
Select objects: *stop selecting objects by selecting <enter>*
Specify first point of mirror line: *select the first end of the mirror line*
Specify second point of mirror line: *select the second end of the mirror line*
Delete source objects? [Yes/No] <N>: *select Y or N*

ORIGINAL

FIRST END
MIRROR LINE

MIRRORED
IMAGE

2ND END
MIRROR LINE

FILLET

The FILLET command will create a radius between two objects. The objects do not have to be touching. If two parallel lines are selected, it will construct a full radius.

1. Select the FILLET command using one of the following:

> **TYPE = F**
> **PULLDOWN = MODIFY / FILLET**
> **TOOLBAR = MODIFY**

The following will appear on the command line:

2. SET THE RADIUS OF THE FILLET
Command: _fillet
Current settings: Mode = TRIM, Radius = 0.000
Select first object or [Polyline/Radius/Trim]: *select "Radius" <enter>*
Specify fillet radius <0.000>: *type the radius <enter>*

3. NOW FILLET THE OBJECTS
Select first object or [Polyline/Radius/Trim]: *select the first object to be filleted*
Select second object: *select the second object to be filleted*

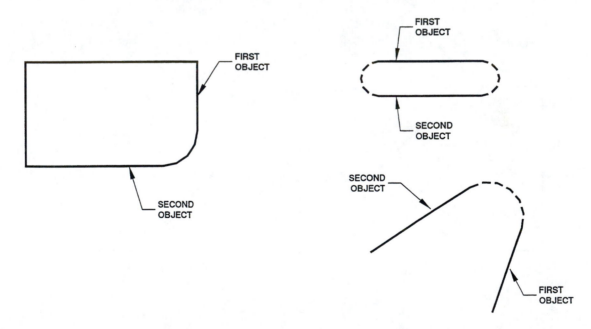

TRIM / NO TRIM OPTION: This option controls whether the original lines are trimmed to the end of the Arc or remain the original length.

POLYLINE: This option allows you to fillet all intersections of a Polyline in one operation. Such as a 4 corners of a rectangle.

CHAMFER

The **CHAMFER** command allows you to create a chamfered corner on two lines.
There are two methods: **Distance and Angle**.

1. Select the CHAMFER command using one of the following:

    TYPE = CHA
    PULLDOWN = MODIFY / CHAMFER
    TOOLBAR = MODIFY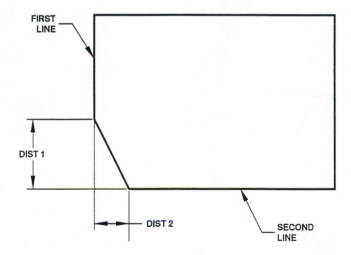

2. <u>**DISTANCE METHOD:**</u> requires input of a distance for each side of the corner.
    (Note: the Angle method is on the next page)

Command: _chamfer
(TRIM mode) Current chamfer Dist1 = 0.000, Dist2 = 0.000
Select first line or [Polyline/Distance/Angle/Trim/Method]: *select "Distance"*
Specify first chamfer distance <0.000>: *type the distance <enter>*
Specify second chamfer distance <1.000>: *type the distance <enter>*

3. **NOW CHAMFER THE OBJECT**
Select first line or [Polyline/Distance/Angle/Trim/Method]: *select the (first line) to be*
chamfered. (dist1)
Select second line: *select the (second line) to be chamfered. (dist2)*

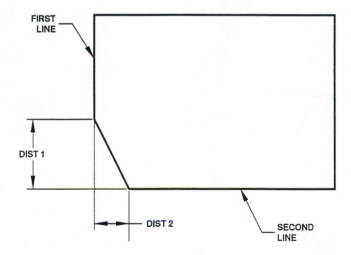

TRIM / NO TRIM OPTION: This option controls whether the original lines are trimmed to the end of the Arc or remain the original length.

POLYLINE: This option allows you to fillet all intersections of a Polyline in one operation. Such as a 4 corners of a rectangle.

CHAMFER (continued)

ANGLE METHOD

1. Select the CHAMFER command

2. **ANGLE METHOD:** requires input for the length of the line and an angle.

Command: _chamfer
(TRIM mode) Current chamfer Dist1 = 1.000, Dist2 = 1.000
Select first line or [Polyline/Distance/Angle/Trim/Method]: *select "A" for Angle <enter>*
Specify chamfer length on the first line <0.000>: *type the chamfer length <enter>*
Specify chamfer angle from the first line <0>: *type the angle <enter>*

3. **NOW CHAMFER THE OBJECT**
Select first line or [Polyline/Distance/Angle/Trim/Method]: *select the (first line) to be chamfered. (length)*
Select second line: *select the (second line) to be chamfered. (Angle)*

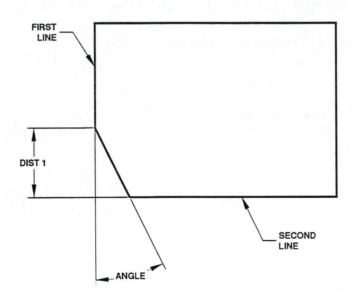

TRIM / NO TRIM OPTION: This option controls whether the original lines are trimmed to the end of the Arc or remain the original length.

POLYLINE: This option allows you to fillet all intersections of a Polyline in one operation. Such as a 4 corners of a rectangle.

EXERCISE 7A

INSTRUCTIONS:

1. Start a **New** file using **1 class template.dwt**.
2. **Draw** the rectangle below using:
   Draw / Rectangle
3. **Round** the corners using the FILLET command
4. **Save** this drawing as **EX7A**

BEFORE FILLET

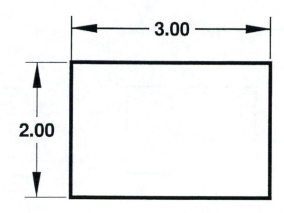

AFTER FILLET

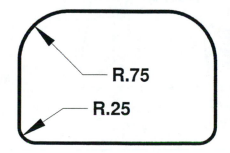

R.75
R.25

EXERCISE 7B

INSTRUCTIONS:

1. Start a **New** file **1 class template.dwt**.
2. **Draw** the rectangles below using:
    Draw / Rectangle
3. **CHAMFER** the corners using the CHAMFER command
4. **Save** this drawing as **EX7B**

BEFORE CHAMFER

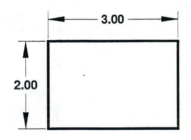

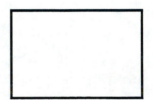

AFTER CHAMFER

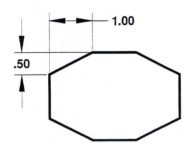

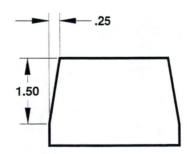

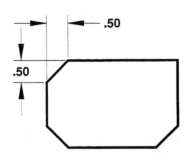

7-8

EXERCISE 7C

INSTRUCTIONS:

1. Start a **New** file **1 class template.dwt** .
2. **Draw** the rectangle below using:
     Draw / Rectangle
3. **CHAMFER** the corners using the CHAMFER command
4. **Save** this drawing as **EX7C**

BEFORE CHAMFER

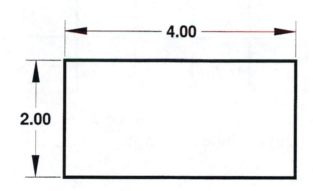

AFTER CHAMFER

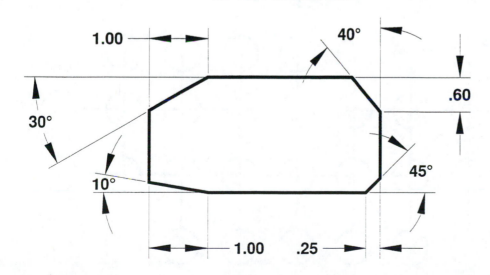

EXERCISE 7D

INSTRUCTIONS:

1. Start a **New** file **1 class template.dwt** .
2. **Draw** the Lines and one Circle as shown below

BEFORE COPY

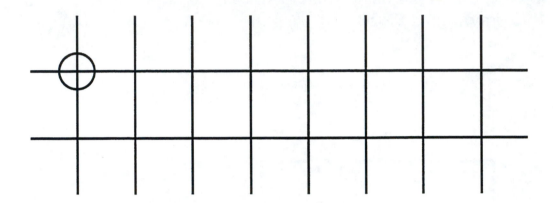

3. Complete the drawing as shown below using:
   a. Copy
   b. Select the Circle
   c. Select Multiple
   d. Select the basepoint on the Original circle. (Notice the basepoints are not all the same)
   e. Select the New location (2nd point of displacement)
4. Save this drawing as **EX7D**

AFTER COPY

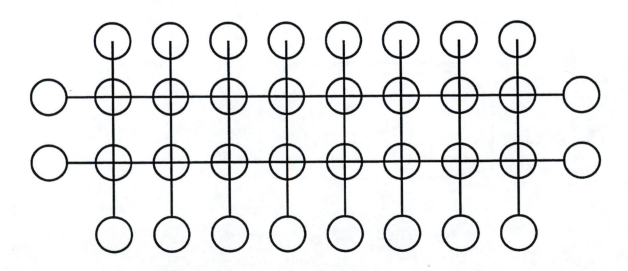

EXERCISE 7E

INSTRUCTIONS:

1. Start a **New** file.
2. Draw the half house below using:
   Lines, Circles and Rectangles
3. Use at least 4 different layers.

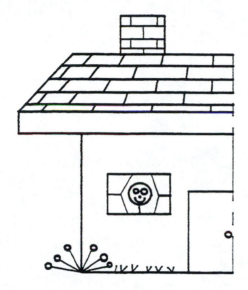

4. Now create a MIRRORED IMAGE of the half house using:
   a. Modify / Mirror
   b. Select the objects to be mirrored
   c. Select the 1st endpoint of the mirror line
   d. Select the 2nd endpoint of the mirror line
   e. Answer **No** to "Delete old objects?"

5. Save this drawing as **EX7E**

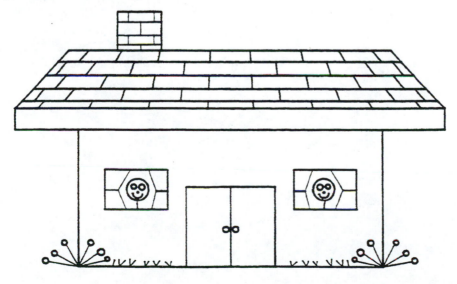

NOTES:

7-12

LEARNING OBJECTIVES

After completing this lesson, you will be able to:

1. Add a "Single Line" of text to your drawing.
2. Add a paragraph, using "Multiline Text".
3. Control the way the text is inserted.
4. Edit text already in the drawing.
5. Scaling the Text

LESSON 8

SINGLE LINE TEXT

SINGLE LINE TEXT allows you to draw one or more lines of text. The text is visible as you type. To place the text in the drawing, you may use the default **START POINT** (the lower left corner of the text), or use one of the many styles of justification described on the next page.

USING THE DEFAULT START POINT

1. Select the **SINGLE LINE TEXT** command using one of the following:

TYPE = DT or TEXT
PULLDOWN = DRAW / TEXT / SINGLE LINE TEXT
TOOLBAR = DRAW [A]

    Command: _dtext
    Current text style: "STANDARD" Text height: 0.250
2. Specify start point of text or [Justify/Style]: ***select the location where you want the text to begin***
3. Specify height <0.250>: ***type the height of your text***
4. Specify rotation angle of text <0>: ***type the rotation angle or <enter> for 0***
5. Enter text: ***type the text string; press enter at the end of the sentence***
6. Enter text: ***type the text string; press enter at the end of the sentence***
7. Enter text: ***type the next sentence or press <enter> to stop***

USING JUSTIFICATION

If you need to be very specific, where your text is located, you must use the Justification option. For example if you want your text in the middle of a rectangular box, you would use the justification option "Middle".

The following is an example of Middle justification.

1. Draw a Rectangle 6" wide and 3" high.
2. Draw a Diagonal line from one corner to the diagonal corner.
        3. Select the SINGLE LINE TEXT command

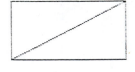

    Command: _dtext
    Current text style: "STANDARD" Text height: 0.250
4. Specify start point of text or[Justify/Style]: ***type "J"***
5. Enter an option [Align/Fit/Center/Middle/Right/TL/ TC/TR/ML/MC/MR/BL/BC/BR]: ***type M***

6. Specify middle point of text: ***snap to the midpoint of the diagonal line***
7. Specify height <0.250>: ***1 <enter>***
8. Specify rotation angle of text <0>: ***0 <enter>***
9. Enter text: ***type: HHHH <enter>***
10. Enter text: ***press <enter> to stop***

OTHER JUSTIFICATION OPTIONS:

ALIGN
Aligns the line of text between two points specified.
The height is adjusted automatically.

FIT
Fits the text between two points specified.
The height is specified by you and does not change.

CENTER HyyHHyyHHyy
This is a tricky one. Center is located at the bottom center of Upper Case letters.

MIDDLE HHHHHHHHHH   HHyyHHyyHH
If only uppercase letters are used: located in the middle, horizontally and vertically.
If both uppercase and lowercase letters are used: located in the middle, horizontally and
vertically, of the lowercase letters.

RIGHT HyyHHyyHHyy
Bottom right of upper case text.

TL, TC, TR HyyHHyyHHyy
Top left, Top center and Top right of upper and lower case text

ML, MC, MR HyyHHyyHHyy
Middle left, Middle center and Middle right of upper case text.

BL, BC, BR HyyHHyyHHyy
Bottom left, Bottom center and Bottom right of lower case text.

MULTILINE TEXT or MTEXT

MULTILINE TEXT has more editing options than Single Line text. You can underline, bold, italic, change the font , etc.
When using Multiline text you must define a text boundary. The text boundary is basically a rectangle that specifies the width of the paragraph. The paragraph is considered one object.

USING MULTILINE TEXT

1. Select the MULTILINE TEXT command using one of the following:

    TYPE = MT
    PULLDOWN = DRAW / TEXT / MULTILINE TEXT
    TOOLBAR = DRAW [A]

    Mtext Current text style: "STANDARD"   Text height: .250
2. Specify first corner: ***Pick the location of the upper left corner of the new text area.***
3. Specify opposite corner or [Height / Justify / Line Spacing / Rotation / Style / Width]: ***Pick the opposite corner of the new text area***

4. The **Multiline Text Editor** will appear.
    Enter the desired text. (The text will *wrap* based on the width you defined.)
    Then select OK button. The text will now be entered into the drawing.

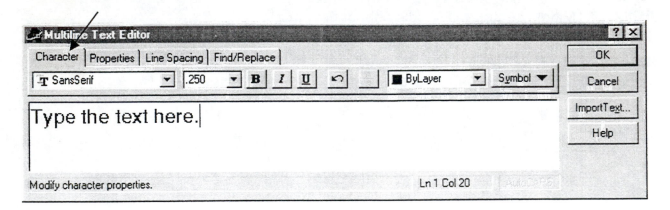

CHARACTER TAB

The Character tab allows you to change individual characters.

You can change the FONT, HEIGHT, BOLD, ITALIC, UNDERLINE or COLOR.

The STACKED button allows you to stack or unstack text or fractions. To use this option you must place a ^ (caret) before the bottom text. (numerator^denominator).

The SYMBOL button allows you to select three common symbols. The plus/minus, diameter and degree.

MULTILINE TEXT continued

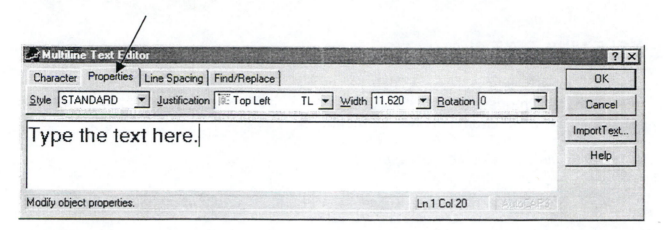

PROPERTIES TAB

The Properties tab allows you to change the entire paragraph.
You can change the TEXT STYLE, JUSTIFICATION, WIDTH and the ROTATION.

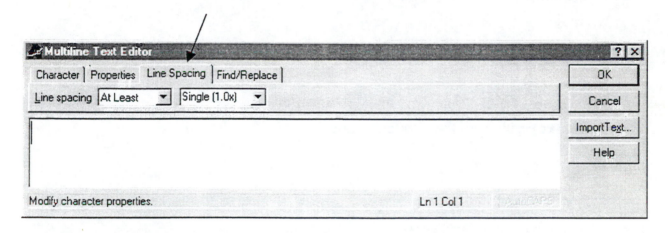

LINE SPACING TAB

The Line Spacing tab allows you to select the spacing between the lines.

FIND / REPLACE

This is an advanced option and will not be discussed at this time.

Note: Creating new text styles will be discussed in Lesson 25.

EDITING TEXT

SINGLE LINE TEXT

1. Select the line of text you want to edit.
2. Press the right mouse button.
3. Select **"Text Edit"** from the shortcut menu.

   The following dialog box will appear:

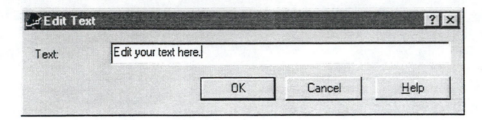

4. Make the changes then select the OK button.
5. Select an annotation object>/Undo: **select the next text to be edited or press <enter> to stop**

MULTILINE TEXT

1. Select the Multiline text you want to edit.
2. Then press the right mouse button.
3. Select **"Mtext Edit"** from the shortcut menu.

The following dialog box will appear:

4. Highlight the text that you want to change. Make the changes then select the OK button.

Note: You may also type **"DDEDIT"** on the command line, then select the text you want to edit. This method works with Single or Multiline Text.

SCALING TEXT

The **Scaletext** command allows you to scale <u>Single or Multiline</u> text using **height**, **factor** or **match** a previously drawn text. The text will be scaled proportionately in the X and Y axis. In other words, it gets larger or smaller all over. You must select a "base point" from which the text will enlarge or reduce. The base point is a justification option. If you would like it to scale from the middle, you will select "middle" as the base point. If you would like the text to scale from the top, you will select "TC". Most of the time you will simple use "existing". Existing is the justification used when the text was originally created.

Select the **SCALETEXT** command using one of the following:

TYPE = scaletext
PULLDOWN = MODIFY / OBJECT / TEXT / SCALE
TOOLBAR = DRAW

HEIGHT
1. Select the line of text you want to edit.
2. Select objects: *select more text or <enter> to stop selecting*
3. Enter a base point option for scaling
   [Existing/Left/Center/Middle/Right/TL/TC/TR/ML/MC/MR/BL/BC/BR]
   <Existing>:*select the base point*
4. Specify new height or [Match object/Scale factor] <.250>:*type new height <enter>*

MATCH OBJECT
1. Select the line of text you want to edit.
2. Select objects: *select more text or <enter> to stop selecting*
3. Enter a base point option for scaling
   [Existing/Left/Center/Middle/Right/TL/TC/TR/ML/MC/MR/BL/BC/BR]
   <Existing>:*select the base point*
4. Specify new height or [Match object/Scale factor] <.250>:*select Match*
5. Select a text object with the desired height: *select the text to match*
   Height = *the new height will be shown here*

SCALE FACTOR
1. Select the line of text you want to edit.
2. Select objects: *select more text or <enter> to stop selecting*
3. Enter a base point option for scaling
   [Existing/Left/Center/Middle/Right/TL/TC/TR/ML/MC/MR/BL/BC/BR]
   <Existing>:*select the base point*
4. Specify new height or [Match object/Scale factor] <.250>:*select Scale factor*
5. Specify scale factor or [Reference] <2.000>: *type the factor*

EXERCISE 8A

INSTRUCTIONS:

1. Start a new drawing using **1 class template.dwt**
2. Duplicate the text shown below using SINGLE LINE text.
3. Use Layer Object.
4. Select **DRAW / TEXT / SINGLE LINE**
5. Follow the instructions in each block of text.

DO NOT DUPLICATE NOTES WITH ARROWS

THIS TEXT IS CENTERED
ON 6.25, 8.00
HT. = .50

TEXT EXERCISE

THIS TEXT'S START POINT IS .75, 7.50
AND THE HEIGHT IS .13.

THIS TEXT IS JUSTIFIED, RIGHT.
THE ENDPOINT IS 11.50, 7.50.
THE HEIGHT IS .13.
THE TEXT WILL LOOK A LITTLE STRANGE
BECAUSE IT IS ALL HANGING OFF THE
RIGHT HAND SIDE OF THE SCREEN RIGHT
NOW. BUT IT WILL MOVE AFTER YOU
PRESS RETURN TWICE.

THIS TEXT IS ALIGNED BETWEEN .75, 5.50 AND 11.50, 5.50. REMEMBER TO PRESS ENTER TWICE WHEN DONE TYPING.

THIS TEXT IS ALSO ALIGNED BUT BETWEEN .75, 4.75 AND 11.75, 5.25. NO HEIGHT OR WIDTH IS REQUIRED.

THESE NUMBERS ARE IN THE MIDDLE OF THE
CIRCLE. THE HEIGHT IS .50. THE CIRCLE IS 1.50 DIA.
USE OBJECT SNAP CENTER TO LOCATE MIDDLE. IT
WILL NOT APPEAR IN THE MIDDLE UNTIL YOU PRESS
ENTER TWICE.

**THIS TEXT IS FIT BETWEEN
1.00, 4.00 AND 5.00, 4.00**
THE TEXT ONLY COMPRESSES IF IT EXTENDS
BEYOND THE 5.00, 4.00 POINT. IT STRETCHES
IF SHORTER. HT = .13

22

CENTER LOCATION
7.00,3.75

THIS TEXT IS
ROTATED 45 DEGREES.
THE HEIGHT IS .20
START POINT IS 8.5, 1.25.

1.00, .50

THIS FITS

THIS TEXT IS FIT INTO
A 1 X 4 RECTANGLE
THE HEIGHT IS 1.00

5.00, .50

EXERCISE 8B

INSTRUCTIONS:

1. Start a new drawing using **1 Class template.dwt**
2. Duplicate the text shown below using MULTILINE text.
3. Select **DRAW / TEXT / MULTILINE**
4. Specify first corner: 0, 0 <enter>
5. Specify opposite corner: 11.5, 3 <enter>
6. Change the font to **Sans Serif**
7. Change the text height to .250
8. Use **Bold**, *italic* where shown.
9. Type this paragraph as one continuous line. Do not press enter at the end of the sentences. (You defined the width of the paragraph when you specified the opposite corner.)

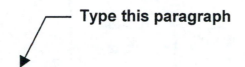

Type this paragraph

AutoCAD 2002 brings big changes for users at every level. From the ***novice*** who is just drawing lines to the ***advanced 3D expert*** manipulating *complex solids*, everyone will find important improvements that affect the way they work with ***AutoCAD***.

EXERCISE 8C

INSTRUCTIONS:

1. Start a new drawing using **1 Class template.dwt**
2. Draw a 6" wide by 3" high rectangle.
3. Draw a diagonal line from corner to corner, as shown.
   Use endpoint snap to be accurate.
4. Place the text <u>accurately</u> in the middle of the box. Text height = 1"

Hint: Use Single Line Text, Justify – Middle and Midpoint snap

EXERCISE 8D

INSTRUCTIONS:

1. Start a new drawing using **1 Class template.dwt**

2. Draw two 6" long lines as shown.

3. Select Draw / Text / Single Line Text
   a. Select **Justify - Center**.
   b. Use Midpoint snap to place the justification point at the midpoint of the line.
   c. Use text height 1" and rotation angle 0.
   d. Type the word "Happy" <enter> <enter>

4. Select Draw / Text / Single Line Text again.
   a. This time select **Justify - BC**. (bottom center)
   b. Use Midpoint snap to place the justification point at the midpoint of the line.
   c. Use text height 1" and rotation angle 0.
   d. Type the word "Happy" <enter> <enter>

Notice the difference between <u>Center</u> and <u>Bottom Center</u>?

EXERCISE 8E

INSTRUCTIONS:

1. Select Draw / Text / Multiline Text
2. Specify the size of the multiline paragraph by entering the coordinates for the first corner and then the coordinates for the opposite corner:
   First corner Type: 0,0 <enter> Opposite Corner Type: 7, 3 <enter>
3. In the Multiline Editor:
   Change the text style to: Sanserif   and the Height to .250 if necessary
4. Type the following as one continuous line. Do not press <enter>.
   When you are finished typing, select OK.

Today is the day that I will learn how to use
AutoCAD's text editing features. I will be a
good student and practice **all** the features
because I **really** want to learn!

Hopefully your text appears the same as the text shown above.

Now we are going to change the width of this paragraph.

5. Select the multiline editor by double clicking on the paragraph.
6. Select the "Properties" tab.
7. Change the "Width" to 4 and select OK.

Today is the day that I will
learn how to use
AutoCAD's text editing
features. I will be a good
student and practice **all**
the features because I
really want to learn!

See how easily you can manipulate the Multiline text.

LEARNING OBJECTIVES

After completing this lesson, you will be able to:

1. Understand the ORIGIN.
2. Draw Objects using Coordinate Input.
3. Understand the difference between Absolute and Relative coordinates.
4. LIST information about objects.
5. Determine the distance between two points.
6. Identify a location in the drawing.
7. Create your own 11 x 17 Master Border.
8. Plot 11 x 17 drawings in Model Space.

LESSON 9

COORDINATE INPUT

Autocad uses the *Cartesian Coordinate System* with an **X** and **Y** axis **(Z** is for 3D). The **X** axis is the Horizontal axis. The **Y** axis is the Vertical axis. The location where the X, Y, and Z axes intersect is called the **ORIGIN.** (0,0,0)

ABSOLUTE COORDINATES   (The format is: **X, Y)**
Absolute coordinates come *from the ORIGIN* and are typed as follows: **5, 8 .** The first number represents the **X-axis** (horizontal) distance from the Origin and the second number represents the **Y-axis** (vertical) distance from the Origin. The two numbers must be separated by a **comma.**

An absolute coordinate of **4, 2** will be **4** units to the right (horizontal) and **2** units up (vertical) from the current location of the Origin.

An absolute coordinate of **-4, -2** will be **4** units to the left (horizontal) and **2** units down (vertical) from the current location of the Origin.

The following are examples. Notice where the Origin is located in each example.

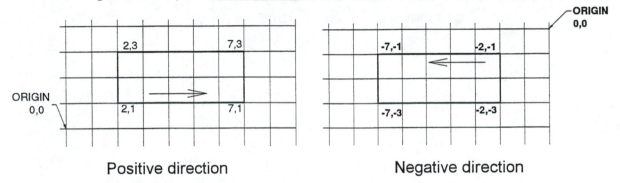

Positive direction   Negative direction

RELATIVE COORDINATES   (The format is: **@X, Y**)
Relative coordinates come *from the last point entered.* The first number represents the **X-axis** (horizontal) and the second number represents the **Y-axis** (vertical). The two numbers are separated by a **comma.** To distinguish between Absolute and Relative, use the **@** symbol and then the X and Y coordinates.

A Relative coordinate of **@5, 2** will go to the **right** 5 units and **up** 2 units from the last point entered.

A Relative coordinate of **@-5, -2** will go to the **left** 5 units and **down** 2 units from the last point entered.

The following is an example of Relative input.

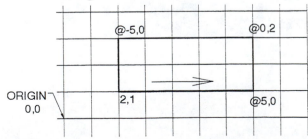

DIRECT DISTANCE ENTRY (DDE)

DIRECT DISTANCE ENTRY is a combination of keyboard entry and mouse movement. **DDE** is used to specify distances in the horizontal or vertical axes from the last point entered. **DDE** is a *Relative Input.* Since it is used for Horizontal and Vertical movements, **Ortho** must be **ON**.

(Note: to specify distances on an angle, refer to Lesson 11)

Using DDE is simple. Just move the cursor and type the distance.
Negative and positive is understood automatically by moving the cursor up (positive), down (negative), right (positive) or left (negative) from the last point entered. No minus sign necessary.

Moving the cursor to the right and typing 5 and <enter> tells AutoCAD that the 5 is positive and Horizontal.
Moving the cursor to the left and typing 5 and <enter> tells AutoCAD that the 5 is negative and Horizontal.
Moving the cursor up and typing 5 and <enter> tells AutoCAD that the 5 is positive and Vertical.
Moving the cursor down and typing 5 and <enter> tells AutoCAD that the 5 is negative and Vertical.

EXAMPLE:

1. <u>Ortho must be ON</u>.
2. Select the Line command.
3. Type: 1, 2 <enter> to enter the first endpoint using Absolute coordinates.
4. Now move your cursor to the right and type: 5 <enter>
5. Now move your cursor up and type: 4 <enter>
6. Now move your cursor to the left and type: 5 <enter> <enter> to stop

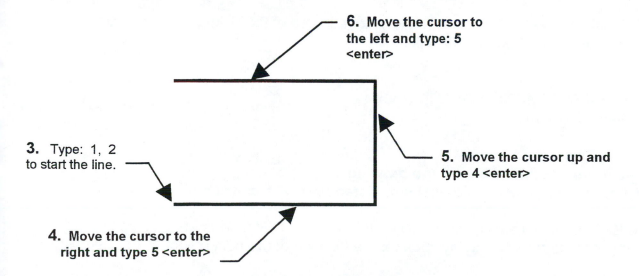

6. Move the cursor to the left and type: 5 <enter>

3. Type: 1, 2 to start the line.

5. Move the cursor up and type 4 <enter>

4. Move the cursor to the right and type 5 <enter>

INQUIRY

The INQUIRY command allows you to Inquire about objects on the screen. There are 8 commands in the inquiry menu but we will only discuss 3 of those commands at this time. The remaining 5 commands will be discussed in the "Advanced" workbook.

LIST
The LIST command will list what kind of object it is, X,Y location, layer, color, length and linetype.

TYPE = LIST
PULLDOWN = TOOLS / INQUIRY / List
TOOLBAR = STANDARD

Select the LIST command
Select the object: *select the object*
Select the object: *press <enter> to stop*

DISTANCE
The DISTANCE command will list the distance between two points that you select.

TYPE = DI
PULLDOWN = TOOLS / INQUIRY / Distance
TOOLBAR = STANDARD

Select the DISTANCE command
First point: *select the first point*
Second point: *select the second point*
Distance = *distance between the two points will be listed here*

ID POINT
The ID POINT command will list the X and Y coordinates of the point that you selected. The coordinates will be from the ORIGIN.

TYPE = ID
PULLDOWN = TOOLS / INQUIRY / ID Point
TOOLBAR = STANDARD

Select the ID POINT command
Point: *select a point anywhere on the drawing*
X =*coordinate listed here* Y = *coordinate listed here* Z = *coordinate listed here*

Note: the **ID POINT** can also be used to create a **LAST POINT**. This enables you to use Relative coordinates (the @ symbol) for the location of the next object.

EXERCISE 9A

INSTRUCTIONS:

1. Start a **New** drawing using:
   9A Template.Dwt
   (If you do not have this template refer page 2-2)

2. Set **UNITS** using:
   Format / Units
   Units = Decimal
   Precision = 0.000

3. Set **DRAWING LIMITS** using:
   Format / Drawing Limits
   Lower Left Corner = 0,0
   Upper Rt. Corner = 17, 11

4. Show the new limits using:
   View / Zoom / All

5. Set **GRIDS** and **SNAP** using:
   Tools / Drafting Settings
   Grids = ON = .500
   Snap = ON = .250

6. **Draw the border below** to scale using the dimensions shown.
   Use layer **BORDER**.

7. Place the **TEXT** as shown.
   Use Layer = **Text-Hvy**
   Text Ht. = .25

8. **Save** this border as **BSIZE**.

9. **PLOT** using:
   File / Plot
   Refer to "Basic Plotting from Model Space" on the next page.

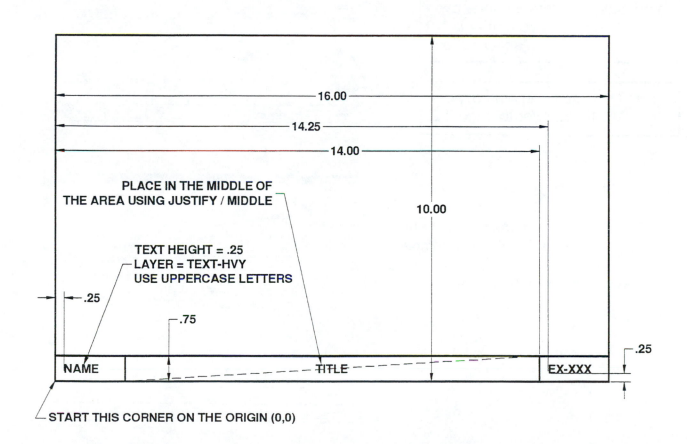

PLACE IN THE MIDDLE OF
THE AREA USING JUSTIFY / MIDDLE

TEXT HEIGHT = .25
LAYER = TEXT-HVY
USE UPPERCASE LETTERS

16.00

14.25

14.00

10.00

.25

.75

.25

NAME

TITLE

EX-XXX

START THIS CORNER ON THE ORIGIN (0,0)

BASIC PLOTTING FROM MODEL SPACE

Note: More Advanced plotting methods will be explained in Lessons 26 and 27.

1. Open the drawing you want to plot.
2. Make sure that the Model tab is active. (Active Model tab)
3. Select the **Plot** command by "Right clicking" on the "Model" tab or using one of the following methods listed below:

> **Type = Print or Plot**
> **Pulldown = File / Plot**
> **Tool bar = Standard**

The Plot dialog box below should appear.

4. Select **Class Page Setup** from the list.

5. Select the **"Plot Device"** tab.

Note: This printer should appear. If not, it needs to be configured. Refer to Appendix A

You may configure a printer even though your computer is not attached to it.

Note: This .ctb file should appear. If not, refer to page 2-2.

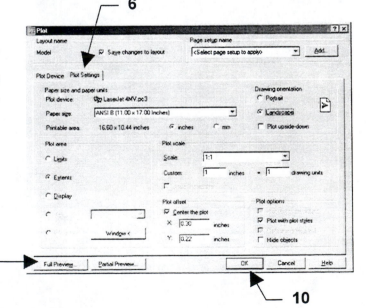

6. Select the **"Plot Settings"** tab.

7. Check all the settings to make sure they match the workbook example.

8. Select **Full Preview** button.

9. If your drawing appears approximately like the display shown below, press <enter>.

10. Select the **OK** button to send the drawing to the printer or <u>select **Cancel** if you do not want to print the drawing at this time or if you are not attached to this printer.</u>

If your drawing did not appear approximately the same as shown below, recheck your settings.
Do you have the correct printer configured, paper size and plot area? Remember, you do not have to be attached to the printer configured. Refer to Appendix A, Add a Printer / Plotter.
Did you forget to open the drawing before attempting to print?

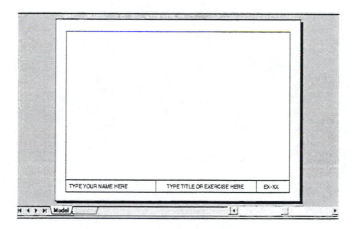

Note: The instructions above are to be used when plotting while in "Model Space". In lesson 26 you will learn how to plot in "Layout" or what is commonly referred to as Paperspace. But you have much more to learn first. Let's just take it step by step and not get confused. You will learn it all by the end of this workbook.

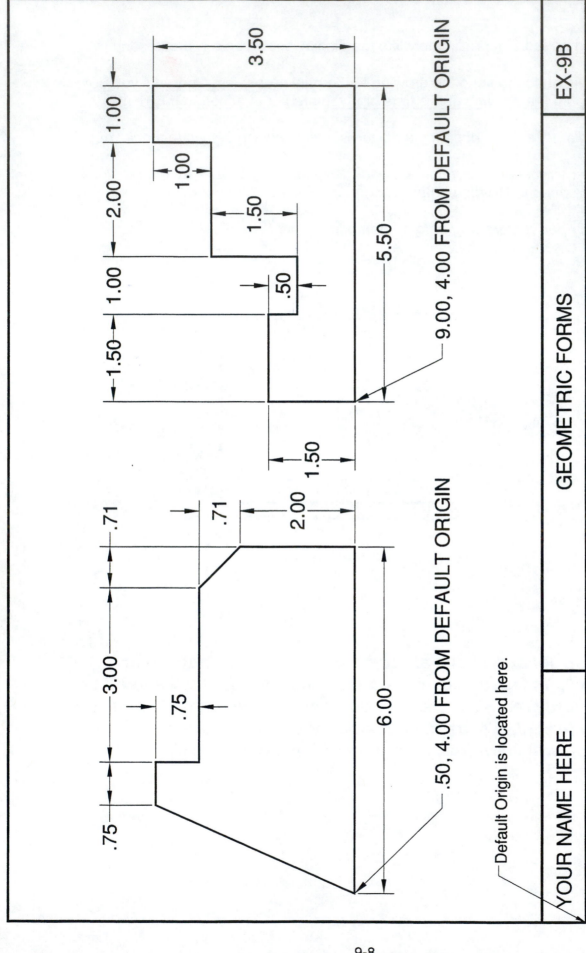

3.50

1.00

1.00

2.00

1.50

1.00

.50

1.50

5.50

9.00, 4.00 FROM DEFAULT ORIGIN

1.50

.71

.71

2.00

3.00

.75

6.00

.50, 4.00 FROM DEFAULT ORIGIN

.75

Default Origin is located here.

YOUR NAME HERE

GEOMETRIC FORMS

EX-9B

EXERCISE 9B

INSTRUCTIONS:
1. Open border **BSIZE.**
2. Draw the objects above by typing the **X** and **Y** coordinates.
3. Use Layer = **Object.**
4. Edit the Title Block text (Refer to page 8-6) <u>Do not erase and replace!</u>
5. Do not dimension.
6. Save as **9B** and **Plot.**

LEARNING OBJECTIVES

After completing this lesson, you will be able to:

1. Move the Origin.
2. Turn the UCS Icon On and Off.
3. Command the UCS Icon to move with the Origin.

LESSON 10

MOVING THE ORIGIN

The ORIGIN is where the X, Y, and Z axes intersect. The Origin's (0,0,0) default location is in the lower left-hand corner of the drawing. But we can move the Origin anywhere on the screen using the UCS command.

You may move the Origin many times while creating a drawing. It will make it much easier to draw objects in the correct locations. You will understand this more after completing 10A, 10B and 10C.

To MOVE the Origin

1. Select one of following:

> **TYPING = UCS <enter>   M <enter>**
> **PULLDOWNS = TOOLS / Move UCS**
> **UCS TOOLBAR =**

Command: _ucs
Current ucs name: *NO NAME*
Enter an option [New/Move/orthoGraphic/Prev/Restore/Save/Del/Apply/?/World]
<World>: *m <enter>*

2. Specify new origin point or [Zdepth]<0,0,0>: *type coordinate or use the cursor to place.*

To RETURN the Origin to the "default" location (the lower left corner):

1. Select one of the following:

> **TYPING = UCS <enter>   W <enter>**
> **PULLDOWNS = TOOLS / New UCS / World**
> **UCS TOOLBAR =**

DISPLAYING THE UCS ICON

The UCS icon is merely a drawing aid. You control how it is displayed.
It can be visible (on) or invisible (off). It can move with the Origin or stay in the default location. You can even change it's appearance.

Select the following pull-down menu:

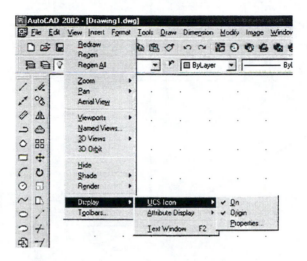

ON: A check mark beside the word ON means the Origin icon will be Visible.
Remove the check mark and the Origin icon will disappear.
It is a good practice to have the Origin Icon "On" most of the time. You will need it as you learn more about AutoCAD. (Set to ON for the workbook exercises)

ORIGIN: A check mark beside the word Origin will move the Origin Icon with the Origin each time you move the Origin. Remove the check mark and the icon will not move. I find it very helpful to know where the Origin is at all times by merely looking for the Origin icon. (Use this setting for the workbook exercises)

PROPERTIES: This setting allows you to change the appearance of the Origin icon.
When you select this option the dialog shown below will appear.
You may change the Style, Size and Color.

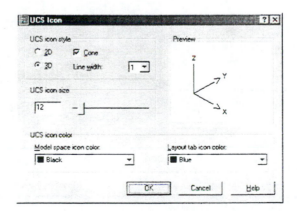

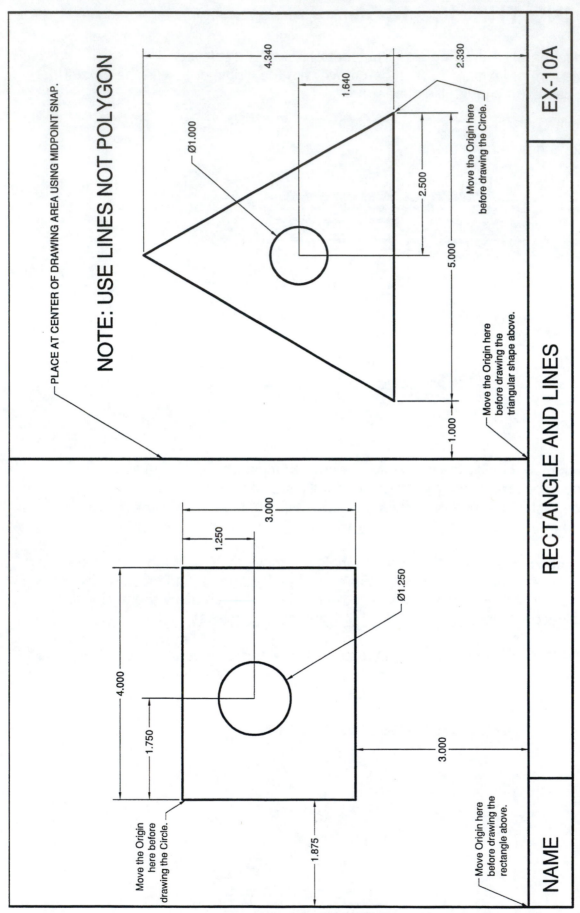

NOTE: USE LINES NOT POLYGON

PLACE AT CENTER OF DRAWING AREA USING MIDPOINT SNAP.

Ø1.000

4.340

1.640

2.330

2.500

5.000

Move the Origin here before drawing the Circle.

1.000

Move the Origin here before drawing the triangular shape above.

3.000

1.250

4.000

1.750

Ø1.250

3.000

1.875

Move the Origin here before drawing the Circle.

Move Origin here before drawing the rectangle above.

RECTANGLE AND LINES

EX-10A

NAME

EXERCISE 10A

INSTRUCTIONS:

1. Open **BSIZE**.
2. Move the Origin to the locations noted, then type X and Y coordinates.
3. Use Layer: **OBJECT**
4. Do not dimension.
5. Edit the Title Block text
6. Save as **10A** and **Plot**.

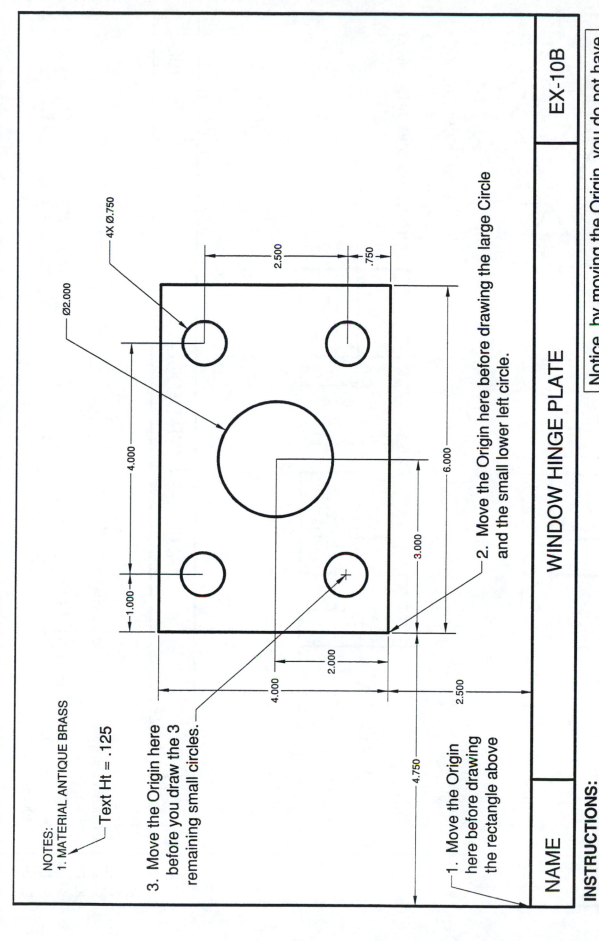

NOTES:
1. MATERIAL ANTIQUE BRASS

Text Ht = .125

Ø2.000

4X Ø.750

2.500

.750

4.000

1.000

6.000

3.000

2.000

4.000

2.500

4.750

3. Move the Origin here before you draw the 3 remaining small circles.

2. Move the Origin here before drawing the large Circle and the small lower left circle.

1. Move the Origin here before drawing the rectangle above

Notice, by moving the Origin, you do not have to add or subtract dimensions. You merely type the X and Y coordinates.

EXERCISE 10B

WINDOW HINGE PLATE

EX-10B

NAME

INSTRUCTIONS:
1. Open **BSIZE.**
2. Move the Origin then type the X and Y coordinates.
3. Use Layer: **OBJECT** and **TXT-LIT** (for the note in the upper left corner).
4. Do not dimension.
5. Edit the Title Block text.
6. Save as **10B** and **Plot.**

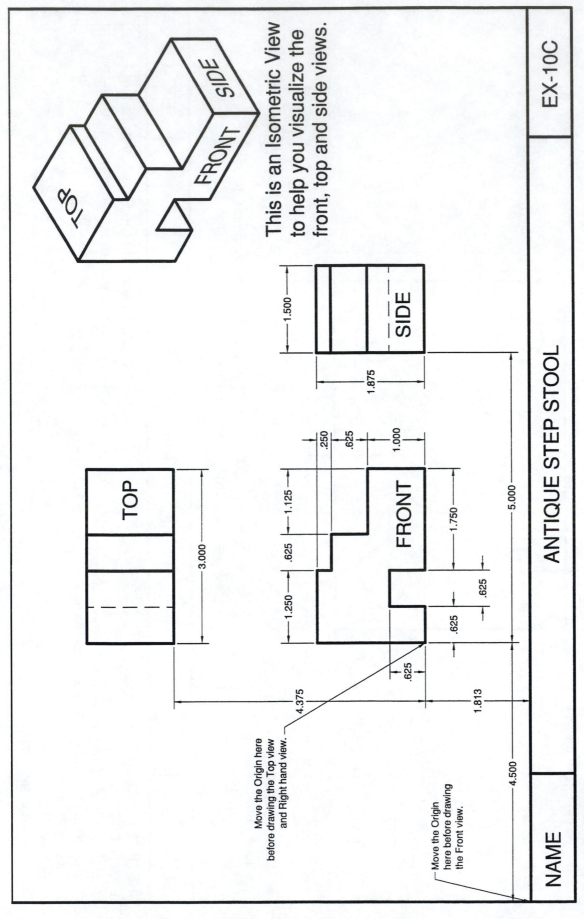

This is an Isometric View to help you visualize the front, top and side views.

Move the Origin here before drawing the Top view and Right hand view.

Move the Origin here before drawing the Front view.

EX-10C

ANTIQUE STEP STOOL

NAME

EXERCISE 10C

INSTRUCTIONS:

1. Open **BSIZE**.
2. Move the origin and enter X and Y coordinates and DDE.
3. Do not dimension.
4. Use Layer: **OBJECT** and **HIDDEN** (for hidden lines).
5. Edit the Title Block text.
6. Save as **10C** and **Plot**.

10-6

LEARNING OBJECTIVES

After completing this lesson, you will be able to:

1. Understand the Polar Degree Clock.
2. Draw Lines to a specific length and angle
3. Draw Objects using Polar Coordinate Input.
4. Use Polar Tracking.
5. Construct an Isometric view.

LESSON 11

POLAR COORDINATE INPUT

In Lesson 9 we learned to control the length and direction of horizontal and vertical lines using Relative Input and Direct Distance Entry. Now we will learn how to control the length and **ANGLE** of a line using **POLAR COORDINATE INPUT**.

UNDERSTANDING THE *"POLAR DEGREE CLOCK"*

Previously when drawing Horizontal and Vertical lines you controlled the direction using a <u>Positive</u> or <u>Negative</u> input. ***Polar Input is different.*** The Angle of the line will determine the direction. For example: to draw a line at a 45 degree angle toward the upper right corner, use the angle 45. But to draw a line at a 45 degree angle toward the lower left corner, use the angle 225. You may also use Polar Input for Horizontal and Vertical lines using the angles 0, 90, 180 and 270. No negative input is required.

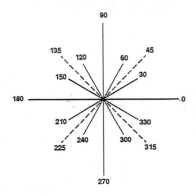

DRAWING WITH *POLAR COORDINATE INPUT*

A Polar coordinate may come ***from the last point entered*** or ***from the Origin,*** depending upon whether you use the @ symbol or not. The first number represents the **Distance** and the second number represents the **Angle**. The two numbers are separated by the **less than (<) symbol**.
The format is: **distance < angle**

A Polar coordinate of **@6<45** will be 6 units long and at an angle of 45 degrees ***from the last point entered.***

A Polar coordinate of **6<45** will be 6 units and 45 degrees from the ***Origin.***

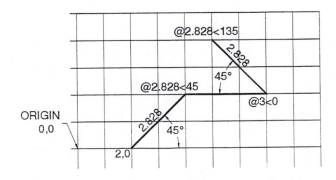

POLAR TRACKING

Polar Tracking can be used in place of **ORTHO**. When *Polar Tracking* is "**ON**", a dotted *"tracking"* line and a *"tool tip"* box appear and "snaps" to a **preset angle increment** when the cursor approaches one of the preset angles. The word *"Polar"*, followed by the *"distance"* and *"angle"* from the last point, appears in the box. (A step by step example is described on the next page.)

SETTING THE ANGLE INCREMENT

1. Right Click on the POLAR button on the Status Bar and select "**SETTINGS**" or Select **Tools / Drafting Settings / Polar Tracking** tab. The following dialog box will appear:

2. Set the Increment Angle to: 15

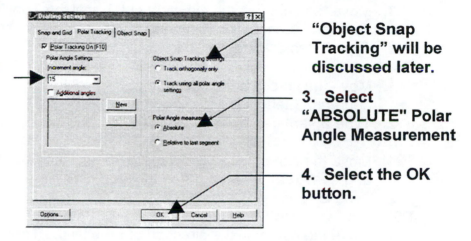

"Object Snap Tracking" will be discussed later.

3. Select "ABSOLUTE" Polar Angle Measurement

4. Select the OK button.

POLAR ANGLE SETTINGS

Increment Angle   Choose from a list of Angle increments including 90, 45, 30, 22.5, 18, 15,10 and 5. You will be able to "snap" to multiples of that angle.

Additional Angles   Check this box if you would like to use an angle other than one listed above.

New   You may add an angle by selecting the "New" button. You will be able to snap to this new angle in addition to the incremental Angle selected. But you will not be able to snap to it's multiple.

Delete   Deletes an Additional Angle. Select the Additional angle to be deleted and then the Delete button.

POLAR ANGLE MEASUREMENT

ABSOLUTE   Polar tracking <u>angles</u> are relative to the UCS.

RELATIVE TO LAST SEGMENT   Polar tracking <u>angles</u> are relative to the last segment.

USING POLAR TRACKING AND DIRECT DISTANCE ENTRY

1. Use the Polar Tracking Settings from the previous page.
2. Set the Status Bar as follows: | SNAP | GRID | ORTHO | | POLAR | OSNAP | OTRACK | LWT | | MODEL |

| OFF | ON | OFF | ON | OFF | OFF | OFF | ON |

3. **Select the Line command**:
   P1
   1. Start the Line anywhere on the in the drawing area.
   P2
   1. Move the cursor in the direction of P2 until the Tool Tip box displays 30 degrees. (Length is not important yet)
   2. Type 2 <enter> (for the length)
   P3
   1. Move the cursor in the direction of P3 until the Tool Tip box displays 90 degrees. (Length is not important yet)
   2. Type 2 <enter> (for the length)
   P4
   1. Move the cursor in the direction of P4 until the Tool Tip box displays 0 degrees. (Length is not important yet)
   2. Type 2 <enter> (for the length)
   P5
   1. Move the cursor in the direction of P5 until the Tool Tip box displays 150 degrees. (Length is not important yet)
   2. Type 2 <enter> (for the length)
   P6
   1. Move the cursor in the direction of P6 until the Tool Tip box displays 180 degrees. (Length is not important yet)
   2. Type 2 <enter> (for the length)
   3. Then type C for close.

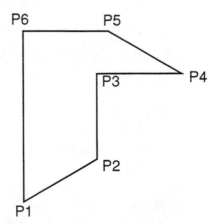

POLAR TRACKING ON or OFF

You may toggle Polar Tracking On or Off using one of the following:
- Left click on the POLAR button on the Status Bar
- Press F10

POLAR SNAP

Polar Snap is used with Polar Tracking to make the cursor snap to specific ***distances*** and ***angles***. If you set Polar Snap distance to 1 and Polar Tracking to angle 30 you can draw lines 1, 2, 3, 4 units... long at an angle of 30, 60, 90 etc. without typing anything on the command line. You just move the mouse and watch the tool tips. (A step by step example is described on the next page)

SETTING THE ANGLE INCREMENT

1. Right Click on the POLAR button on the Status Bar and select "SETTINGS" or select **Tools / Drafting Settings / Polar Tracking** tab.
   The following dialog box will appear:

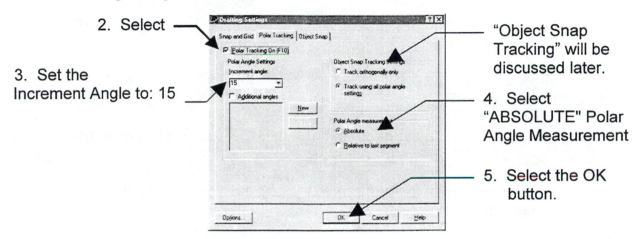

2. Select

3. Set the Increment Angle to: 15

"Object Snap Tracking" will be discussed later.

4. Select "ABSOLUTE" Polar Angle Measurement

5. Select the OK button.

SETTING THE POLAR SNAP

1. Right Click on the SNAP button on the Status Bar and select "SETTINGS" or select **Tools / Drafting Settings / Snap and Grid** tab.
   The following dialog box will appear:

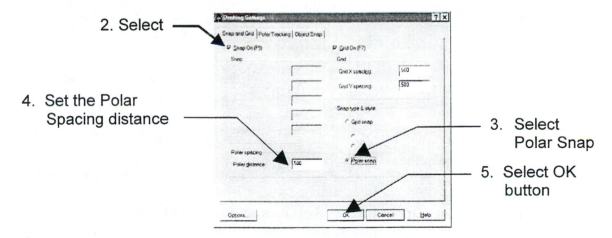

2. Select

4. Set the Polar Spacing distance

3. Select Polar Snap

5. Select OK button

SNAP AND GRID   Sets standard snap and grid information
POLAR SPACING   Increment Snap distance when Polar Snap is ON.
STYLE   This setting will be taught in the Advanced course.
TYPE   Sets the Snap to Polar or Grid

USING POLAR TRACKING AND POLAR SNAP

Now let's draw the objects below again, but this time with "Polar Snap" instead of Direct Distance Entry.

1. Use the Polar Tracking and Polar Snap Settings from the previous page.

2. Set the Status Bar as follows: |SNAP|GRID|ORTHO||POLAR|OSNAP|OTRACK|LWT||MODEL|

    ON   ON OFF   ON OFF   OFF   OFF   ON

3. Select the Line command:
    P1
    1. Start the Line anywhere in the drawing area.

    P2
    1. Move the cursor in the direction of P2 until the Tool Tip box displays **Polar 2.00 <30°**

    P3
    1. Move the cursor in the direction of P3 until the Tool Tip box displays **Polar 2.00 <90°**

    P4
    1. Move the cursor in the direction of P4 until the Tool Tip box displays **Polar 2.00 <0°**

    P5
    1. Move the cursor in the direction of P5 until the Tool Tip box displays **Polar 2.00 <150°**

    P6
    1. Move the cursor in the direction of P6 until the Tool Tip box displays **Polar 2.00 <180°**
    2. Then type C for close.

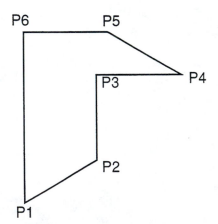

NOTE: You may OVERRIDE the Polar Settings at any time by typing:
@ Length< Angle   at the Command line.

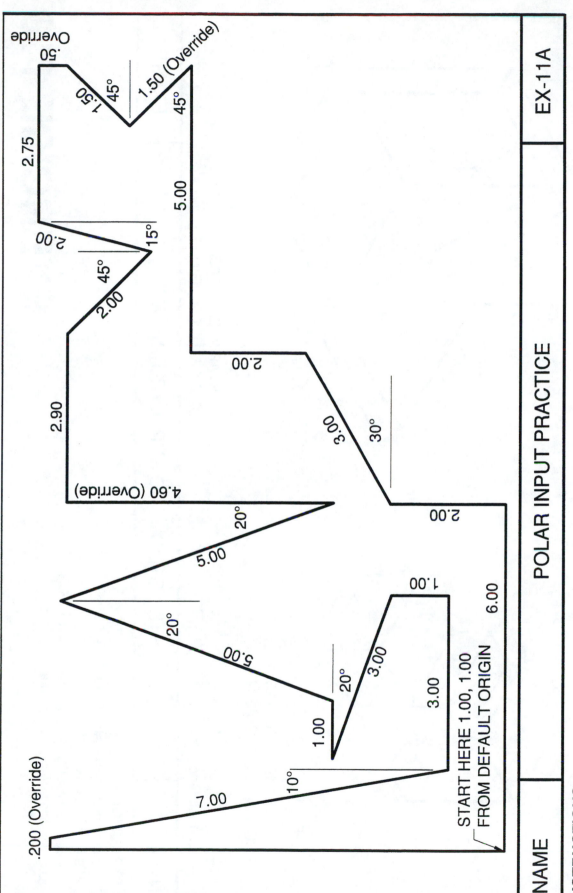

NAME

POLAR INPUT PRACTICE

EX-11A

EXERCISE 11A

INSTRUCTIONS:

1. Draw the lines above using POLAR TRACKING.
2. Start the first endpoint using ABSOLUTE COORDINATES.
3. Set the Polar Angle to 10° and Polar Distance to 1.00.
4. You may have to Override some of the settings. (Read Note on bottom of page 11-5)
5. Save as 11A and Plot.

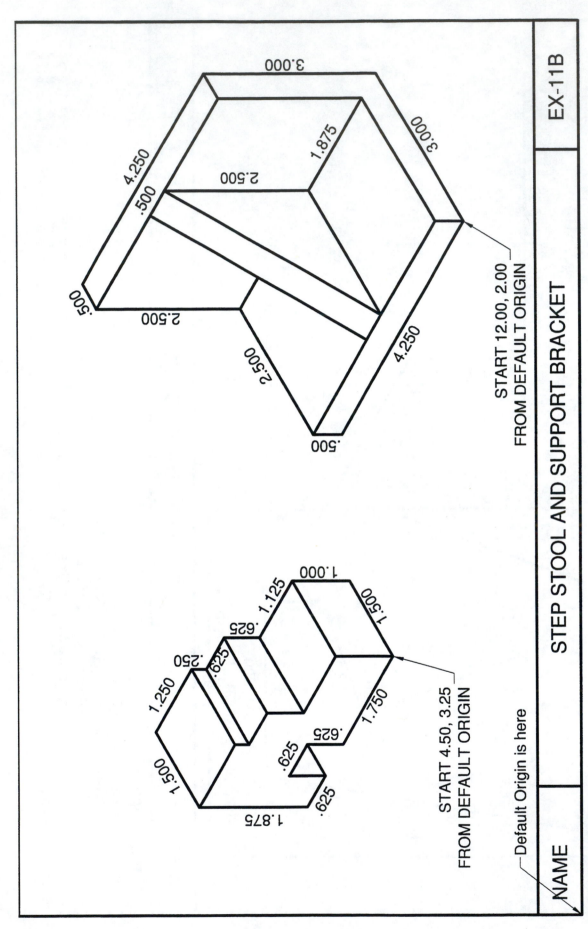

EXERCISE 11B

EX-11B

STEP STOOL AND SUPPORT BRACKET

Diagram labels (top figure):
- 3.000
- 4.250
- 1.875
- 2.500
- .500
- 3.000
- .500
- 2.500
- 2.500
- .500
- 4.250
- .500
- START 12.00, 2.00 FROM DEFAULT ORIGIN

Diagram labels (bottom figure):
- 1.000
- 1.125
- .625
- .250
- .625
- 1.250
- 1.500
- 1.500
- .625
- .625
- 1.750
- 1.875
- .625
- .625
- START 4.50, 3.25 FROM DEFAULT ORIGIN

— Default Origin is here

NAME

INSTRUCTIONS:

1. Draw the lines above using POLAR TRACKING.
2. The Isometric lines are 30°.
3. You decide what POLAR DISTANCE or use DDE.
4. Location and size must be accurate.

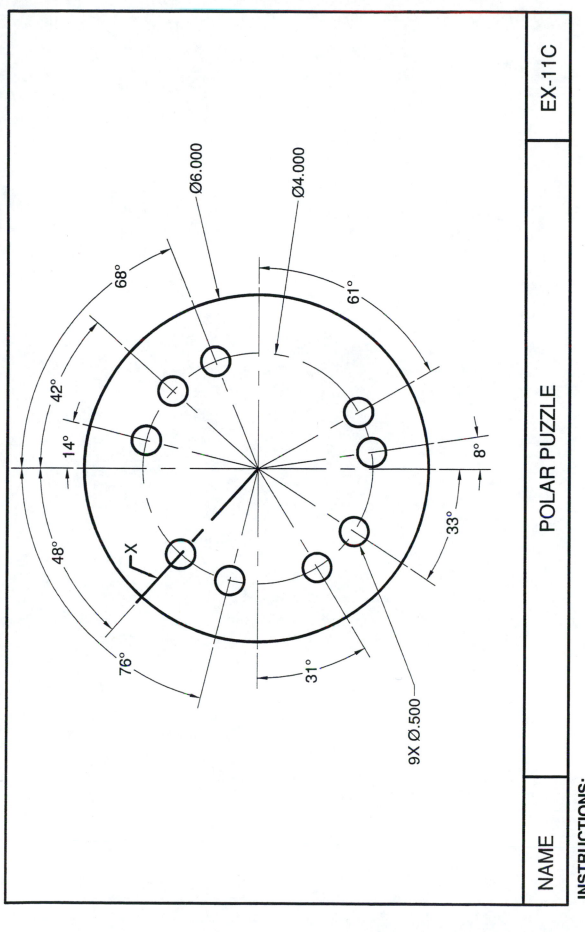

Ø6.000

Ø4.000

68°

61°

42°

14°

48°

76°

8°

33°

31°

X

9X Ø.500

| NAME | POLAR PUZZLE | EX-11C |

EXERCISE 11C

INSTRUCTIONS:

This time polar snap and tracking will not be helpful. You will have to use basic polar coordinates. For example, the line marked "X" can be drawn as follows:

1. Place the first endpoint by snapping to the "center" of the Circle.
2. Now type @3.125<138 <enter>.

The length is .125 beyond the radius of the circle and the angle is 90 +48=138 (adding in the CCW direction).

Now see if you can figure out the remaining angles. (Refer to 11-2 for angles)

NOTES:

LEARNING OBJECTIVES

After completing this lesson, you will be able to:

1. Duplicate an object at a specified distance away.
2. Make changes to an object's properties.

LESSON 12

OFFSET

The **OFFSET** command duplicates an object parallel to the original object at a specified distance away. The new object will retain the same color, layer and linetype of the original.

1. Select the OFFSET command using one of the following:

   TYPING = OFFSET
   PULLDOWN = MODIFY / OFFSET
   TOOLBAR = MODIFY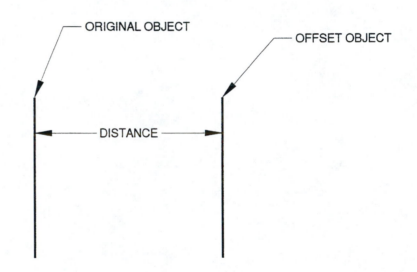

2. Specify offset distance or [Through] <Through>: *type the offset distance*
3. Select object to offset or <exit>: *select the object to offset*
4. Specify point on side to offset: *Select which side of the original you want the duplicate to appear, by placing your cursor and clicking.*
5. Select object to offset or <exit>: *Press <enter> to stop.*

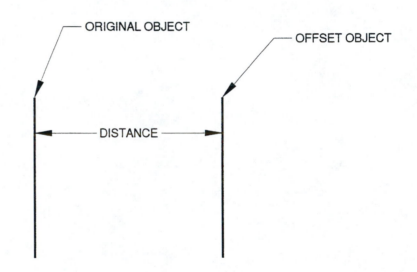

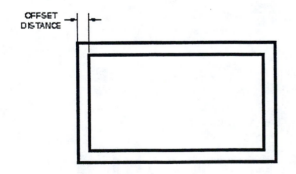

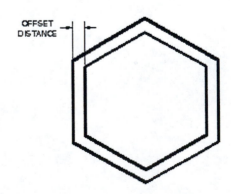

MODIFY PROPERTIES

The Properties dialog box, shown below, makes it possible to change an object's properties. You simply open the modify properties dialog box and you can change any of the properties that are displayed.

To open the Modify Properties dialog box, double click on the object that you want to change. You may view the properties by Category or Alphabetic.

Once the dialog box is opened, it remains on the screen until you close it by clicking on the "**X**" in the upper right corner or press Ctrl + 1.
Ctrl + 1 can be used to toggle the Properties dialog box Open or Close.

Open the Properties dialog box by double clicking on an object or use one of the following:

TYPING = PROPERTIES or PROPS or CH
PULLDOWN = MODIFY / PROPERTIES
TOOLBAR = OBJECT PROPERTIES
KEYS = CTRL + 1

Click here to close
or Ctrl + 1

MODIFY PROPERTIES
Dialog Box

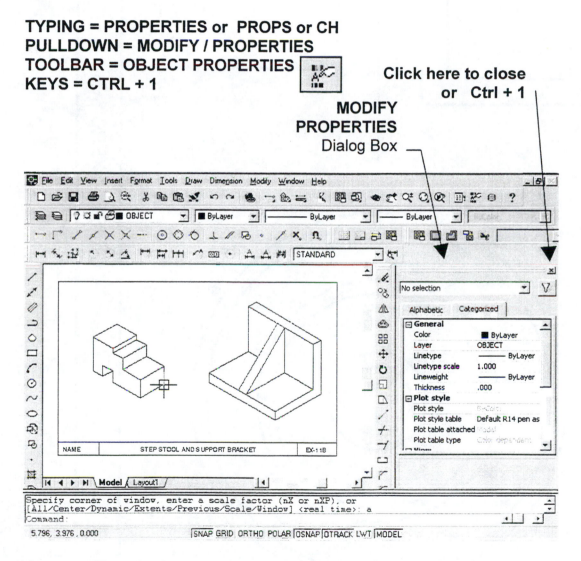

*Note: You must "Deselect" a previously selected object before selecting another object to change, unless the changes are the same for both objects. To "**Deselect an object**", press the ESC key or press the right mouse button and select "Deselect" from the short cut menu.*

EXERCISE 12A

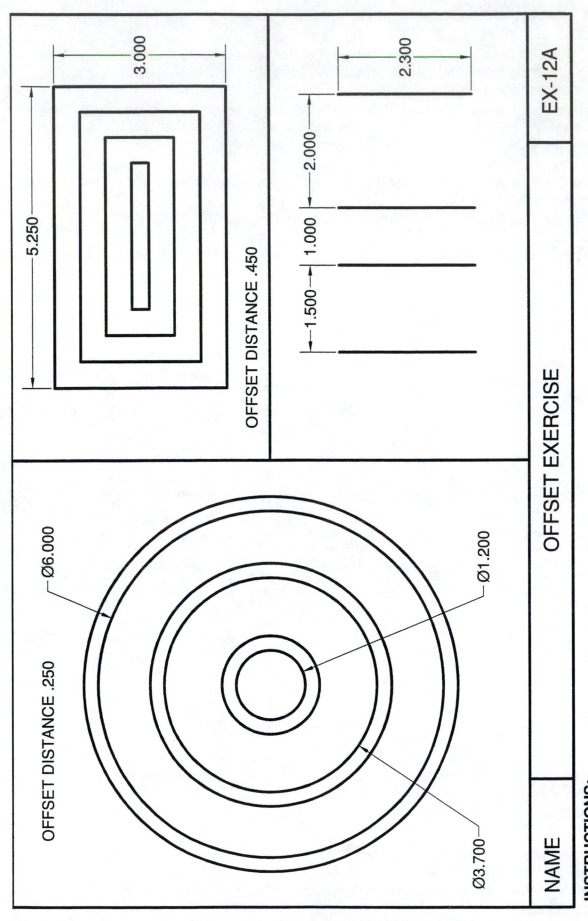

3.000

2.300

5.250

2.000

1.000

1.500

OFFSET DISTANCE .450

EX-12A

Ø6.000

Ø1.200

Ø3.700

OFFSET DISTANCE .250

OFFSET EXERCISE

NAME

INSTRUCTIONS:

1. Draw the objects above using:
   Circles, Rectangles, Lines and Offset.

2. Save as: **EX-12A**

WINDOW SCHEDULE

SYM	SIZE	TYPE	GLAZING
A	5'-0" X 4'-0"	WOOD FIXED	3/16" SHEET
B	3'-0" X 4'-0"	WOOD FIXED	3/16" SHEET
C	3'-0" X 3'-0"	WOOD FIXED	3/16" SHEET
D	2'-0" X 3'-0"	ALUMINUM SLIDER	3/16" SHEET

TEXT HT. = 3/16"

TEXT HT. = 1/8"

TEXT HT. = 1/8"

6-1/4"

3/8" 1/2" 1/4"

1/16"

1/2" 1-3/4" 2-1/2" 1-1/2" 1/16"

HOW TO LOCATE THE MIDDLE OF EACH AREA.
Draw a diagonal line from corner to corner of each area. Use justification MIDDLE. Snap to Midpoint of the diagonal line.

SIZE

EX-12B

EXERCISE 12B

NAME		WINDOW SCHEDULE

INSTRUCTIONS:

1. Draw the Window Schedule above using:

   Line, Offset and Text (**Use** Single line text. **Do not** use Multiline text)

2. Use Layer: Border for lines. Layer: Text-Hvy for Titles. Layer: Text-lit for descriptions.

3. Save as: **EX-12B**

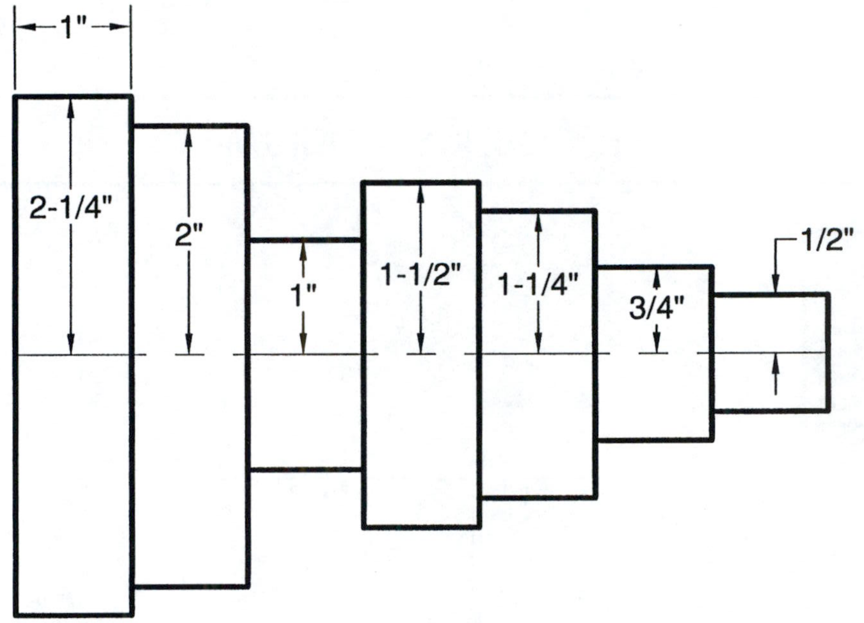

OFFSET AND MIRROR EXERCISE

EXERCISE 12C

EX-12C

NAME

12-6

INSTRUCTIONS:

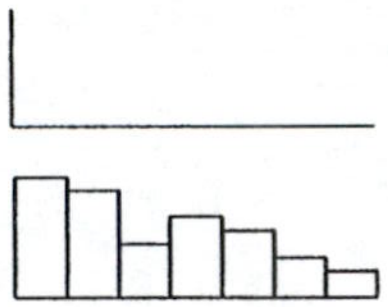

1. Draw a horizontal and vertical line.
2. Draw the upper half using OFFSET.
3. Trim all excess lines.
4. MIRROR the upper half.
5. Change the layer of the center line using MODIFY / PROPERTIES.
6. Save as: EX-12C.

Dimensions shown on drawing:
1/2"
3/4"
1-1/4"
1-1/2"
1"
2"
2-1/4"
1"

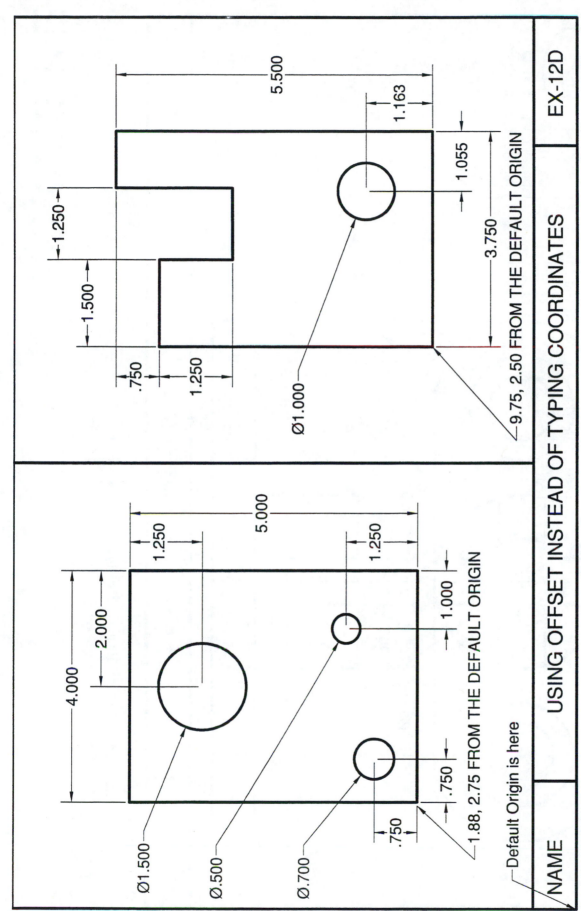

EXERCISE 12D

5.500

1.163

1.055

3.750

1.250

1.500

.750

1.250

Ø1.000

9.75, 2.50 FROM THE DEFAULT ORIGIN

5.000

1.250

1.250

2.000

4.000

1.000

.750

.750

Ø1.500

Ø.500

Ø.700

1.88, 2.75 FROM THE DEFAULT ORIGIN

Default Origin is here

| NAME | USING OFFSET INSTEAD OF TYPING COORDINATES | EX-12D |

INSTRUCTIONS:

1. Draw the Objects above using:
   Offset, Line, Circle and Trim.
   (Do not type coordinates. Create Intersections by offsetting the lines)

2. Save as: **EX-12D**

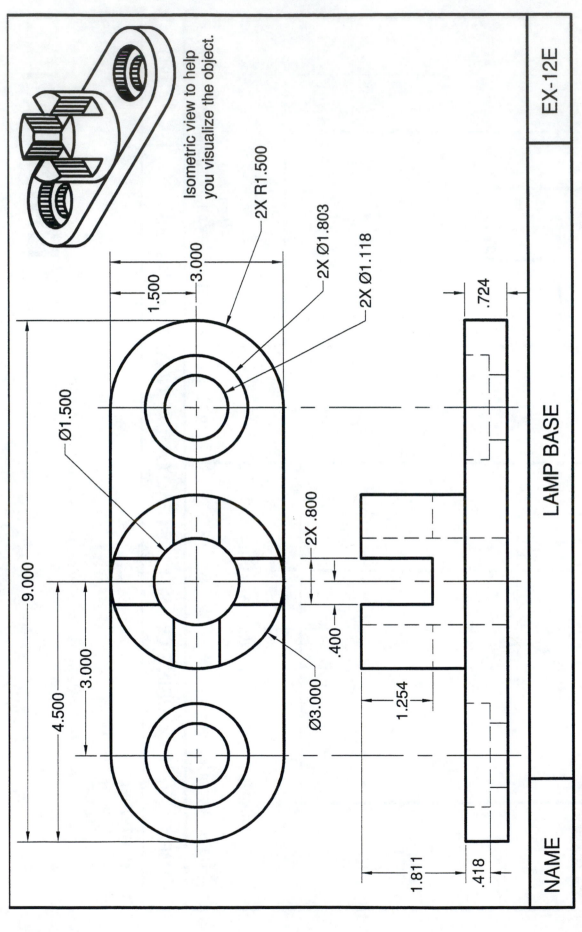

Isometric view to help you visualize the object.

2X R1.500

2X Ø1.803

2X Ø1.118

3.000

1.500

Ø1.500

9.000

4.500

3.000

Ø3.000

2X .800

.400

1.254

1.811

.418

.724

LAMP BASE

EX-12E

EXERCISE 12E

INSTRUCTIONS:

1. Draw the Objects above. You decide the best method.
   Note: It is Symmetrical.

2. Save as: **EX-12E**

NAME

LEARNING OBJECTIVES

After completing this lesson, you will be able to:

1. Create multiple copies in a rectangular or Circular pattern.

LESSON 13

ARRAY

The ARRAY command allows you to make multiple copies in a **RECTANGULAR** or Circular **(POLAR)** pattern. The maximum limit of copies per array is 100,000. This limit can be changed but should accommodate most users.

RECTANGULAR ARRAY
The method allows you to make multiple copies of object(s) in a rectangular pattern. You specify the number of rows (horizontal), columns (vertical) and the offset distance between the rows and columns. The offset distances will be equally spaced.

Offset Distance is sometimes tricky to understand. *Read this carefully*. The offset distance is the distance from a specific location on the original to that same location on the invisible copy. It is not just the space in between the two. Refer to the example below.

To use the rectangular array command you will select the object(s), specify how many rows and columns desired and the offset distance for the rows and the columns. **Step by step instructions on page 13-3.**

Example of Rectangular Array:

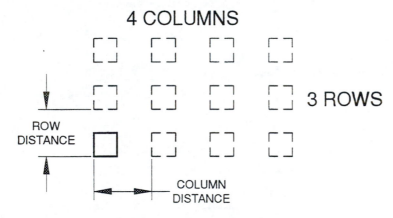

Example of Rectangular Array on an angle.
Notice the copies do not rotate. The Angle is only used to establish the placement.

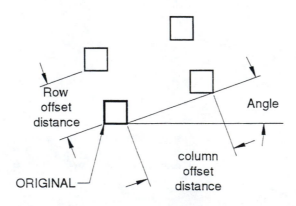

ARRAY (Continued)

RECTANGULAR ARRAY

1. Select the ARRAY command using one of the following:

> **TYPE = ARRAY**
> **PULLDOWN = MODIFY / ARRAY**
> **TOOLBAR = MODIFY**

The dialog shown below will appear.

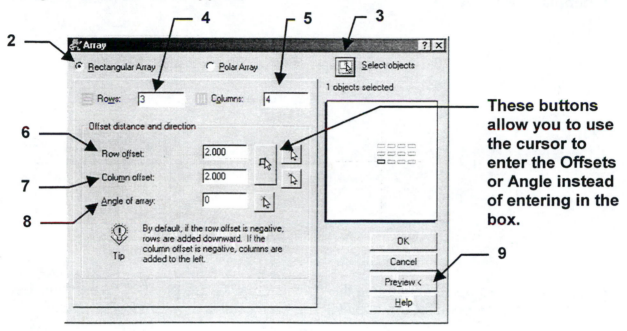

These buttons allow you to use the cursor to enter the Offsets or Angle instead of entering in the box.

2. Select "**Rectangular Array**"

3. Select the **"Select Objects"** button.
   This will take you back to your drawing. Select the objects to Array then <enter>

4. Enter the number of rows.

5. Enter the number of columns.

6. Enter the row offset. (The distance from a specific location on the original to that same specific location on the future copy) See example on pg. 13-2.

7. Enter the column offset. (The distance from a specific location on the original to that same specific location on the future copy) See example on pg. 13-2.

8. Enter an angle if you would like the array to be on an angle.

9. Select the Preview button.
   If it looks correct, select the Accept button. If it is not correct, select the Modify button, make the necessary corrections and preview again.
   (Note: if the Preview button is gray, you have forgotten to "Select objects"- #3)

ARRAY (continued)

POLAR ARRAY

This method allows you to make multiple copies in a circular pattern. You specify the total number of copies to fill a specific Angle or specify the angle between each copy and angle to fill.

To use the polar array command you select the object(s) to copy, specify the center of the array, specify the number of copies or the angle between the copies, the angle to fill and if you would like the copies to rotate as they are copied.

Example of Polar Array

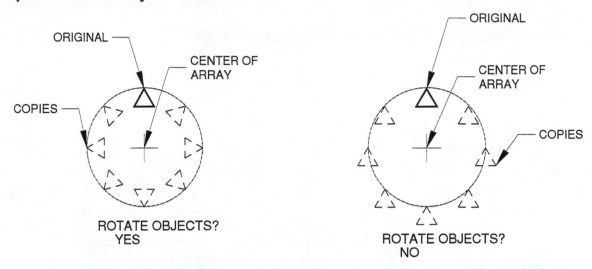

Note: the two examples above use the objects default base point. The example below specifies the base point for the copies. The end result is different from the example above right.

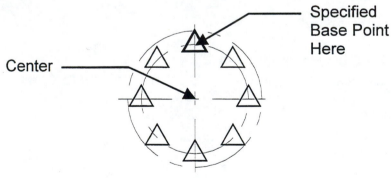

The difference between "Center Point" and "Objects Base Point" is sometimes confusing. When specifying the Center Point, try to visualize the copies already there. Now focus on the center of that array. In other words, it is the Pivot Point from which the copies will be placed around. The Base Point will be located on the original object.

ARRAY (continued)

POLAR ARRAY

1. Select the ARRAY command using one of the following:

> **TYPE = ARRAY**
> **PULLDOWN = MODIFY / ARRAY**
> **TOOLBAR = MODIFY**

The dialog shown below will appear.

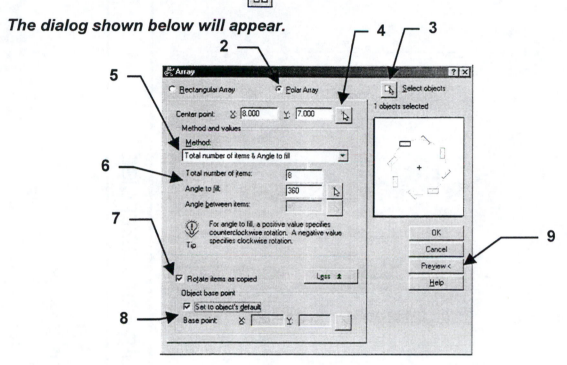

2. Select " **Polar Array"**

3. Select the **"Select Objects"** button.
   This will take you back to your drawing. Select the objects to Array then <enter>

4. Press the "Center Point" button and select the center point with the cursor or enter the X and Y coordinates in the "Center Point" boxes.

5. Select the method.

6. Enter the "Total number of items", "Angle to fill" and or "Angle between items".

7. Select whether you want the items rotated as copied or not. (See pg. 13-4 for explanation)

8. Accept the objects default base point or enter the X and Y coordinates.

9. Select the Preview button.
   If it looks correct, select the Accept button. If it is not correct, select the Modify button, make the necessary corrections and preview again.
   (Note: if the Preview button is gray, you have forgotten to select objects #3)

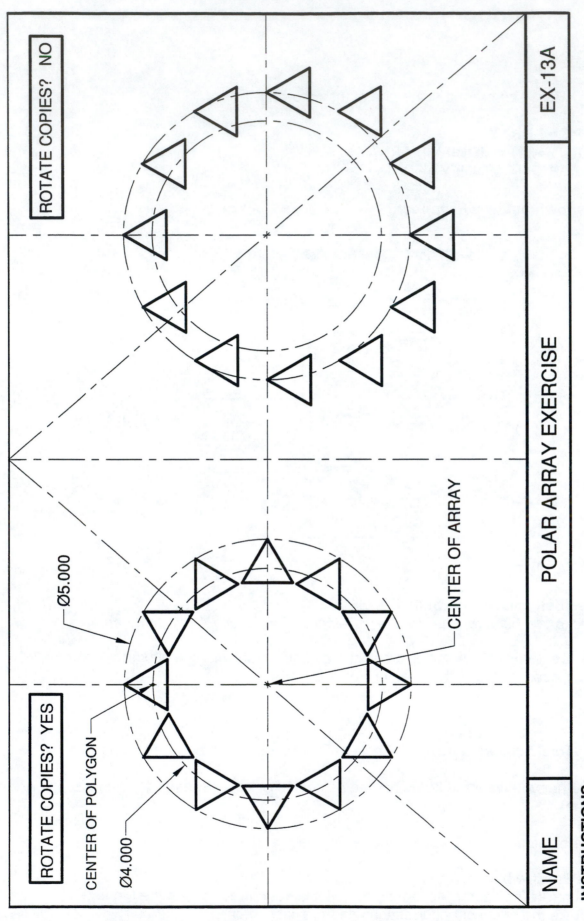

EXERCISE 13A

ROTATE COPIES? NO

ROTATE COPIES? YES

CENTER OF POLYGON

Ø5.000

Ø4.000

CENTER OF ARRAY

NAME

POLAR ARRAY EXERCISE

EX-13A

INSTRUCTIONS:

1. Draw the Centerlines and Circles first. (layer: Center)
2. Draw the **Original Polygon** (Inscribed, R.1/2") at the **12:00 position.**
3. Using Polar Array, array the original Polygon.
4. Number of items: **12**
5. Save as: **EX-13A**

13-6

EX-13B

RECTANGULAR ARRAY EXERCISE

EXERCISE 13B

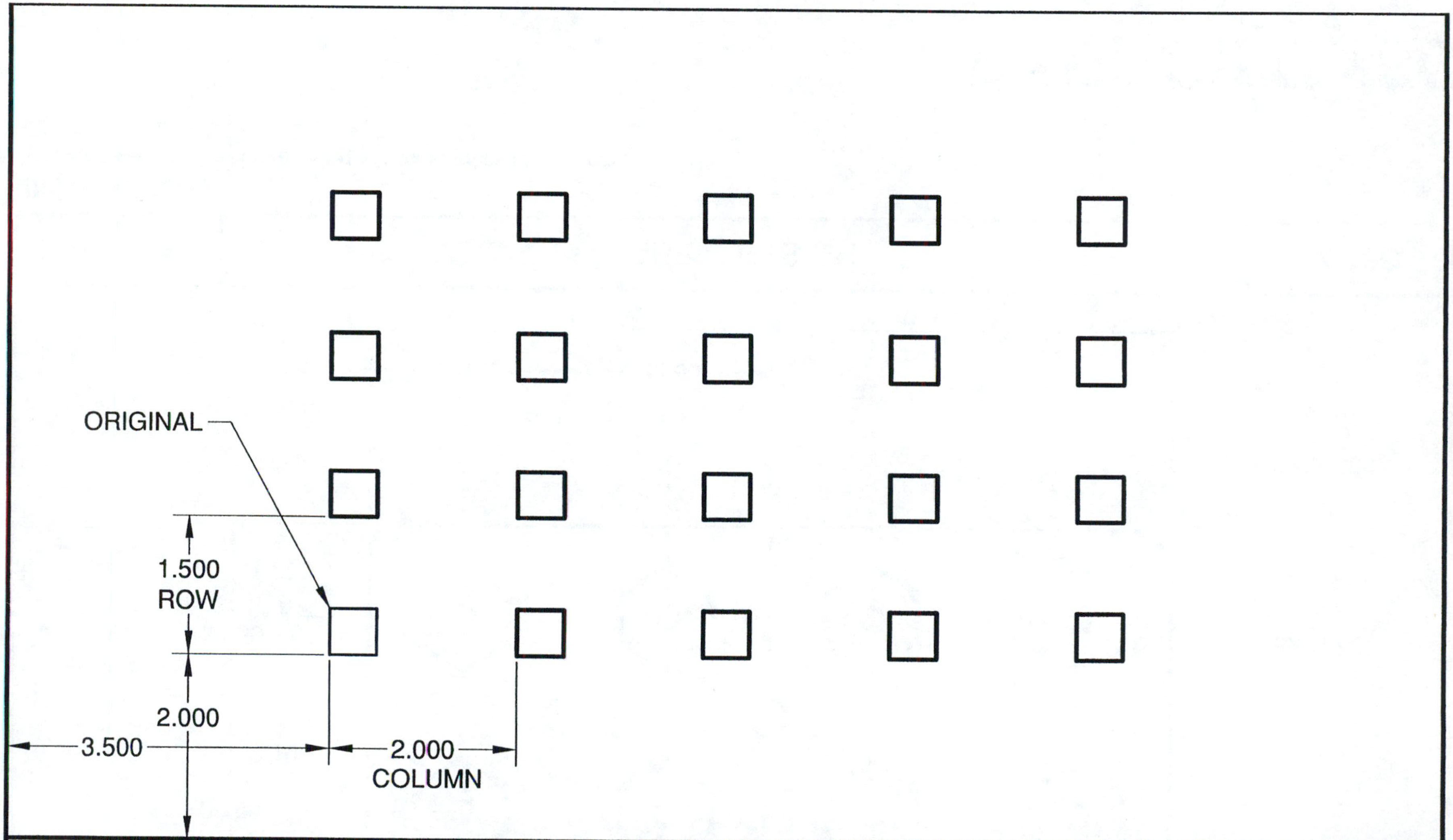

ORIGINAL

2.000
COLUMN

1.500
ROW

2.000

3.500

INSTRUCTIONS:

1. Draw the lower left RECTANGLE first. .500 Square. (layer: Object)
2. Using Rectangular Array, array the original Rectangle as shown.
   No. of Rows = 4   No. of Columns = 5
   Distance between Rows = 1.500   Distance between columns = 2.000
4. Save as: **EX-13B**

NAME

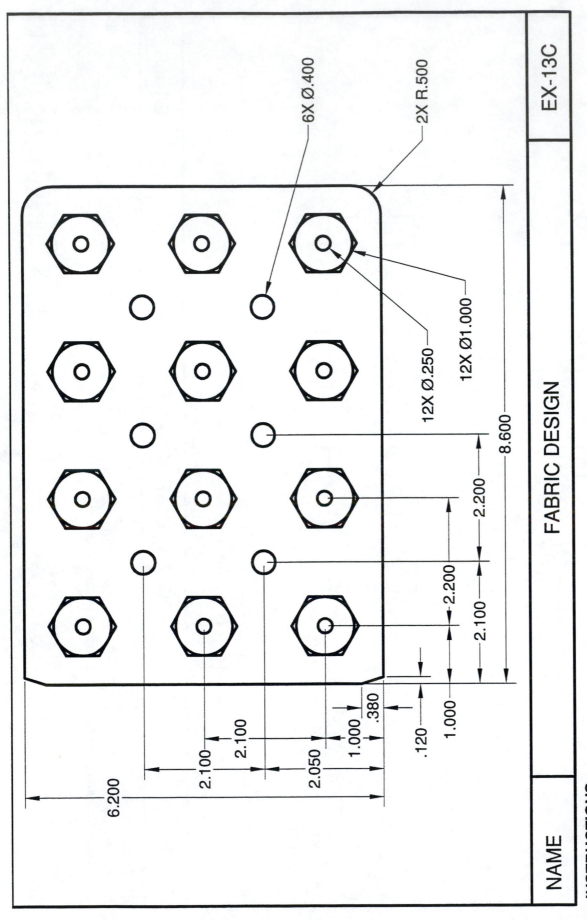

EXERCISE 13C

EX-13C

6X Ø.400

2X R.500

12X Ø.250

12X Ø1.000

8.600

2.200

2.200

2.100

6.200

2.100

2.100

2.050

1.000

.380

.120

1.000

FABRIC DESIGN

NAME

INSTRUCTIONS:

1. Draw the objects above using the most efficient methods.

2. Save as: **EX-13C**

13-8

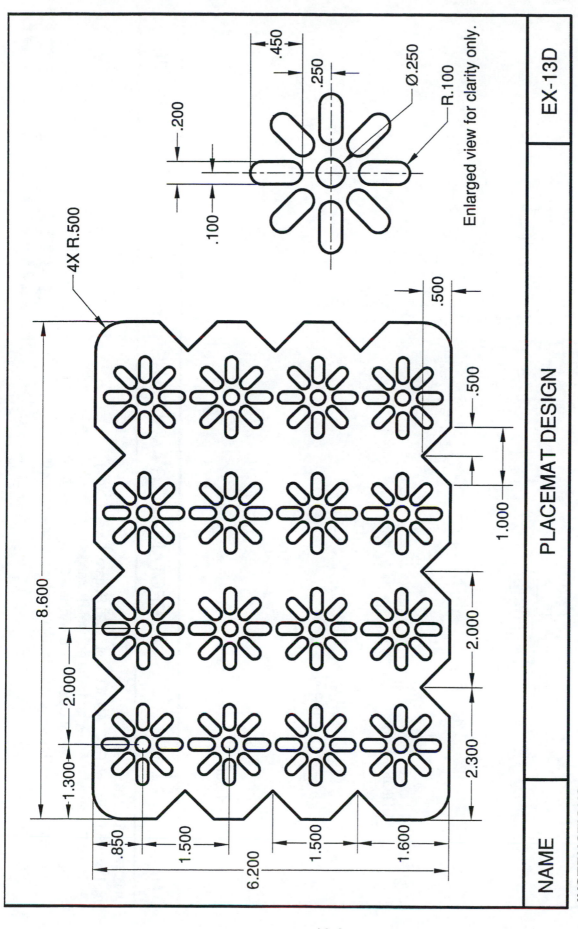

.450

.200

.250

Ø.250

R.100

.100

Enlarged view for clarity only.

4X R.500

8.600

.500

.500

1.000

2.000

2.000

2.300

.850

1.500

1.500

1.600

6.200

1.300

EX-13D

PLACEMAT DESIGN

NAME

EXERCISE 13D

INSTRUCTIONS:

1. Draw the objects above using the most efficient methods.
2. Save as: **EX-13D**

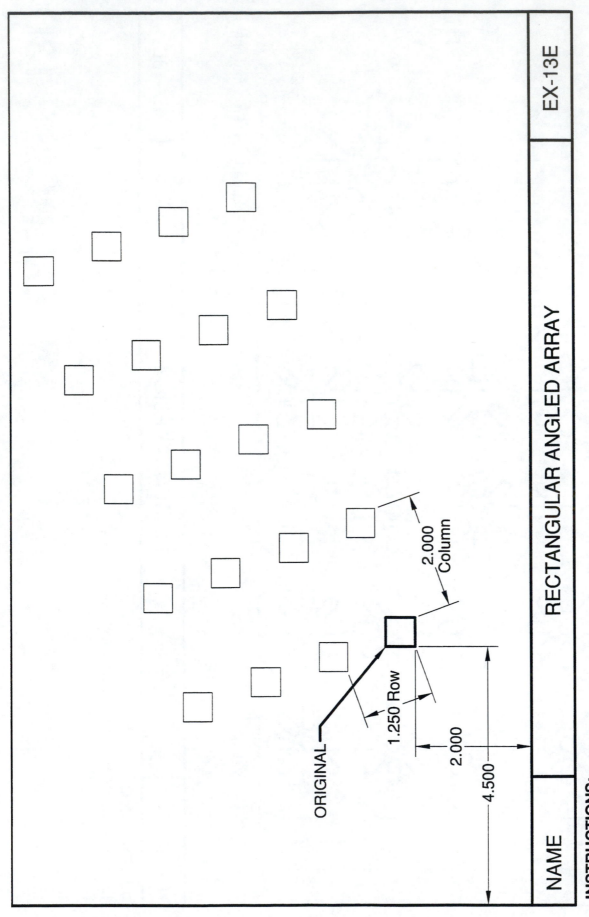

EXERCISE 13E

NAME	RECTANGULAR ANGLED ARRAY	EX-13E

INSTRUCTIONS:

1. Draw the lower left RECTANGLE first. .500 Square. (layer: Object)
2. Using Rectangular Array, array the original Rectangle as shown.
   No. of Rows = 4   No. of Columns = 5   Angle = 20
   Distance between Rows = 1.250   Distance between columns = 2.000
4. Save as: **EX-13E**

2.000
Column

ORIGINAL

1.250 Row

2.000

4.500

13-10

LEARNING OBJECTIVES

After completing this lesson, you will be able to:

1. Make an existing object larger or smaller proportionately.
2. Stretch or compress an existing object.
3. Rotate an existing object to a specific angle.

LESSON 14

SCALE

The **SCALE** command is used to make objects larger or smaller <u>proportionately</u>. You may scale using a scale factor or a reference length. You must also specify a base point. Think of the base point as a stationary point from which the objects scale. It does not move.

Select the SCALE command using one of the following:

> **TYPE = SCALE**
> **PULLDOWN = MODIFY / SCALE**
> **TOOLBAR = MODIFY**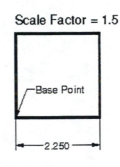

SCALE FACTOR

Command: _scale
2. Select objects: *select the object(s) to be scaled*
3. Select objects: *select more object(s) or <enter> to stop*
4. Specify base point: *select the stationary point on the object*
5. Specify scale factor or [Reference]: *type the <u>scale factor </u><enter>*

If the scale factor is greater than 1, the objects will increase in size. If the scale factor is less than 1, the objects will decrease in size.

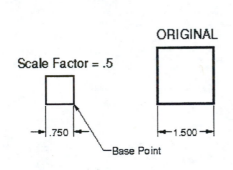

REFERENCE

Command: _scale
2. Select objects: *select the object(s) to be scaled*
3. Select objects: *select more object(s) or <enter> to stop*
4. Specify base point: *select the stationary point on the object*
5. Specify scale factor or [Reference]: *select Reference*
6. Specify reference length <1>: *specify a <u>reference</u> length*
7. Specify new length: *specify the new length*

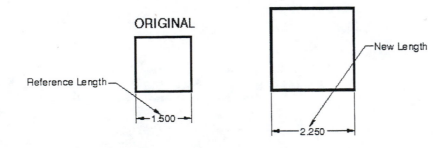

STRETCH

The **STRETCH** command allows you to stretch or compress object(s). Unlike the Scale command, you can alter an objects proportions with the Stretch command. In other words, you may increase the length without changing the width and vice versa.

Stretch is a very valuable tool. Take some time to really understand this command. It will save you hours when making corrections to drawings.

When selecting the object(s) you must use a **CROSSING** window.
Objects that are crossed, will *stretch.*
Objects that are totally enclosed, will *move*.

1. Select the STRETCH command using one of the following:

   TYPE = S
   PULLDOWN = MODIFY / STRETCH
   TOOLBAR = MODIFY

   Command: _stretch
2. Select objects to stretch by crossing-window or crossing-polygon...
3. Select objects: *select the first corner of the crossing window*
4. Specify opposite corner: *specify the opposite corner of the crossing window*
5. Specify base point or displacement: *select a base point (where it stretches from)*
6. Specify second point of displacement: *type coordinates or place location with cursor*

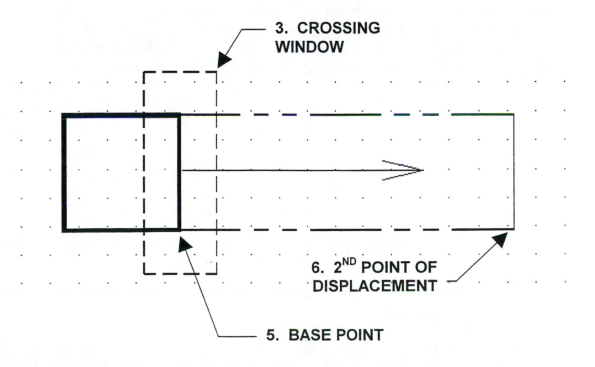

3. CROSSING WINDOW

6. 2ND POINT OF DISPLACEMENT

5. BASE POINT

ROTATE

The **ROTATE** command is used to rotate objects around a Base Point. (pivot point)
After selecting the objects and the base point, you will enter the rotation angle or select a reference angle followed by the new angle.
A **Positive** rotation angle revolves the objects **Counter- Clockwise**.
A **Negative** rotation angle revolves the objects **Clockwise**.

Select the ROTATE command using one of the following:

> **TYPE =RO**
> **PULLDOWN = MODIFY / ROTATE**
> **TOOLBAR = MODIFY**

ROTATION ANGLE OPTION
Command: _rotate
1. Current positive angle in UCS: ANGDIR=counterclockwise ANGBASE=0
2. Select objects: *select the object to rotate*
3. Select objects: *select more object(s) or <enter> to stop*
4. Specify base point: *select the base point (pivot point)*
5. Specify rotation angle or [Reference]: *type the angle of rotation*

REFERENCE OPTION
Command: _rotate
1. Current positive angle in UCS: ANGDIR=counterclockwise ANGBASE=0
2. Select objects: *select the object to rotate*
3. Select objects: *select more object(s) or <enter> to stop*
4. Specify base point: *select the base point (pivot point)*
5. Specify rotation angle or [Reference]: *select Reference*
6. Specify the reference angle <0>: *Snap to the reference object (1) and (2)*
7. Specify the new angle: *drag the object and snap to the new angle*

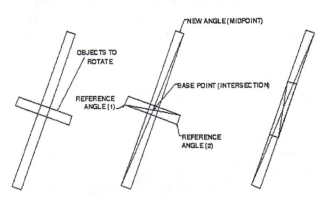

ANGDIR and **ANGBASE** are system variables. The values shown indicate the current status of these system variables.
ANGDIR controls the **CCW** or **CW** rotation.
ANGBASE controls the use of a base angle.
These variables can be changed, but it is best to leave them in the default mode for now.

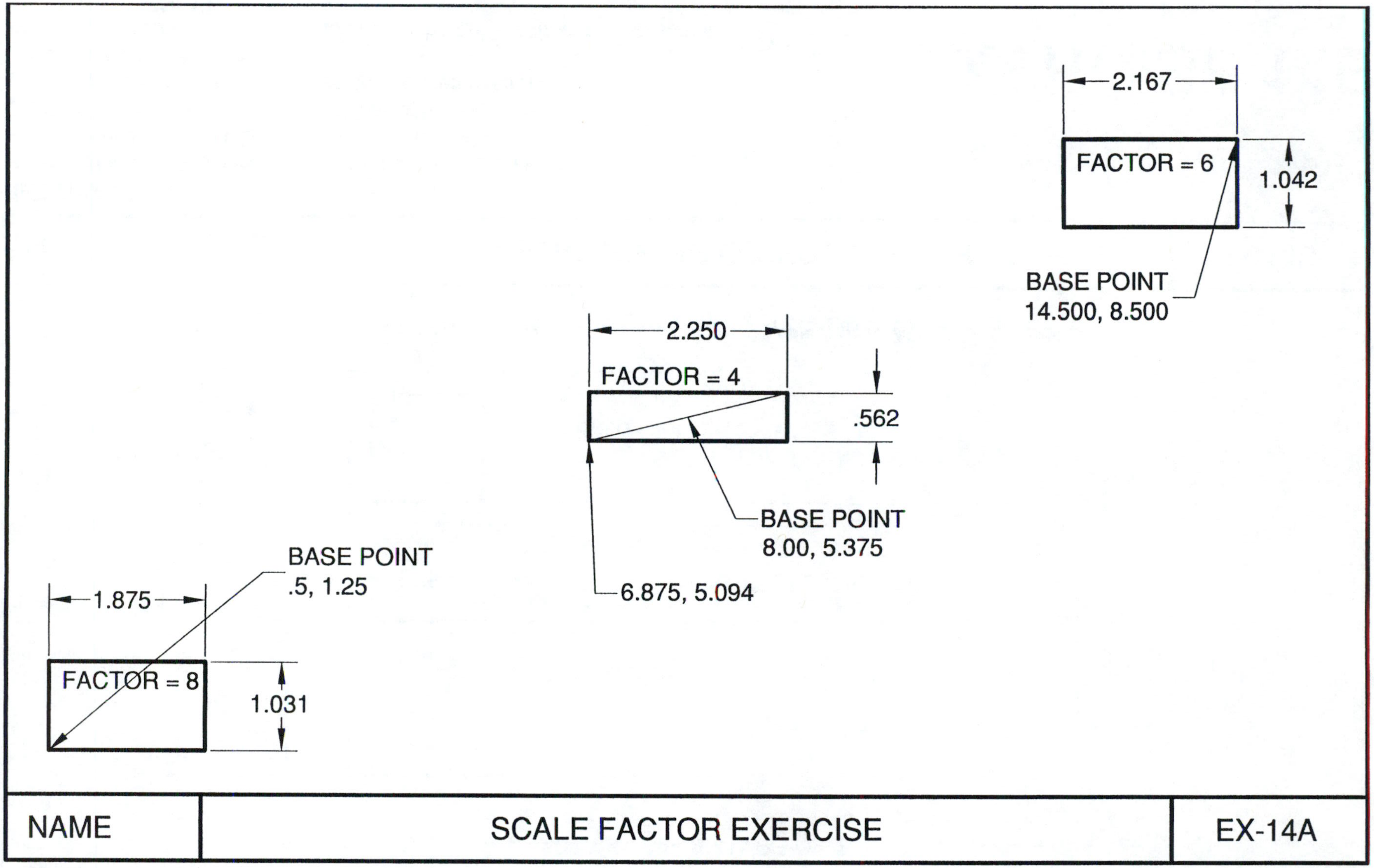

2.167

1.042

FACTOR = 6

BASE POINT
14.500, 8.500

.562

2.250

FACTOR = 4

BASE POINT
8.00, 5.375

6.875, 5.094

BASE POINT
.5, 1.25

1.031

1.875

FACTOR = 8

EXERCISE 14A

SCALE FACTOR EXERCISE

EX-14A

NAME

INSTRUCTIONS:

1. Draw the 3 Rectangles above.
   (Size and location is very important)

2. Scale each Rectangle using:

   a. Modify / Scale   b. Use Factors and Base points shown.

3. Save as: **EX-14A**

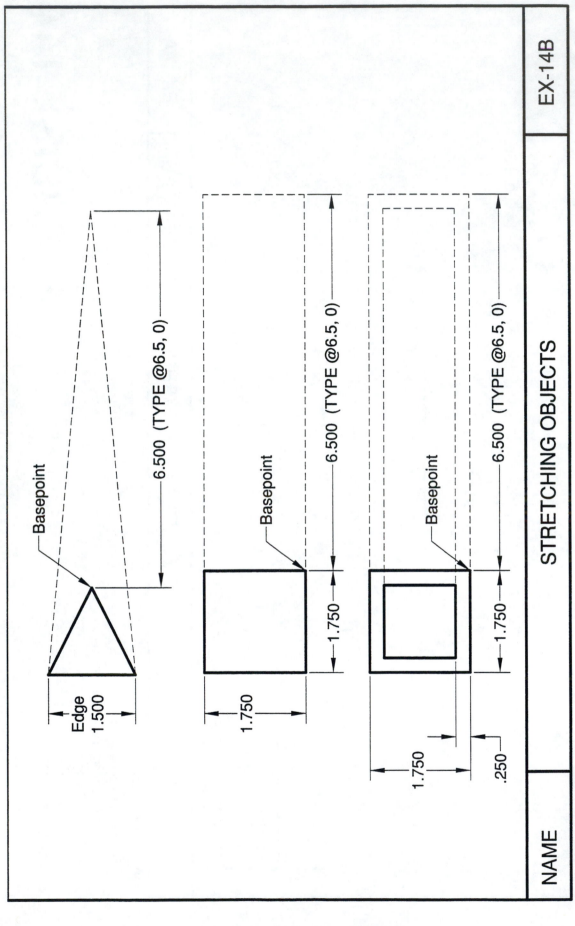

EXERCISE 14B

STRETCHING OBJECTS

Basepoint

Edge
1.500

6.500 (TYPE @6.5, 0)

Basepoint

1.750

6.500 (TYPE @6.5, 0)

1.750

Basepoint

1.750

.250

1.750

6.500 (TYPE @6.5, 0)

NAME

EX-14B

INSTRUCTIONS:

1. Draw the 3 dark objects on the left, then STRETCH them
   to the new lengths following steps a thru c below.
   (New lengths are indicated with dashed lines)
   a. Use "crossing window" to select the area to stretch
   b. Select the Basepoint
   c. Input how much you want to stretch the objects "from the basepoint".
2. Save as: **EX-14B.**

14-6

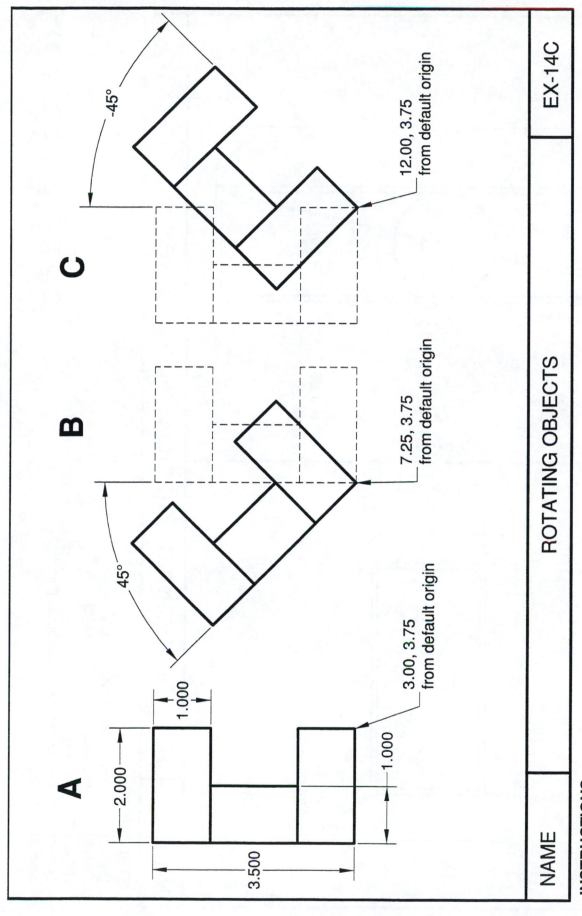

EXERCISE 14C

A

2.000

1.000

1.000

3.500

3.00, 3.75
from default origin

B

45°

7.25, 3.75
from default origin

C

-45°

12.00, 3.75
from default origin

NAME	ROTATING OBJECTS	EX-14C

INSTRUCTIONS:

1. Draw the object at position A.
2. Copy the first drawing to positions B and C.
   (Copy location represented with dashed lines)
3. Rotate the copies as shown.
4. Save as: **EX-14C.**

14-7

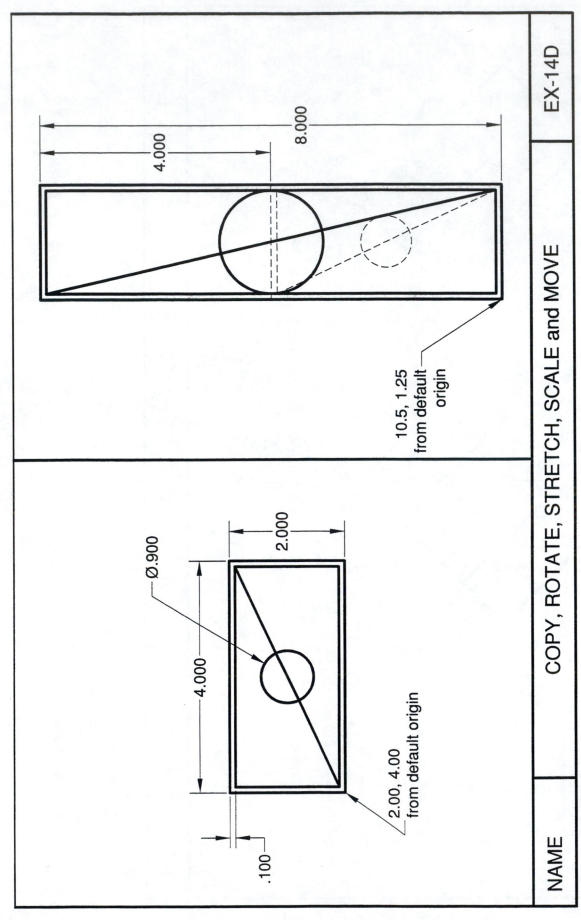

8.000

4.000

10.5, 1.25
from default
origin

2.000

Ø.900

4.000

2.00, 4.00
from default origin

.100

EX-14D

EXERCISE 14D

COPY, ROTATE, STRETCH, SCALE and MOVE

NAME

INSTRUCTIONS:

1. Draw the objects on the left. (layer: Object)
2. Copy these objects and move to the right side.
3. Rotate 90° and Stretch.
4. Move the Circle to proper location and Scale. (factor: 2)
5. Save as: **EX-14D.**

LEARNING OBJECTIVES

After completing this lesson, you will be able to:

1. Cross hatch a section view.
2. Solidly fill an area.
3. Make changes to cross hatch already in the drawing.
4. Make selected layers temporarily disappear.

LESSON 15

HATCH

The **BHATCH** command is used to create hatch lines for section views or filling areas with specific patterns.

To draw **hatch** you must start with a closed boundary. A closed boundary is an area completely enclosed by objects. A rectangle would be a closed boundary. You simply pick inside the closed boundary. BHATCH locates the area and automatically creates a temporary polyline around the outline of the hatch area. After the hatch lines are drawn in the area, the temporary polyline is automatically deleted. (Polylines are discussed in Lesson 23)

A Hatch set is one object. If you explode it, it will return to many objects.

1. Select the BHATCH command using one of the following:

   TYPE = BH
   PULLDOWN = DRAW / HATCH
   TOOLBAR = DRAW

   The following dialog box appears:

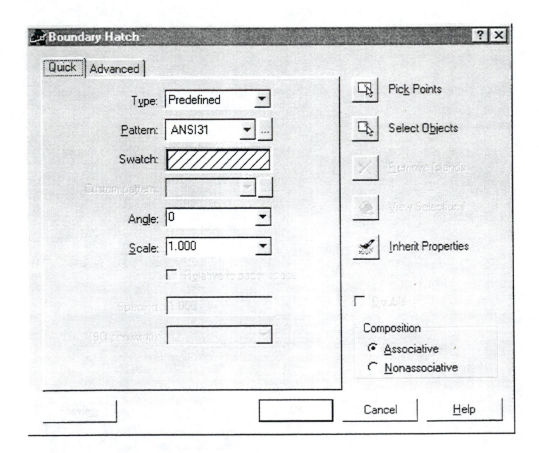

HATCH (continued)

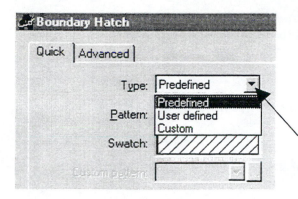

2. Select the hatch "TYPE"
Select one of the following:
PREDEFINED, USER DEFINED or CUSTOM
(Descriptions of each are listed below.)

2. Click on the "Type" down arrow.

a. *PREDEFINED*
AutoCAD has many predefined hatch patterns. These patterns are stored in the acad.pat and acadiso.pat files. (You may also purchase patterns from other software companies.)

Note: Using Hatch patterns will greatly increase the size of the drawing file. So use them conservatively.

To select a pattern by name, click on the "Pattern" down arrow. A drop-down list of available patterns will appear.

To select a pattern by appearance, click on the (...) button. This will display the "Hatch Pattern Palette" dialog box.

Predefined Pattern Properties

Pattern
This box displays the name of the Pattern you selected.

Swatch
The selected pattern is displayed here.

Angle
This determines the rotation angle of the pattern. A pre-designed pattern has a default angle of 0. If you change this Angle it will rotate the pattern relative to it's original design.

Scale
The value in this box is the scale factor. A good starting point would be to enter the scale factor of the drawing. Such as: If the drawing will be plotted at ¼" = 1, "4" is the scale factor. (Drawing Scale factors will be discussed in Lesson 29)

HATCH (continued

b. *USER DEFINED*
This selection allows you to simply draw continuous lines. (No special pattern) You specify the Angle and the Spacing between the lines. (This selection does not increase the size of the drawing file like Predefined)

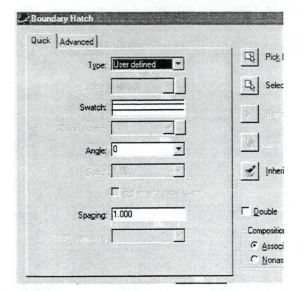

User-defined Pattern Properties

Swatch
A sample of the angle and spacing settings is displayed here.

Angle
Specify the actual angle of the hatch lines.
(0 to 180)

Spacing
Specify the actual distance between each hatch line.

Double
If this box is checked, the hatch set will be drawn first at the angle specified, then a second hatch set will be drawn rotated 90 degrees relative to the first hatch set, creating a criss-cross affect.

c. *CUSTOM*
See the AutoCAD Customization Guide for information on creating and saving custom hatch patterns.

3. Select the Composition Associative or Non Associative.

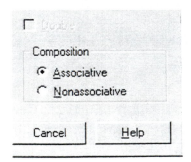

a. Associative: The hatch set is one entity and if the boundary size is changed the hatch will automatically change to the new boundary shape.

b. Non Associative: The hatch set is exploded into multiple entities and if the boundary shape is changed the hatch set will not change.

HATCH (continued)

4. Select the Area you want to Hatch using "Pick Points or Select Objects.

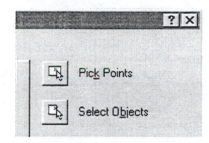

a. PICK POINTS
Select the **PICK POINTS** box then select a point inside the area you want to hatch. A boundary will automatically be determined.

b. SELECT OBJECTS
Select the boundary by selecting the object(s). The objects must form a closed shape with no gaps or overlaps.

5. Preview the Hatch.
   a. After you have selected the boundary, press the right mouse button and select "**Preview**". This option allows you to preview the hatch set before it is actually applied to the drawing.
   b. Press the right mouse button again.
   c. The hatch dialog box should reappear. If the preview is not what you expected, make the changes and preview again. When you are satisfied, select the **OK** button.

Note: It is always a good idea to take the extra time to preview the hatch. It will actually save you time in the long run.

AutoCAD Hatch Patterns

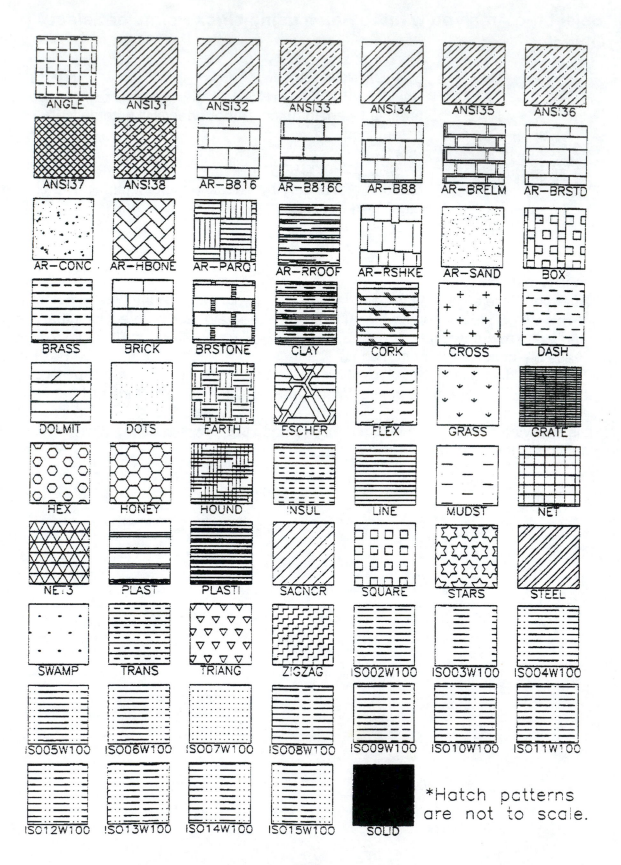

*Hatch patterns are not to scale.

EDITING HATCH

TYPE = HE
PULLDOWN = MODIFY / HATCH   **(Version LT uses MODIFY / OBJECT / HATCH)**
TOOLBAR = MODIFY II

HATCHEDIT allows you to edit an existing hatch pattern in the drawing.
You simply select the hatch pattern that you want to change, the hatch dialog box will appear. Make the changes and preview. Your changes should be displayed. Right click and select OK.

LAYER MANAGEMENT

ON and OFF

If a layer is **ON** it is **visible**. If a layer is **OFF** it is **not visible**.
Only layers that are **ON** can be **edited** or **plotted**.

Warning: Objects on a Layer that have been turned OFF can be accidentally erased.
When you are prompted to "select objects" and instead of selecting the objects with the
cursor, you type <u>ALL</u> on the command line. You will be accidentally be selecting the
objects on the layer that is turned OFF also.

FREEZE and THAW

Freeze and **Thaw** are very similar to On and Off. If a layer is Frozen it is not visible.
Thawed layers are visible. Only thawed layers can be edited or plotted.
But Freeze and Thaw have additional features.
a. Objects on a Frozen layer **can not** be accidentally erased by typing <u>ALL</u>
b. Freezing also speeds up regeneration time, when working with large and complex
     drawings, because frozen layers are not **regenerated**.

LOCK and UNLOCK

Locked layers are visible but can not be edited.

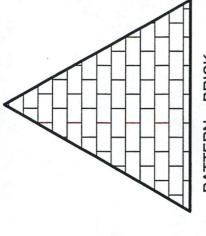

PATTERN = BRICK
SCALE = 1
ANGLE = 0

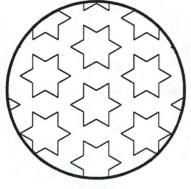

PATTERN = STARS
SCALE = 2
ANGLE = 0

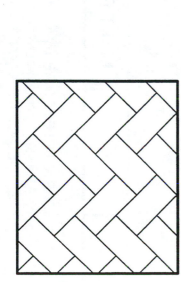

PATTERN = AR-HBONE
SCALE = .125
ANGLE = 0

INSTRUCTIONS:

1. Draw the **RECTANGLE, CIRCLE AND POLYGON** above approximately as shown. (Use layer = Object)
2. Select the **BHATCH** command. (Use Layer = Hatch)
3. Select Type: **PREDEFINED.**
4. Select the pattern listed above.
5. Select the **PICK POINTS** button.
   a. Place the cursor inside the hatch area and click.
6. Right click and select Preview.
   a. Right click again.
7. If not ok, make changes to the hatch options and preview again.
8. If ok, select the **OK** button.

| NAME | BEGINNING HATCH | EX-15A |

INSTRUCTIONS:

1. Follow the directions above.
2. Save as: **EX-15A.**

EXERCISE 15A

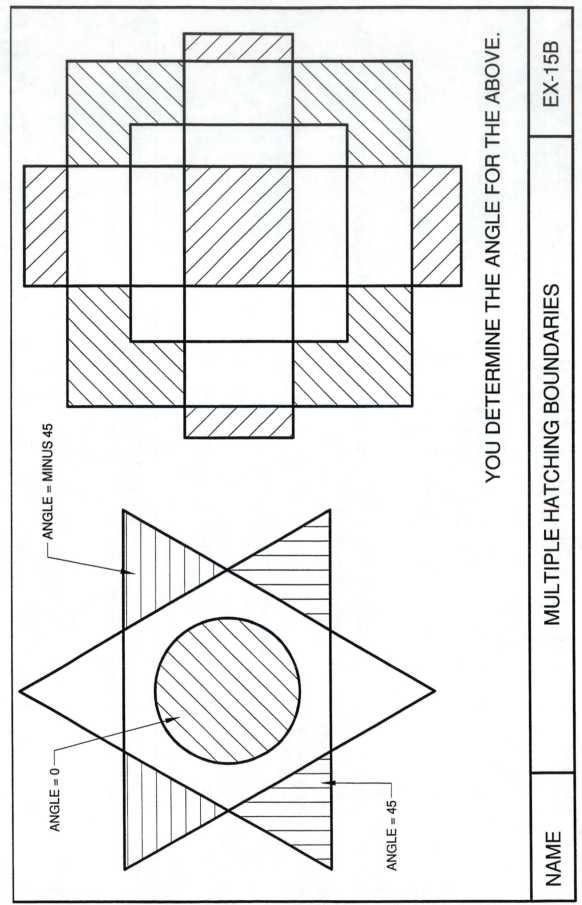

YOU DETERMINE THE ANGLE FOR THE ABOVE.

ANGLE = MINUS 45

ANGLE = 0

ANGLE = 45

EXERCISE 15B

EX-15B

MULTIPLE HATCHING BOUNDARIES

NAME

INSTRUCTIONS:

1. Draw the POLYGONS, CIRCLE AND RECTANGLES above.
2. HATCH as shown. (Use step by step procedure on EX-15A)
3. PATTERN = ANSI 31   SCALE = 2   ANGLE = noted above
4. Save as: EX-15B.

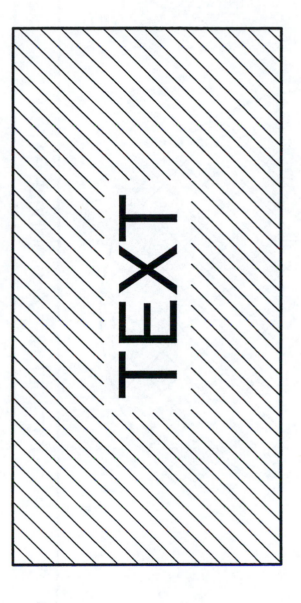

NAME

HATCHING AROUND TEXT AUTOMATICALLY

EX-15C

EXERCISE 15C

INSTRUCTIONS:

1. Draw the RECTANGLE above (Layer = Object)
2. Place 1.00 Ht. text in the middle of the Rectangle.   (Layer = Object)
3. Select options: Pattern = ANSI 31   Scale = 2   Angle = 0
4. Click on the SELECT OBJECTS button and select the Rectangle and Text.
5. Preview and OK.
6. Save as: **EX-15C.**

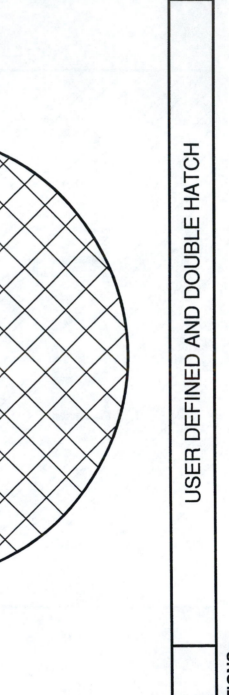

EX-15D

USER DEFINED AND DOUBLE HATCH

EXERCISE 15D

INSTRUCTIONS:

1. Draw the CIRCLE above (Layer = Object)
2. Draw the hatch using Type: **USER DEFINED** (Layer = Hatch)
3. Select options: Spacing = .50   Angle = 45
4. Select the **DOUBLE** box.
5. Select **PICK POINTS** button and click inside of the circle.
6. Preview, OK and Save as: **EX-15D.**

NAME

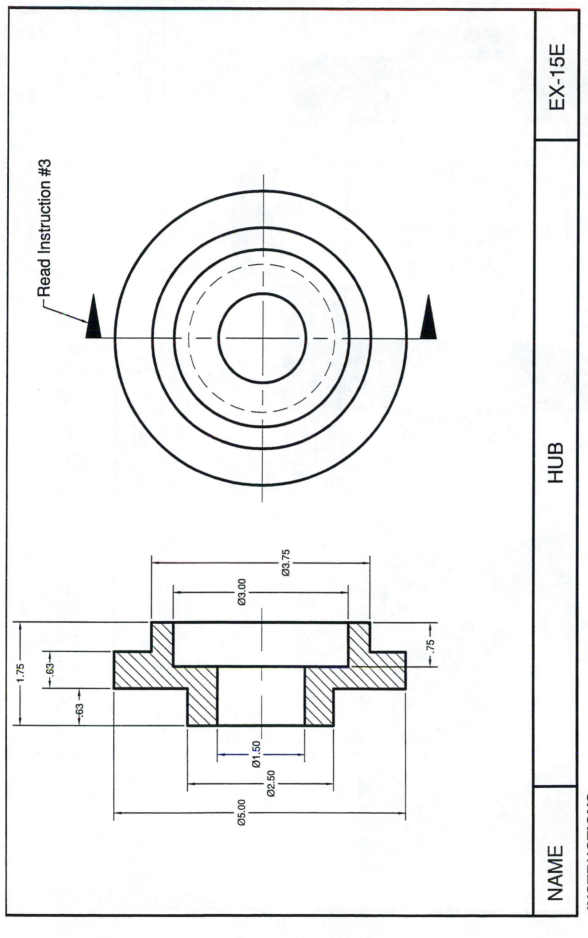

Read Instruction #3

Ø3.75
Ø3.00
1.75
.63
.63
.75
Ø1.50
Ø2.50
Ø5.00

NAME

HUB

EX-15E

INSTRUCTIONS:

1. Draw the HUB above (Layer = Object)
2. Draw the hatch using Pattern = ANSI 31 Scale = 1 Angle = 0 (Layer = Hatch)
3. Draw the section arrow then fill using "Solid" hatch. (Layer = Hatch)
4. Save as: EX-15E.

EXERCISE 15E

EX-15F

EXERCISE 15F

EDITING HATCH PATTERNS

NAME

INSTRUCTIONS:
1. Open drawing 15B and change the exisitng hatch pattern to SOLID.
2. Select MODIFY / HATCH (AutoCAD LT: use MODIFY / OBJECTS / HATCH)
3. Select the hatch sets to be edited.
4. Select hatch pattern SOLID, PREVIEW, OK then APPLY.
5. Save as EX-15F.

LEARNING OBJECTIVES

After completing this lesson, you will be able to:

1. Understand the importance of True Associative dimensioning.
2. Use Grips.
3. Add Linear, Baseline and Continued dimensions to your drawing.
4. Control the appearance of dimensions.
5. Create a New Dimension Style.
6. Compare two Dimension Styles.

LESSON 16

DIMENSIONING

Dimensioning is basically easy, but as always, there are many options to learn. As a result, I have divided the dimensioning process into 5 lessons. (Lessons 16 through 20) So relax and just take it one lesson at a time.

In this Lesson you will learn how to create a dimension style and how to create horizontal and vertical dimensions. But first you need to understand about AutoCAD 2002's new true associative and trans-spatial dimensioning feature.

True Associative and Trans-spatial Dimensioning

True Associative Dimensioning means that the dimensions are actually attached to the objects that they dimension. If you move the object, the dimension will move with it. If you scale or stretch the object, the dimension text value will change also. (Note: It is not parametric. This means, you can not change the dimension text value and expect the object to change.)

Trans-spatial will be discussed in Lesson 26 and 27.

True Associative Dimensioning can be set to ON, OFF or Exploded.

I strongly suggest that you keep true associative dimensioning on. It is truly a very powerful feature and will make editing the objects and dimensions much easier.

On = Dimensions are truly associative. In other words, associated to the objects and will change if the object changes. (This is the new 2002 true associative dimensioning feature)
Off = Dimensions are non-associative. In other words, not associated to the objects and will not change if the object changes. (This setting represents the pre-2002 associative feature)
Exploded = Dimensions are not associated to the objects and are totally separate objects. (arrows, lines and text)

How to turn On or OFF.

There are 2 methods:
Method 1. On the command line type: *dimassoc <enter>,*
     then enter the number *2 for On, 1 for Off* or *0 for Exploded <enter>*

NOTE: The DIMASSOC command has replaced the DIMASO command from previous AutoCAD releases.

Method 2. Select **Tools / Options / User Preferences tab.**
Checked box = On, Unchecked = Off, you can not set Exploded here.

Associative Dimensioning

☑ Make new dimensions associative

The Default setting is "2" or "ON" but check to make sure

When you first enter AutoCAD 2002, the True Associative and Trans-spatial dimensioning feature is "ON". This setting is saved with each individual drawing. It is not a system setting for all drawings, as it has been in past releases. This means, when you open a drawing, it is important to check the **dimassoc** command to verify that True Associative dimensioning is ON. Especially if you open a drawing created with an AutoCAD release previous to 2002. All drawings created previous to release 2002 will be set to "Off".

How to Re-associate a dimension

If a dimension was created with a previous version of AutoCAD or True Associative dimensioning was turned off, you may use the **dimreassociate** command to change the non-associative dimensions into associative dimensions.
(You may use the **Tools / Inquiry / List** command to determine whether a dimension is associative or non-associative.)

1. Select **Dimension / Reassociate Dimensions**. (No icon available)

   Command: _dimreassociate
   Select dimensions to reassociate ...

2. Select objects: *select the dimension to be reassociated*

3. Select objects: *select more dimensions or <enter> to stop*

4. Specify first extension line origin or [Select object] <next>: *an "X" will mark the first extension line; use object snap to select the exact location of the extension line point (If the "X" has a box around it, just press <enter>*

5. Specify second extension line origin <next>: *the "X" will move to another location. Use object snap or <enter>*

6. *Continue until all extension line points are selected.*

Regenerating Associative dimensions

Sometimes after panning and zooming, the associative dimensions seem to be floating or not following the object. The **DIMREGEN** command will move the associative dimensions back into their correct location.
You must type **dimregen <enter>** on the command line. Sorry, AutoCAD did not provide an icon or a pull-down menu.

GRIPS

Grips are little boxes that appear if you select an object when no command is in use. Grips must be enabled by typing "grips" <enter> then 1 <enter> on the command line or selecting the "enable grips" box in the **OPTIONS / SELECTION** dialog box.

Grips can be used to quickly edit objects. You can move, copy, stretch, mirror, rotate, and scale objects using grips.

The following is a quick overview on how to use three of the most frequently used options. Grips have many more options and if you like the example below, you should research them further in the AutoCAD help menu.

1. Select the object (no command can be in use while using grips)
2. Select one of the grips. It will turn solid. This indicates that it is "hot". Hot means that this grip is the basepoint.
3. The editing modes will be displayed on the command line. You may cycle through these modes by pressing the SPACEBAR or ENTER key or use the shortcut menu.
4. <u>After editing you must press the ESC key to deactivate the grips on that object.</u>

Selecting a grip:
When you select a grip it becomes "HOT".

Hot grip

Moving an object:
1. Select the object.
2. Select the grip in the middle of the object.
3. Move the cursor to the new location.
4. Press the ESC key.

1 (Original object)

Move

Coping an object:
1. Select the object.
2. Select the grip.
3. Select the COPY mode from the grip menu.
4. Select the new location for the copy(s).
Note: Grips will allow you to make multiple copies. Press the ESC key to stop.

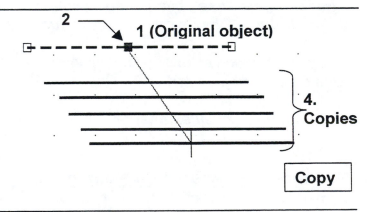

1 (Original object)

4. Copies

Copy

Stretch an object:
1. Select the object
2. Select the grip.
3. Move the cursor to stretch the object or type @X,Y
4. Press the ESC key.

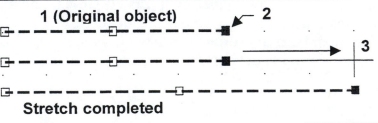

1 (Original object)

Stretch completed

Stretch

LINEAR DIMENSIONING

First open the dimension toolbar. Using the toolbar icons to select the dimension commands is the most efficient method. (Refer to page 2-6 to open toolbar)

<u>Linear dimensioning</u> allows you to create horizontal and vertical dimensions.

1. Select the **LINEAR** command.
   Command:_Linear
   Specify first extension line origin or <select object>: *snap to first extension line origin (P1)*
   Specify second extension line origin: *snap to second extension line origin (P2)*
   Specify dimension line location or [Mtext/Text/Angle/Horizontal/Vertical/Rotated]: *select where you want the dimension line placed. (P3)*
   Dimension text = 2.000 *(the dimension text value will be displayed on the last line)*

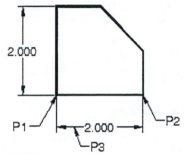

BASELINE DIMENSIONING

<u>Baseline dimensioning</u> allows you to establish a **baseline** for successive dimensions. The spacing between dimensions is automatic and should be set in dimension styles. A Baseline dimension must be used with an existing dimension. If you use Baseline dimensioning immediately after a Linear dimension, you do not have to specify the baseline origin.

1. Create a <u>linear</u> dimension first. (1.400   P1 and P2)
2. Select the **BASELINE** command.
   Command: _dimbaseline
3. Specify a second extension line origin or [Undo/Select] <Select>: *snap to the second extension line origin (P3)*
   Dimension text = 2.588
4. Specify a second extension line origin or [Undo/Select] <Select>: *snap to P4*
   Dimension text = 3.633
5. Specify a second extension line origin or [Undo/Select} <Select>: *select <enter> twice to stop*

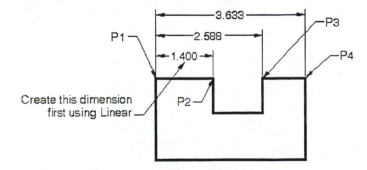

CONTINUE DIMENSIONING

Continue creates a series of dimensions in-line from an existing dimension. If you use the continue dimensioning immediately after a Linear dimension, you do not have to specify the continue extension origin.

1. Create a linear dimension first. (1.400   P1 and P2)
2. Select the Continue command.
    Command: _dimcontinue
    Specify a second extension line origin or [Undo/Select] <Select>: *snap to the second extension line origin (P3)*
    Dimension text = 1.421
    Specify a second extension line origin or [Undo/Select] <Select>: *snap to the second extension line origin (P4)*
    Dimension text = 1.364
    Specify a second extension line origin or [Undo/Select] <Select>: *press <enter> twice to stop*

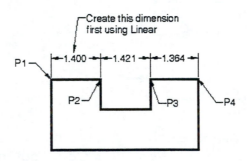

DIMENSION STYLES

Using the "Dimension Style Manager", you can change the appearance of the dimension features such as length of arrowheads, size of the dimension text, etc. There are over 70 different settings.
You can also Create New, Modify, Override and Compare Dimension Styles. All of these are simple by using the Dimension Style Manager described below.

Select the "Dimension Style Manager" using one of the following:

TYPE = DDIM
PULLDOWN = DIMENSION / STYLE
TOOLBAR = DIMENSION

The following dialog box will appear.

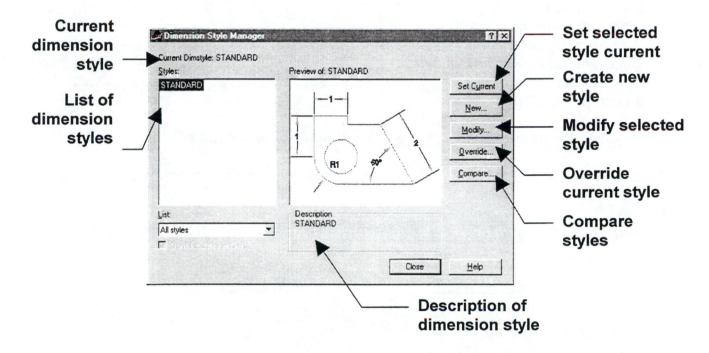

Current dimension style

List of dimension styles

Set selected style current

Create new style

Modify selected style

Override current style

Compare styles

Description of dimension style

Set Current   Select a style from the list of styles and select the **set current** button. (Only Standard is shown unless you have previously created other styles)

New   Select this button to create a new style. When you select this button, the **Create New Dimension Style** dialog box is displayed. (See page 16-8)

Modify   Selecting this button opens the **Modify dimension Style** dialog box which allows you to make changes to the current style. (See page 17-4)

Override   An override is a temporary change to the current style. Selecting this button opens the Override Current Style dialog box. (See page17-5)

Compare   Compares two styles. (See page 16-11)

CREATING A NEW DIMENSION STYLE

When creating a new style you must start with an existing style, such as Standard. Next, assign it a new name, make the desired changes and when you select the OK button, the new style will have been successfully created.

LET'S CREATE A NEW STYLE
A dimension style is a group of settings that has been saved under a name you assign.

1. Open your drawing **BSIZE** and set **DIMASSOC** to **2**
2. Select the **DIMENSION STYLE** command (Ref. page 16-7)
3. Select the **NEW** button. (Ref. page 16-7)
4. Enter **CLASS STYLE** in the "New Style Name" box.
5. **Start With**: we will start with the settings in the STANDARD style and then make some changes.
6. **Use For**: is for creating "family" dimension styles and will be discussed later. For now, leave it set to "All dimensions".
7. Select the **CONTINUE** box.

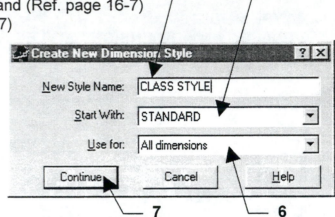

The "New Dimension Style: Class Style" dialog box will appear.

8. Select the **"Primary Units"** tab and make the changes shown below.

NOTE:
REFER TO APPENDIX D FOR DESCRIPTIONS OF ALL DIMENSION SETTINGS

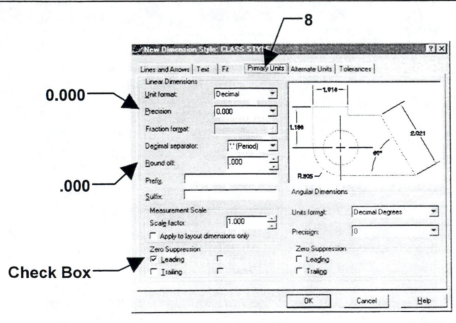

DO NOT SELECT THE OK BUTTON YET

9. Select the *"Lines and Arrows"* tab and make the changes shown below.

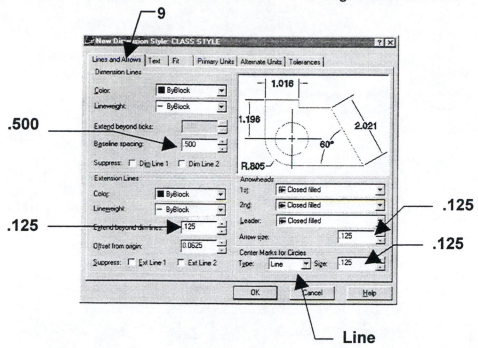

.500

.125

.125

.125

Line

DO NOT SELECT THE OK BUTTON YET.

10. Select the **"Text"** tab and make the changes shown below.

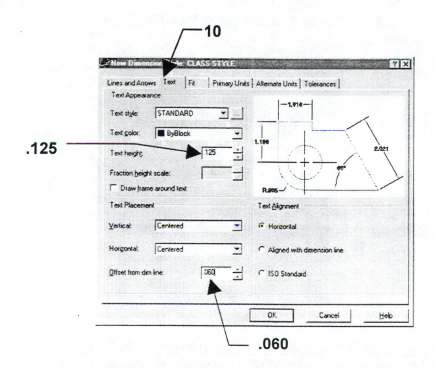

.125

.060

DO NOT SELECT THE OK BUTTON

11. Select the **"Fit"** tab. (Look at it but No changes are necessary.)

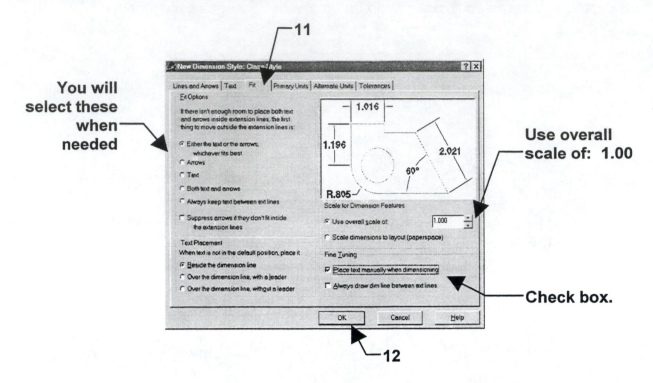

11

**You will
select these
when
needed**

**Use overall
scale of: 1.00**

Check box.

12

12. **NOW** you may select the **OK** button.

13. *Your new style* **"Class Style"** *should be listed*. Select the **"Set Current"** button to make your new style "Class Style" the style that we will use.

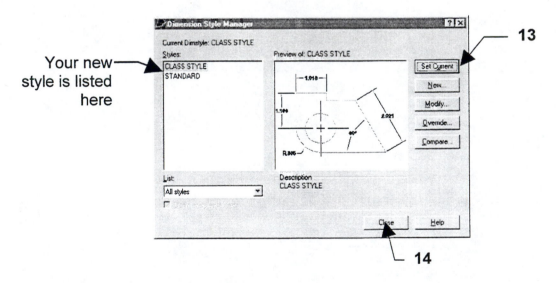

**Your new
style is listed
here**

13

14

14. Select the **Close** button to **exit**.
15. Save your drawing as **BSIZE**.

Note: You have successfully created a new "Dimension Style" called "Class Style". This style will be saved in your BSIZE drawing after you save the drawing. It is important that you understand that this dimension style resides only in the BSIZE drawing. If you open another drawing, this dimension style will not be there.

COMPARE TWO DIMENSION STYLES

Sometimes it is useful to compare the settings of two styles. Compare will compare the two styles and list the differences.

LET'S COMPARE "CLASS STYLE" AND "STANDARD"

1. Select the Dimension Style command.
2. Select the Compare button.

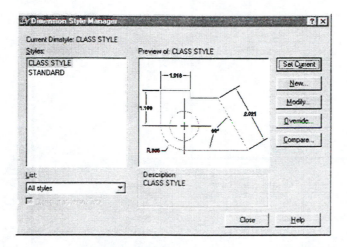

The "Compare Dimension Style" dialog box will appear.

3. Select "Class Style" in the Compare box.
4. Select "Standard" in the With box.
5. AutoCAD found differences and listed them.

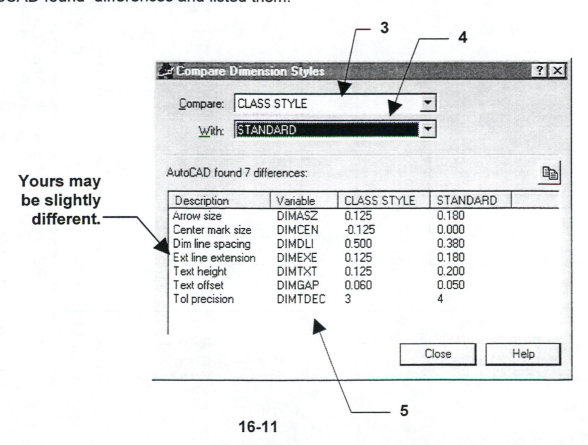

Yours may be slightly different.

AutoCAD found 7 differences:

Description	Variable	CLASS STYLE	STANDARD
Arrow size	DIMASZ	0.125	0.180
Center mark size	DIMCEN	-0.125	0.000
Dim line spacing	DIMDLI	0.500	0.380
Ext line extension	DIMEXE	0.125	0.180
Text height	DIMTXT	0.125	0.200
Text offset	DIMGAP	0.060	0.050
Tol precision	DIMTDEC	3	4

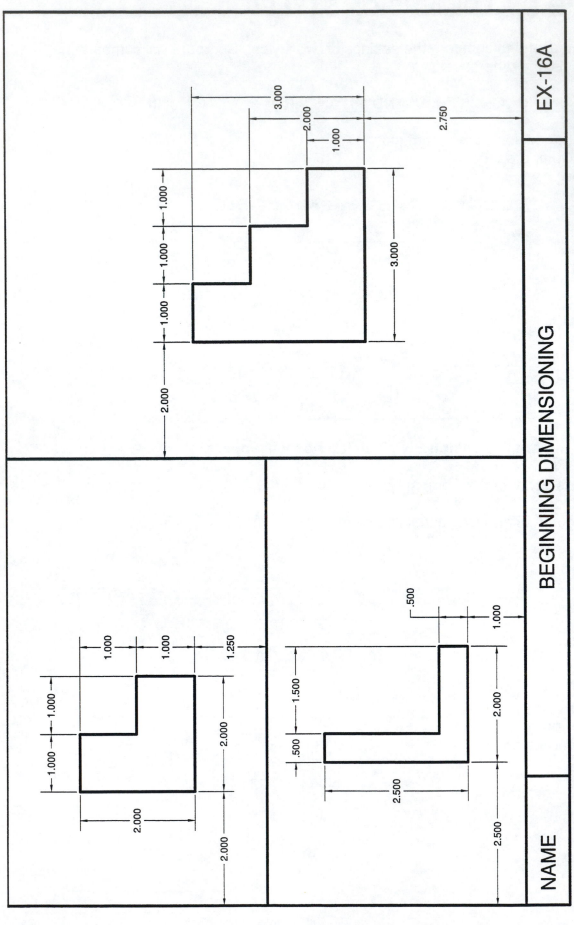

BEGINNING DIMENSIONING

NAME

EX-16A

INSTRUCTIONS: (Before dimensioning this drawing, create a dimension style in your Bsize master drawing.
Follow the instructions on page 16-8 thru 10)

1. Draw the objects above. (Use Layer: Object)
2. Dimension as shown using Dimension Style: Class Style and Linear,
   Baseline and Continue. (Use Layer: Dim)
3. Try to duplicate the dimensions as shown.
4. Save as: **EX-16A**

EXERCISE 16A

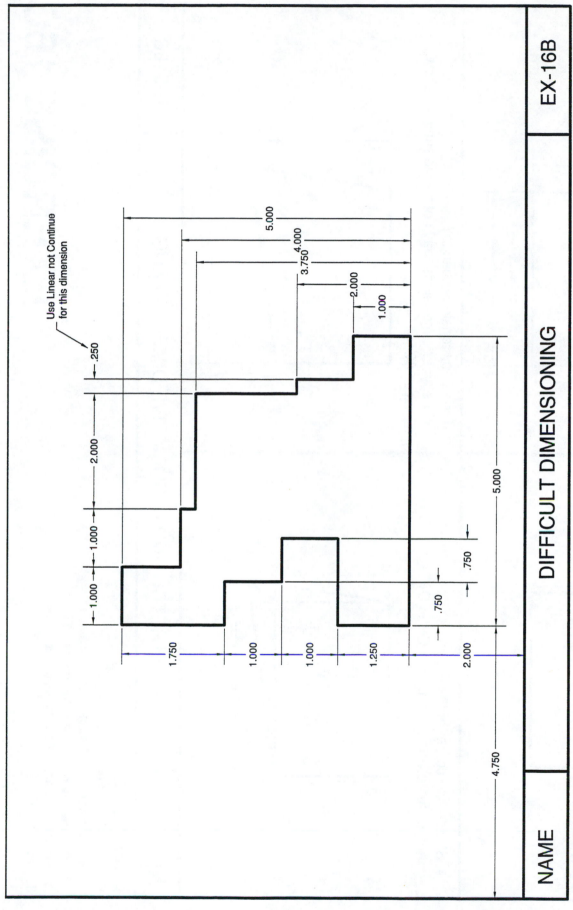

Use Linear not Continue
for this dimension

.250

2.000

1.000

1.000

5.000

4.000

3.750

2.000

1.000

5.000

.750

.750

1.750

1.000

1.000

1.250

2.000

4.750

EXERCISE 16B

| NAME | DIFFICULT DIMENSIONING | EX-16B |

INSTRUCTIONS:

1. Draw the objects above. (Use Layer: Object)
2. Note: The OFFSET command would be more efficient than coordinate input.
3. Dimension as shown using Dimension Style: Class Style and Linear,
   Baseline and Continue. (Use Layer: Dim)
4. Try to duplicate the dimensions as shown.
5. Save as: **EX-16B**

EXERCISE 16C

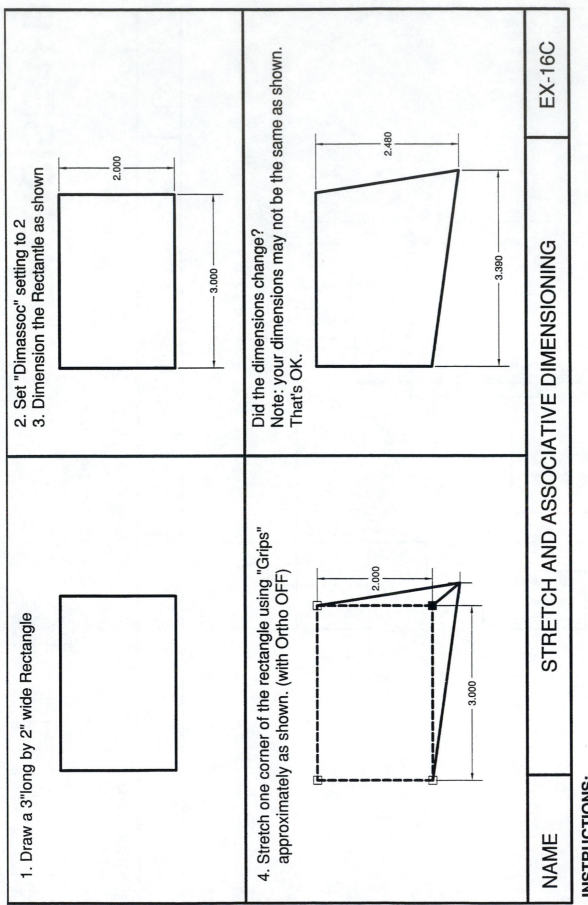

1. Draw a 3"long by 2" wide Rectangle

2. Set "Dimassoc" setting to 2
3. Dimension the Rectantle as shown

2.000

3.000

Did the dimensions change?
Note: your dimensions may not be the same as shown.
That's OK.

2.480

3.390

4. Stretch one corner of the rectangle using "Grips"
approximately as shown. (with Ortho OFF)

2.000

3.000

NAME	STRETCH AND ASSOCIATIVE DIMENSIONING

INSTRUCTIONS:

1. Follow the instructions above.
2. Do not divide your drawing into 4 sections.
   Just draw one rectangle in the middle of your
   drawing area and follow the instructions.
3. Save as: **EX-16C**

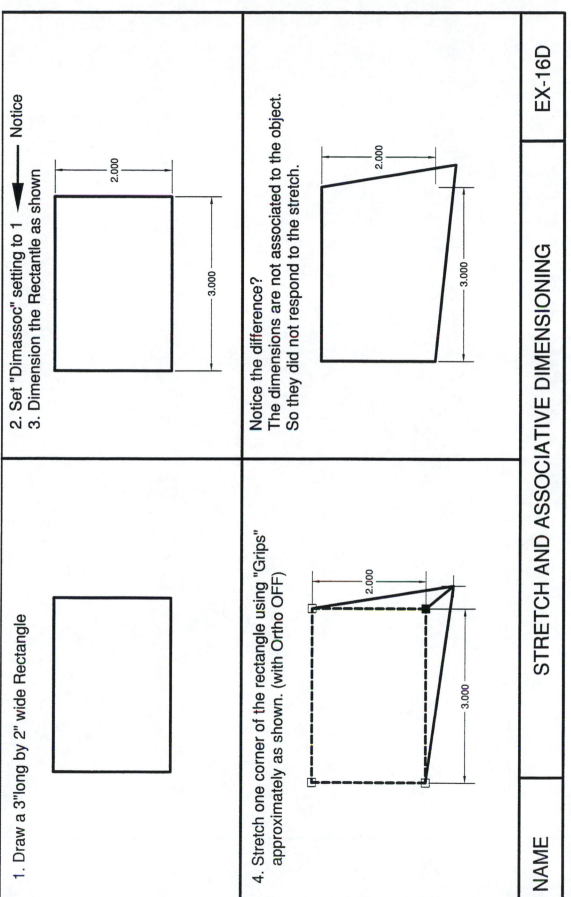

1. Draw a 3"long by 2" wide Rectangle

2. Set "Dimassoc" setting to 1 ← Notice
3. Dimension the Rectantle as shown

2.000

3.000

4. Stretch one corner of the rectangle using "Grips" approximately as shown. (with Ortho OFF)

2.000

3.000

Notice the difference?
The dimensions are not associated to the object.
So they did not respond to the stretch.

2.000

3.000

| NAME | STRETCH AND ASSOCIATIVE DIMENSIONING | EX-16D |

EXERCISE 16D

INSTRUCTIONS:
1. Follow the instructions above.
2. Do not divide your drawing into 4 sections.
   Just draw one rectangle in the middle of your
   drawing area and follow the instructions.
3. Save as: EX-16D

NOTES:

LEARNING OBJECTIVES

After completing this lesson, you will be able to:

1. Edit dimension text values
2. Edit the Dimension position.
3. Modify an entire Dimension Style.
4. Override a dimension style.
5. Edit a dimension using Properties.

LESSON 17

EDITING DIMENSION TEXT VALUES

Sometimes you need to modify the dimension text. You may add a symbol, a note or even change the text of an existing dimension. There are 2 methods.

Example: Add the word "Max." to the existing dimension.

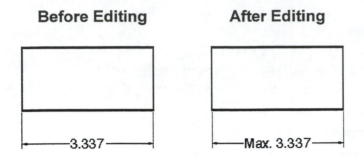

Before Editing   **After Editing**

Method 1.
1. Double click on the dimension that you want to change.
   The Properties box will appear.
2. Scroll down to Text / Text override
   (Notice that the actual measurement is directly above it.)
3. Type the new text and press <enter>

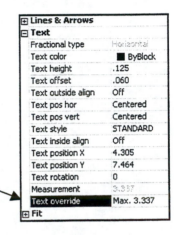

Method 2.
1. Type on the Command line: **DDEDIT** <enter>
2. Select the dimension you want to edit. (Only one at a time)
3. The "Multiline Text Editor" will appear.
   If the dimension is <u>Associative</u>, it will display the dimension text as a symbol <>.
   Do not erase *this symbol. You can add text before or after the symbol.*
4. Select the OK button.

Represents the "Associative" dimension value 3.337

Word added

4

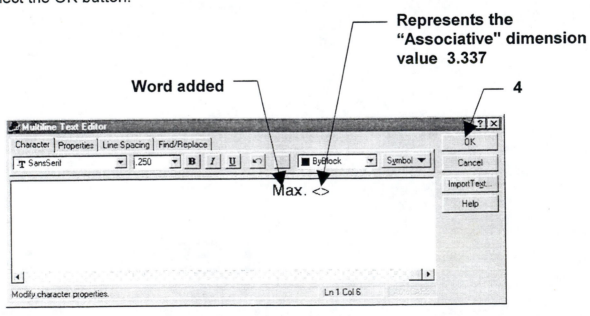

EDITING THE DIMENSION POSITION

You can edit the position of the dimension and / or it's text.
Sometimes dimensions are too close and you would like to stagger the text or you need to move an entire dimension to a new location, such as the examples below.

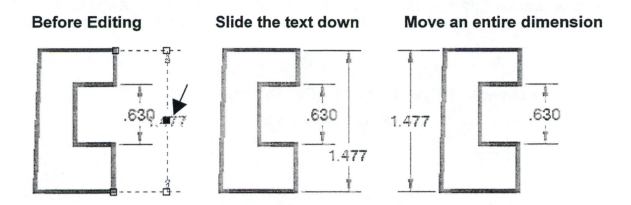

Before Editing   **Slide the text down**   **Move an entire dimension**

1. Select the dimension that you want to change. (Grips will appear)
2. Select the middle grip. (It will become solid and active, hot)
3. Move the cursor and the dimension will respond.
4. Press the left mouse button to place the dimension in the new location.

ADDITIONAL EDITING OPTIONS USING THE SHORTCUT MENU

1. Select the dimension that you want to change.
2. Press the Right Mouse button.
3. Select "Dimension Text Position" from the shortcut menu shown to the right.
4. A sub-menu appears with many editing options.

Experiment with these options. They will be very helpful in the future.

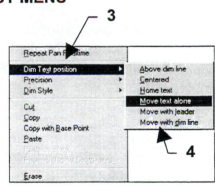

Note: This command will not work with "Non-associative" or Exploded dimensions. You will have to use the "Stretch" command to achieve the same results.

MODIFY AN <u>ENTIRE</u> DIMENSION STYLE

After you have created a Dimension Style, you may find that you have changed your mind about some of the settings. You can easily change the entire Style by using the "Modify" button in the Dimension style Manager dialog box. This will not only change the Style for future use, but it will also update dimensions already in the drawing.

Note: if you do not want to update the dimensions already in the drawing, but want to make a change to the next dimension drawn,   refer to Override, page 17-5

1. Select the Dimension Style command. (Refer to page 16-7)

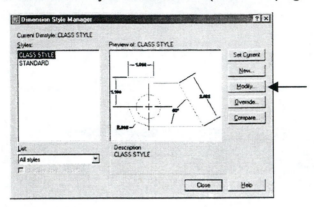

2. Select the Modify button from the Dimension Style Manager dialog box.

3. Make the desired changes to the settings.

4. Select the OK button.

5. Select the Close button.

Now look at your drawing. Have your dimensions updated?

<u>Note: If some of the dimensions have not changed:</u>
1. Select Dimension / Update
2. Select the dimension(s) you wish to update and press <enter>

Note: This feature <u>will not</u> work with "<u>Non-associative</u>" or <u>Exploded</u> dimensions.

OVERRIDE A DIMENSION STYLE

A dimension Override is a **temporary** change to the dimension settings. An override will not affect existing dimensions. It will affect only new dimensions.

Use this option when you want your next dimension just a little different but you don't want to create a whole new dimension style and you don't want to change the existing dimensions.

1. Select **Format / Dimension Style.**

2. Select the **Dimension Style** you want to override.

3. Select the **Override** button from the Dimension Style Manager dialog box.

4. Make the desired changes to the settings.

5. Select the OK button.
   a. Look at the List of styles. Under the Style name, a sub heading of "Style overrides" should be displayed.
   b. The description box should display the style name and the override settings.

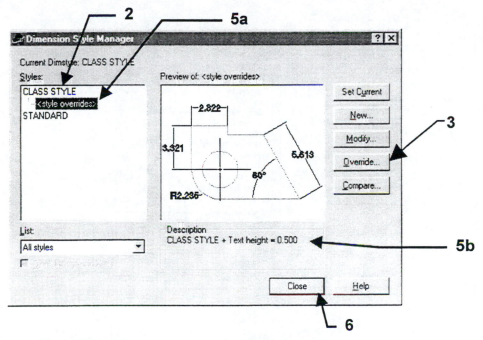

6. Select the Close button.

If you want to return to style "**Class Style**", select it and then select the "**Set Current**" button. Each time you select a different style, you must select the **Set Current** button to activate it.

This command **will not** work with "Non-associative" dimensions.

EDITING A DIMENSION using PROPERTIES

Sometimes you would like to modify the settings of an **individual existing** dimension.
This can be achieved using the Modify Properties command.

1. Double click on the dimension that you wish to change.

   The Properties Window will appear.

2. Select the (+) symbol beside the Setting category you would like to change.
   This will expand the category display.

3. Select and change the desired settings.

4. Press <enter> . *(The change should have taken effect)*

5. Press the <esc> key **or** move the cursor onto the drawing area, right click and select
   "Deselect All" from the shortcut menu.

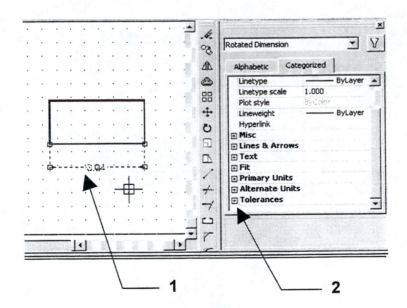

Note: This command <u>will not</u> work with <u>Non-associative</u> or <u>Exploded </u> dimensions.

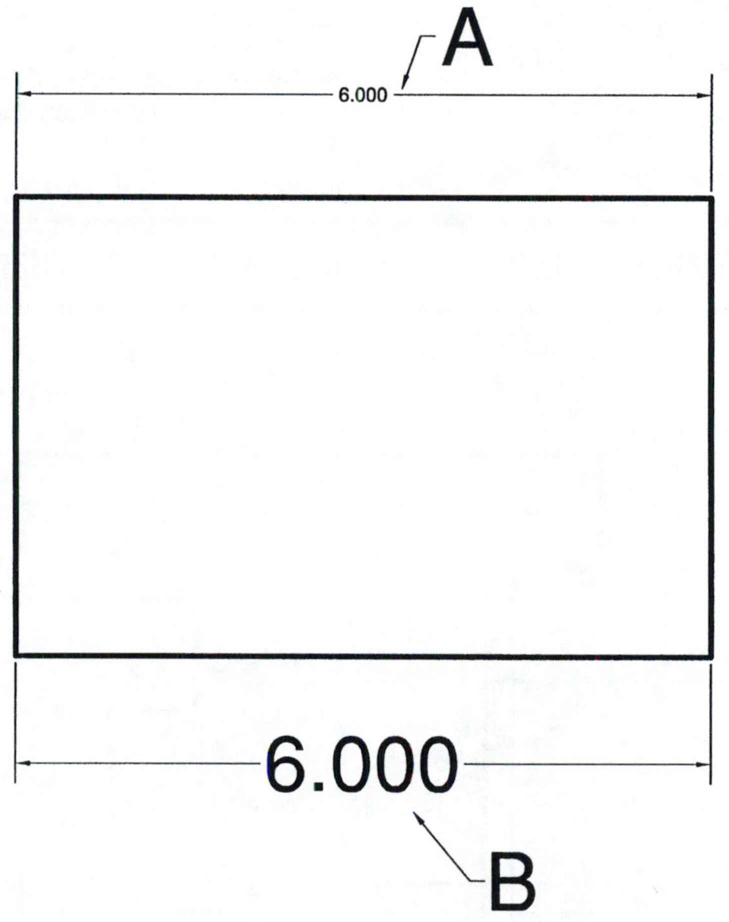

A

6.000

6.000

B

NAME	OVERRIDE	EX-17A

EXERCISE 17A

INSTRUCTIONS:

1. Draw the 6" Long by 4" Wide Rectangle above. (Use Layer: Object)
2. Use dimension style "Class Style" for dimension A. (Use Layer: Dim)
3. Use OVERRIDE for dimension B. Change the setting for Text height to .500.
4. Save as: **EX-17A**

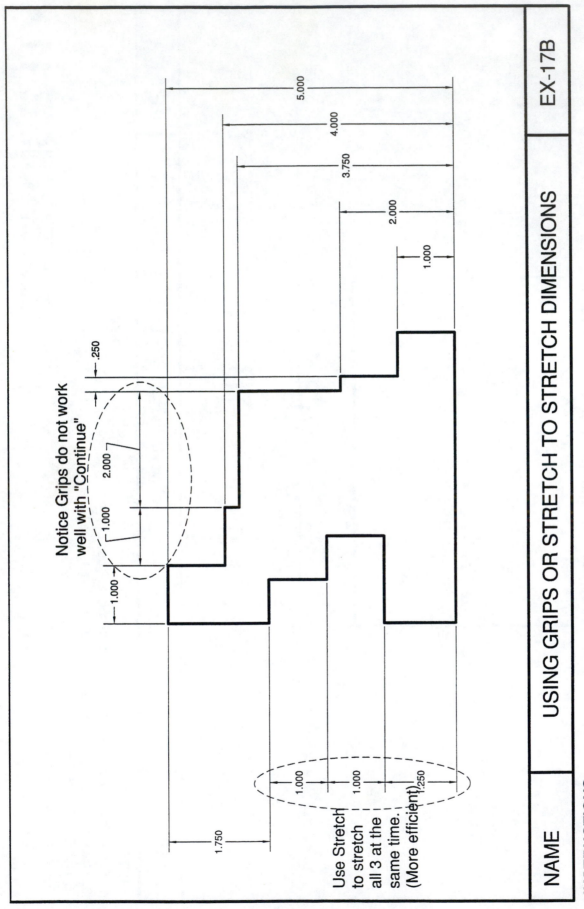

Notice Grips do not work
well with "Continue"

Use Stretch
to stretch
all 3 at the
same time.
(More efficient)

EXERCISE 17B

NAME	USING GRIPS OR STRETCH TO STRETCH DIMENSIONS

INSTRUCTIONS:

1. Open drawing 16B.
2. Try using Grips to stretch the dimensions as shown.
You may find that the STRETCH command works better in some cases.
3. Save as: **EX-17B**

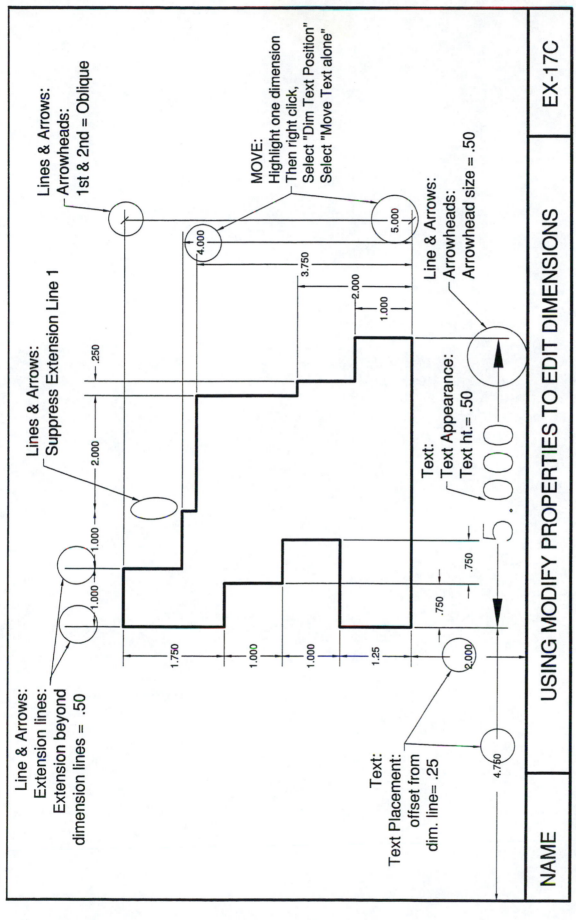

EXERCISE 17C

Lines & Arrows:
Arrowheads:
1st & 2nd = Oblique

MOVE:
Highlight one dimension
Then right click,
Select "Dim Text Position"
Select "Move Text alone"

Lines & Arrows:
Suppress Extension Line 1

Line & Arrows:
Arrowheads:
Arrowhead size = .50

Line & Arrows:
Extension lines:
Extension beyond
dimension lines = .50

Text:
Text Appearance:
Text ht.= .50

Text:
Text Placement:
offset from
dim. line= .25

| NAME | USING MODIFY PROPERTIES TO EDIT DIMENSIONS | EX-17C |

INSTRUCTIONS:
1. Open Drawing 16B.
2. Edit the dimensions using: MODIFY / PROPERTIES.
3. Save as: **EX-17C**

NOTES:

LEARNING OBJECTIVES

After completing this lesson, you will be able to:

1. Add Diameter, Radial and Angular dimensions to your drawing.
2. Draw Center Marks.
3. Control the size and appearance of the Center Marks.
4. Understand the need for Sub-Styles.
5. Create a Sub-Style.

LESSON 18

RADIAL DIMENSIONING

DIAMETER DIMENSIONING

The **DIAMETER** dimensioning command should be used when dimensioning circles and arcs of <u>more than 180 degrees</u>.

<u>Center marks</u> are automatically drawn as you use the diameter dimensioning command. If the circle already has a center mark or you do not want a center mark, set the center mark setting to **NONE** (Dimension Style / Lines and Arrows tab) before using Diameter dimensioning.

1. Select the **DIAMETER** command.
   Command: _dimdiameter
2. Select arc or circle: *click on the arc or circle (P1), location is not important, <u>do not use object snap.</u>*
   Dimension text = *the diameter will be displayed here*
3. Specify dimension line location or [Mtext/Text/Angle]: *place dimension text location (P2)*

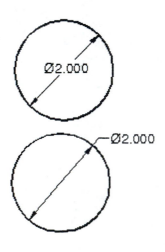

- -

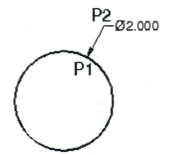

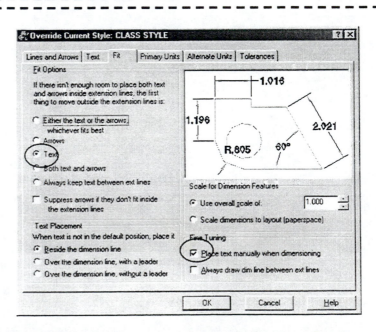

If you would like your Diameter dimensions to appear as shown in the two examples above, you must change the "**Fit Options**" and "**Fine Tuning**" in the **Fit tab** in your Dimension Style.

RADIAL DIMENSIONING (continued)

RADIUS DIMENSIONING

The **RADIUS** dimensioning command should be used when dimensioning arcs of <u>LESS than 180 degrees.</u>

<u>Center Marks</u> are automatically drawn as you use the **RADIUS** dimensioning command. If the circle already has a center mark, set the center mark to **NONE** (in the Dimension Style) before using RADIUS dimensioning. Or create a "sub-style" as shown on page 18-6.

1. Select the **RADIUS** command.
    Command: _dimradius
2. Select arc or circle: ***click on the arc (P1), location is not important, do not use snap.***
    Dimension text = ***the radius will be displayed here***
3. Specify dimension line location or [Mtext/Text/Angle]: ***place dim text location (P2)***

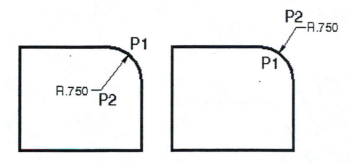

- -

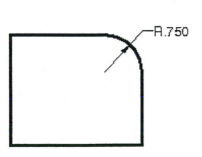

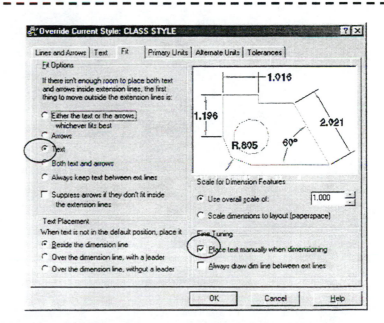

If you would like your Radius dimensions to appear as shown in the example immediately above, you must change the "**Fit Options**" and "**Fine Tuning**" in the **Fit tab** in your Dimension Style.

ANGULAR DIMENSIONING

The **ANGULAR** dimension command is used to create an angular dimension between two lines that form an angle.   All that is necessary is the selection of the two lines and the location for the dimension text.

The **degree symbol** is automatically added as the dimension is created.

1. Select the **ANGULAR** command.
    Command: _dimangular
2. Select arc, circle, line, or <specify vertex>: *click on the first line that forms the angle (P1) location is not important, do not use snap.*
3. Select second line: *click on the second line that forms the angle (P2)*
4. Specify dimension arc line location or [Mtext/Text/Angle]: *place dimension text location*
    Dimension text = *angle will be displayed here*

Any of the 4 angular dimensions shown below can be created by clicking on the 2 lines (P1 and P2) that form the angle.

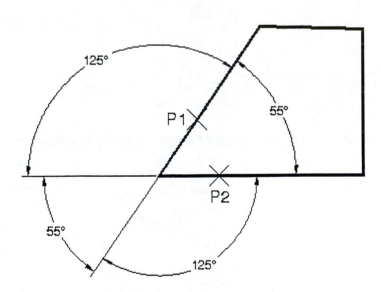

CENTERMARK

CENTERMARKS can ONLY be drawn with circular objects like Circles and Arcs. You set the size and type.

The Center Mark has three types, **None, Mark** and **Line** as shown below.

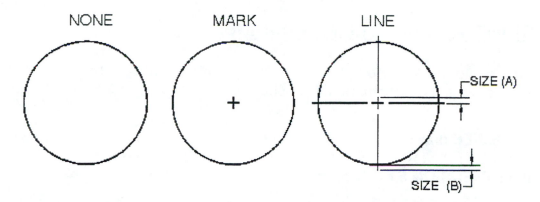

What does "SIZE" mean?

The **size** setting determines both, (A) the length of half of the intersection line and (B) the length extending beyond the circle. (See above)

Where do you set the CENTERMARK "TYPE" and "SIZE"

1. Select the *Dimension Style* command.
2. Select: *New, Modify, or Override.*
3. Select: *LINES and ARROWS* tab
4. Select the *Center mark type*
5. Set the **Size**.

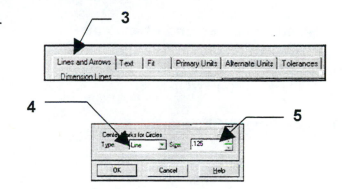

To draw a CENTER MARK

1. Select the **Center mark** command using one of the following:

      TYPING = DIMCENTER or DCE
      PULLDOWN = DIMENSION / CENTERMARK
      TOOLBAR = DIMENSION

2. Select arc or circle: *select the arc or circle with the cursor.*

CREATING A DIMENSION SUB-STYLE

Sometimes when using a dimension style, you would like the Linear, Angular, Diameter and Radius dimensions to have different settings. But you want them to use the same dimension style. To achieve this, you must create a "sub-style".
Sub-styles have also been called "children" of the "Parent" dimension style. As a result, they form a family.
A Sub-style is permanent, unlike the Override command, which is temporary.

LET'S CREATE A SUB-STYLE FOR RADIUS.

We will set the center mark to None for the Radius command only.
The Diameter command center mark will not change.

1. Open your **BSIZE** drawing.

2. Select the **DIMENSION STYLE** command.

3. Select **"Class Style"** from the Style List.

4. Select the **NEW** button.

5. Change the "Use for" to:
   Radius Dimensions

6. Select **Continue**

7. Select the **Lines and Arrows** tab.

8. Change the "Center Marks for Circles" Type: **NONE**

9. Select the **OK** button

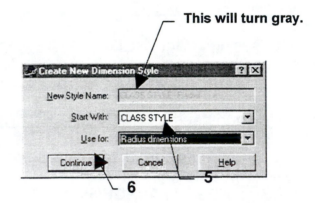

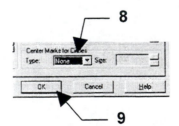

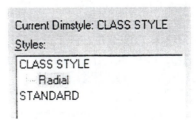

You have now created a sub-style that will automatically override the basic "Class Style" whenever you use the Radius command.

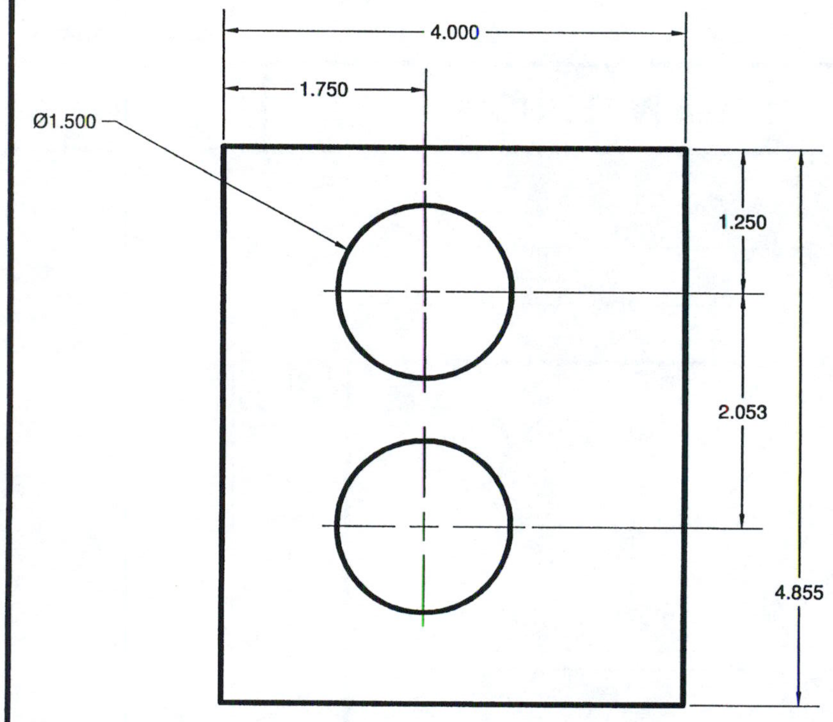
4.000
1.750
Ø1.500
1.250
2.053
4.855

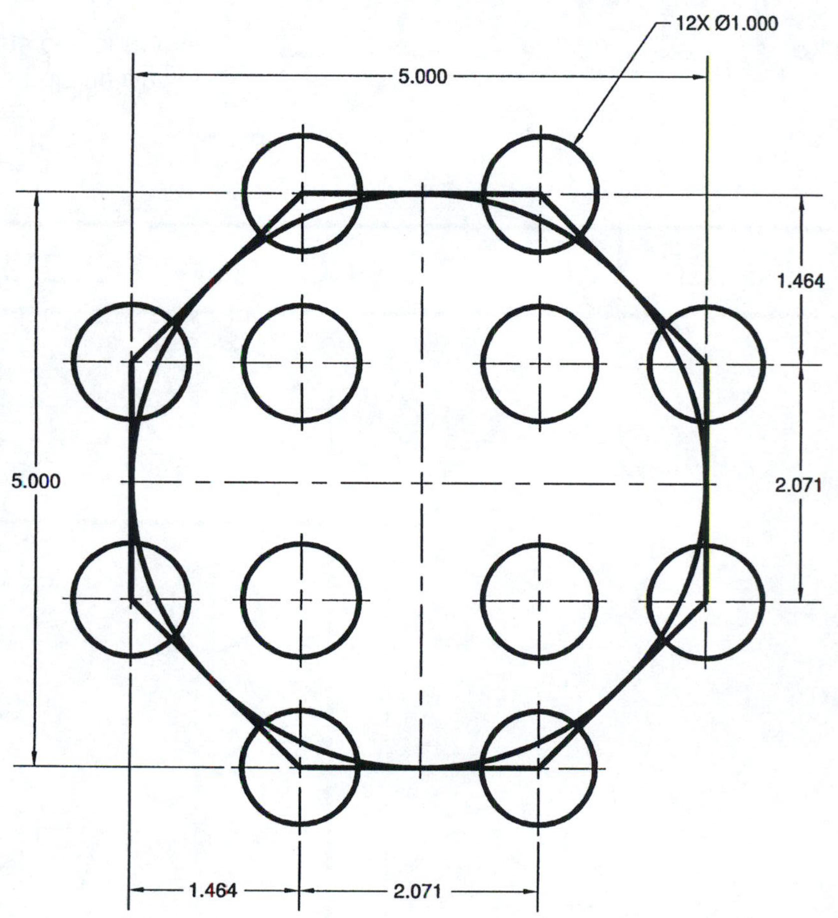
12X Ø1.000
5.000
1.464
5.000
2.071
1.464
2.071

NAME	DIAMETER AND LINEAR DIMENSIONING	EX-18A

INSTRUCTIONS:

1. Draw the objects above.
2. Dimension as shown using LINEAR and DIAMETER dimensioning.
3. NOTE: Dimension the Diameter first, then add the center marks to the remaining circles
   Draw the Linear dimensions last so you can snap to the endpoint of the center marks.
4. Save as: **EX-18A**

EXERCISE 18A

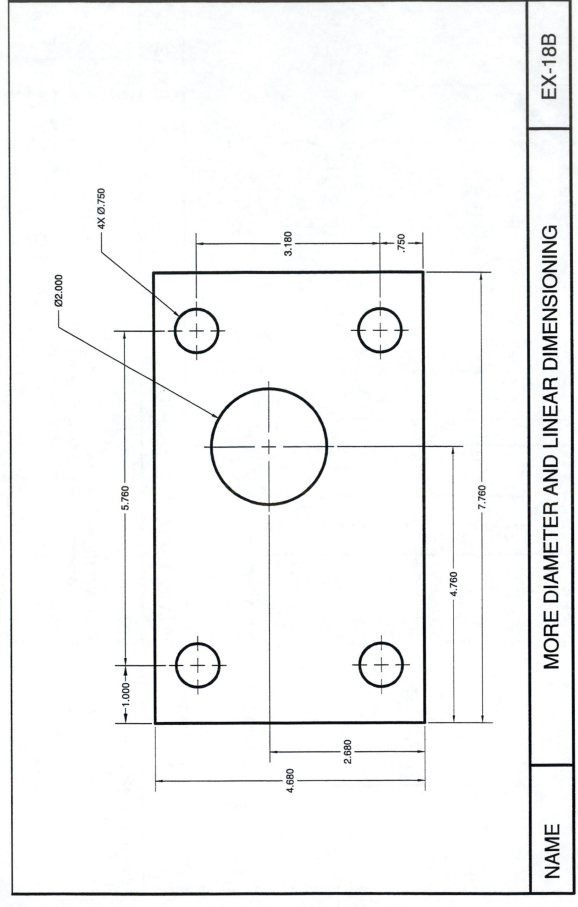

EX-18B

EXERCISE 18B

MORE DIAMETER AND LINEAR DIMENSIONING

NAME

INSTRUCTIONS:

1. Draw the objects shown above.
2. Dimension as shown using LINEAR and DIAMETER dimensioning.
3. NOTE: Dimension the Diameters first, then add center marks to the remaining circles.
   Draw the Linear dimensions last so you can snap to the endpoint of the center marks.
4. Save as: **EX-18B**

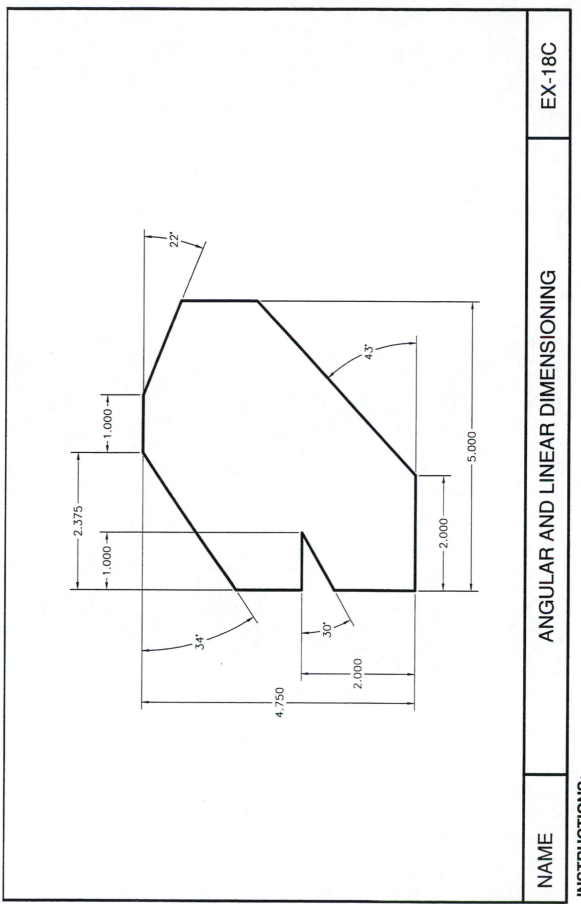

EXERCISE 18C

| NAME | ANGULAR AND LINEAR DIMENSIONING | EX-18C |

INSTRUCTIONS:

1. Open your BSIZE dwg.
2. Draw the object above. Consider using OFFSET instead of coordinate input.
3. Dimension as shown using LINEAR and ANGULAR dimensioning.
4. Dimension Style = Class style   Layer = DIM
5. Save as: **EX-18C**

NOTES:

LEARNING OBJECTIVES

After completing this lesson, you will be able to:

1. Dimension objects that are on an angle.
2. Draw a Leader.
3. Add symbols such as: diameter, plus or minus and degree to text.
4. Pre-assign a prefix or suffix to a dimension.

LESSON 19

ALIGNED DIMENSIONING

The **ALIGNED** dimension command aligns the dimension with the angle of the object that you are dimensioning. The process is the same as Linear dimensioning. It requires two extension line origins and placement of text location. (Example below)

1. Select the **ALIGNED** command using one of the following:

    TYPE = DIMALIGNED or DIMALI or DAL
    PULLDOWN = DIMENSION / ALIGNED
    TOOLBAR = DIMENSION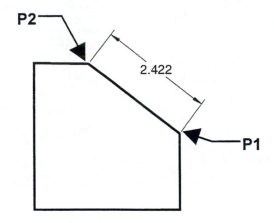

    Command: _dimaligned
2. Specify first extension line origin or <select object>: *select the first extension line origin (P1)*
3. Specify second extension line origin: *select the second extension line origin (P2)*
4. Specify dimension line location or [Mtext/Text/Angle]: *place dimension text location*

    Dimension text = *the dimension value will appear here*

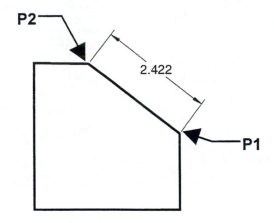

LEADER

The **LEADER** command is primarily used to add a **note** to an object. A Leader's appearance is very similar to a Radial dimension <u>but</u> a Leader <u>should not</u> to be used for Radial dimensioning. A Leader allows you to type a note at the end of the hook. (See example below)

Note: In recent versions of AutoCAD, the Leader command has been called "Quick Leader". So sometimes you will see a "q" associated with the command.

1. Select the **LEADER** command using one of the following.

    TYPE = LE or QLEADER
    PULLDOWN = DIMENSION / LEADER
    TOOLBAR = DIMENSION

    ———— See "Settings" below

    Command: _qleader
2. Specify first leader point, or [Settings]<Settings>: *select the location for the arrowhead (P1)*
3. Specify next point: *select next location (P2)*
4. Specify next point: *select another point or press <enter> to input text*
5. Specify text width <.000>: *press <enter>*
6. Enter first line of annotation text <Mtext>: *type your desired text here*
7. Enter next line of annotation text: *type more text or press <enter> to stop*

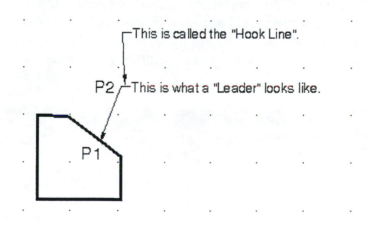

P2 ⌐This is what a "Leader" looks like.

⌐This is called the "Hook Line".

P1

HOOK LINE
The hook line is automatically added to the last line segment (P2) if the leader line is 15 degrees or more from horizontal. The length of the Hook Line is controlled by the arrow length setting in the dimension style.

SETTINGS:
If you would like to make changes to the appearance of the Leader, select **"Settings"** before you place the first point (arrowhead location). Selecting **"Settings"** will display a dialog box with many options. These options will not be discussed in the Advanced Workbook.

SPECIAL TEXT CHARACTERS

Characters such as the **degree symbol, diameter symbol** and the **plus / minus symbols** are created by typing **%%** and then the appropriate "code" letter.
For example: entering 350**%%D** will create: **350°**. The **"D"** is the **"code"** letter.

SYMBOL		CODE
⌀	Diameter	%%C
°	Degree	%%D
±	Plus / Minus	%%P

SINGLE LINE TEXT
If you are using "Single Line Text", type the code in the sentence. While you are typing, the code will appear, in the sentence, on the command line. But when you are finished typing, and press <enter>, the symbol will appear.

MULTILINE TEXT
The code displays the same as single line text if you type your text in the text editor. But multiline text offers another method for inserting special character "symbols". See below.

INSERTING SPECIAL CHARACTERS USING THE *"SYMBOL"* BUTTON IN THE: *"MULTILINE TEXT EDITOR".*
While you are typing in the multiline text editor, instead of typing the code, select the "symbol" button. A drop-down menu will appear. Select the symbol desired and the code or the actual symbol will automatically appear in the sentence. This is not a great time saver but it does relieve you of having to memorize frequently used codes

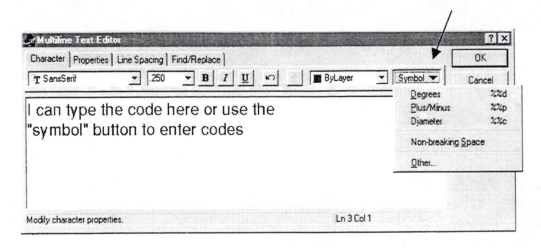

PREFIX and SUFFIX

The **PREFIX** (before) and the **SUFFIX** (after) allows you to preset text to be inserted automatically as you dimension.

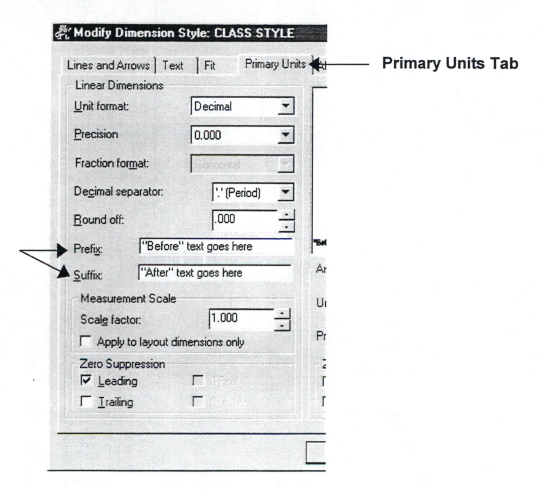

Primary Units Tab

Examples:

If you wanted all of your dimensions to end with *Ref*, you would type **<space>Ref** in the suffix box.

If you wanted all of your dimensions to begin with *2 places*, you would type **2 places** in the prefix box.

Note: If you enter text in the Prefix box when drawing Radial dimensions, the **"R"** for radius or the **diameter symbol**, will not be automatically drawn. You must add the symbol code, also, to the prefix box.

Example: If you would like a diameter dimension to have 2X as a Prefix, you must type the following, in the Prefix box: **2X <space> %%C**.

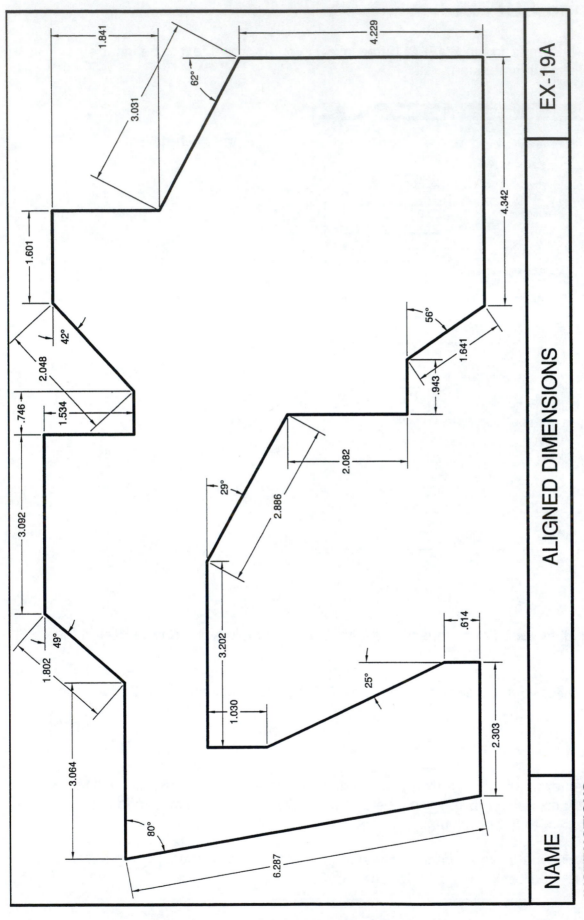

EXERCISE 19A

| NAME | ALIGNED DIMENSIONS | EX-19A |

INSTRUCTIONS:

1. Draw the object shown above. You will get to practice "Polar Coordinates".
2. Dimension using Aligned, Linear and Angular.
3. Use Dimension Style "Class Style".
4. Save as 19A and Plot.

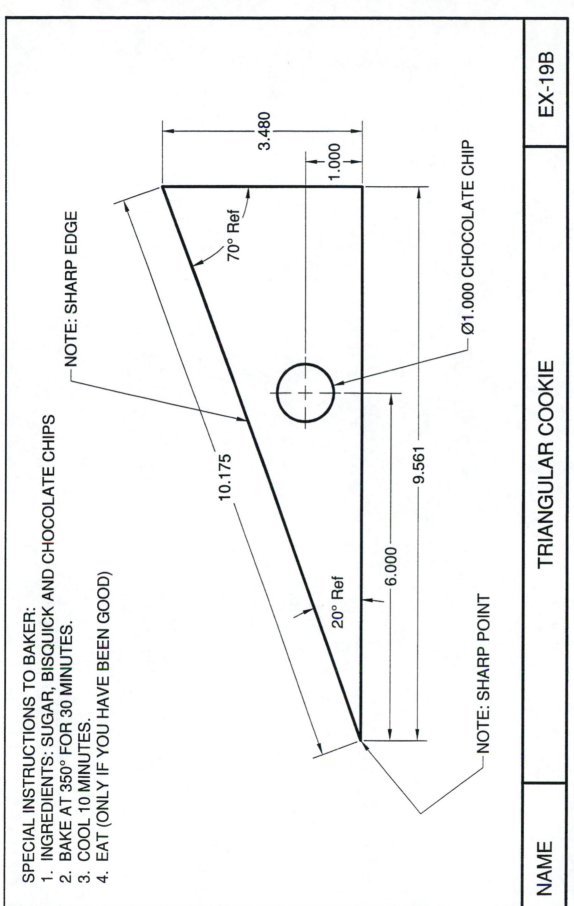

SPECIAL INSTRUCTIONS TO BAKER:
1. INGREDIENTS: SUGAR, BISQUICK AND CHOCOLATE CHIPS
2. BAKE AT 350° FOR 30 MINUTES.
3. COOL 10 MINUTES.
4. EAT (ONLY IF YOU HAVE BEEN GOOD)

NOTE: SHARP EDGE

70° Ref

3.480

1.000

Ø1.000 CHOCOLATE CHIP

10.175

20° Ref

9.561

6.000

NOTE: SHARP POINT

| NAME | TRIANGULAR COOKIE | EX-19B |

EXERCISE 19B

INSTRUCTIONS:
1. Draw the object above.
2. Dimension as shown using:
   LINEAR, ANGULAR, RADIAL, ALIGNED and QUICK LEADER dimensioning.
3. Use Dimension Style "Class Style".
4. For the Note use: Text Ht. = .125   Layer = TXT-LIT
5. Save as: **EX-19B**

NOTES:

LEARNING OBJECTIVES

After completing this lesson, you will be able to:

1. Use Multiple Automatic dimensioning.
2. Edit Multiple dimensions.

LESSON 20

QUICK DIMENSION

Sorry LT users, this command is not available to you. Skip to Lesson 21.

Quick Dimension creates multiple dimensions with one command. Quick Dimension can create Continuous, Baseline, Radius and Diameter dimensions. *(Ordinate will be discussed in the Advanced workbook)*

1. Select the **Quick Dimension** command using one of the following:

TYPE = QDIM
PULLDOWN = Dimension/Quick Dimension
TOOLBAR = DIMENSION

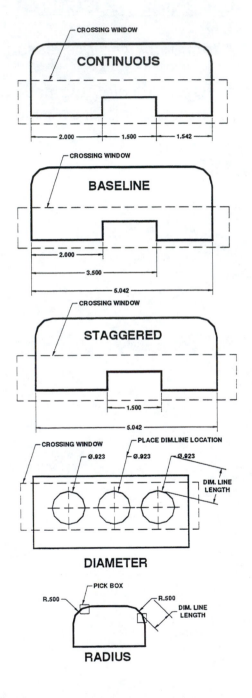

CONTINUOUS

2. Select the objects to be dimensioned with a crossing window or pick each object
3. Press <enter> to stop
4. Select **"C"** <enter> for **Continuous.**
5. Select the location of the dimension line.

BASELINE

2. Select the objects to be dimensioned with a crossing window or pick each object.
3. Press <enter> to stop
4. Select **"B"** <enter> for **Baseline.**
5. Select the location of the dimension line.

STAGGERED

2. Select the objects to be dimensioned with a crossing window or pick each object.
3. Press <enter> to stop
4. Select **"S"** <enter> for **Staggered**.
5. Select the location of the dimension line.

DIAMETER

2. Select the objects to be dimensioned with a crossing window or pick each object (Qdim will automatically filter out any linear dims)
3. Press <enter> to stop
4. Select **"D"** <enter> for **Diameter**
5. Select the location of the dimension line.
(Dimension line length is determined by the "Baseline Spacing" setting)

RADIUS

2. Select the objects to be dimensioned with a crossing window or pick each object.
   (Quick Dimension will automatically filter out any linear dimensions)
3. Press <enter> to stop selecting objects
4. Select **"R"** <enter> for **Radius**.
The dimensions are automatically placed, you do not select the location for the dimension line. *Dimension line length is determined by the "Baseline Spacing" setting)*

EDITING MULTIPLE DIMENSIONS

You can edit existing multiple dimensions using the QDIM / Edit command. The Qdim, edit command will edit all multiple dimensions, no matter whether they were created originally with Qdim or not. All multiple: linear, baseline and continue dimensions respond to this editing command.

1. Select the QDIM command.
2. Select the dimensions to edit.
3. Press <enter> to stop selecting.
4. Select "E" for edit.

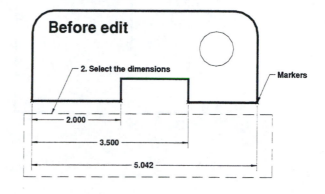

Small *markers* will appear at the extension line origins. These markers are called **"dimension points"**. You can **Add** or **Remove** dimensions by selecting these markers.

REMOVE
AutoCAD assumes that you want to Remove dimensions, so this is the default setting.

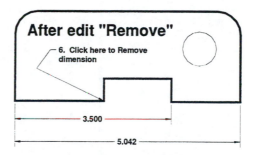

5. Indicate dimension point to remove, or [Add/eXit] <eXit>:.
6. Click on the extension line markers you want to remove.
7. Press "X" to stop selecting.
8. Press "ESC" to stop.

ADD

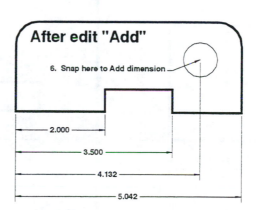

5. Select "A" <enter> for Add
6. Using Object Snap, select the extension line origins of the dimension you want to Add.
7. Press "X" to stop selecting.
8. Place the dimension line location.

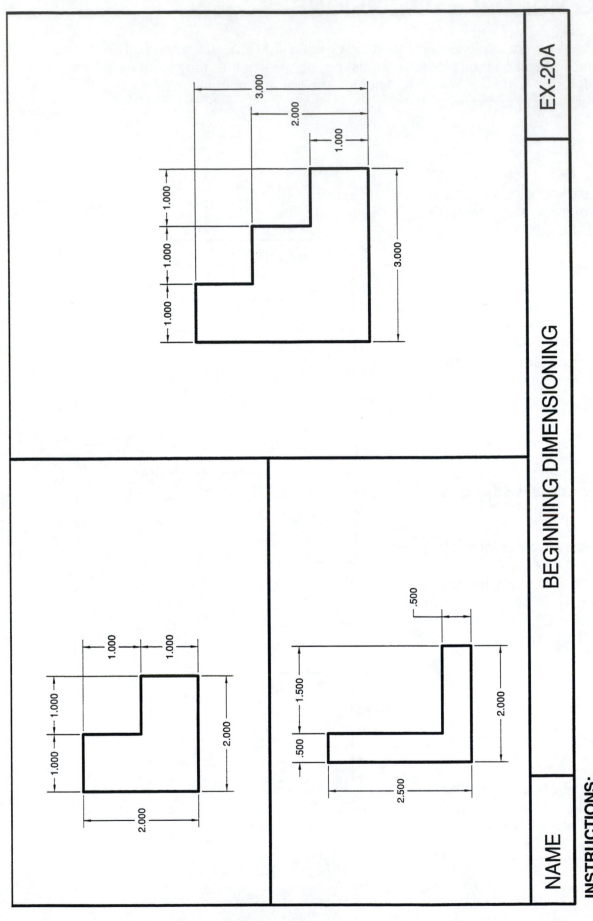

EXERCISE 20A

EX-20A

BEGINNING DIMENSIONING

NAME

INSTRUCTIONS:

1. Open EX-16A
2. Erase all the dimensions
3. Dimension again using QDIM command.
4. Save as: **EX-20A**

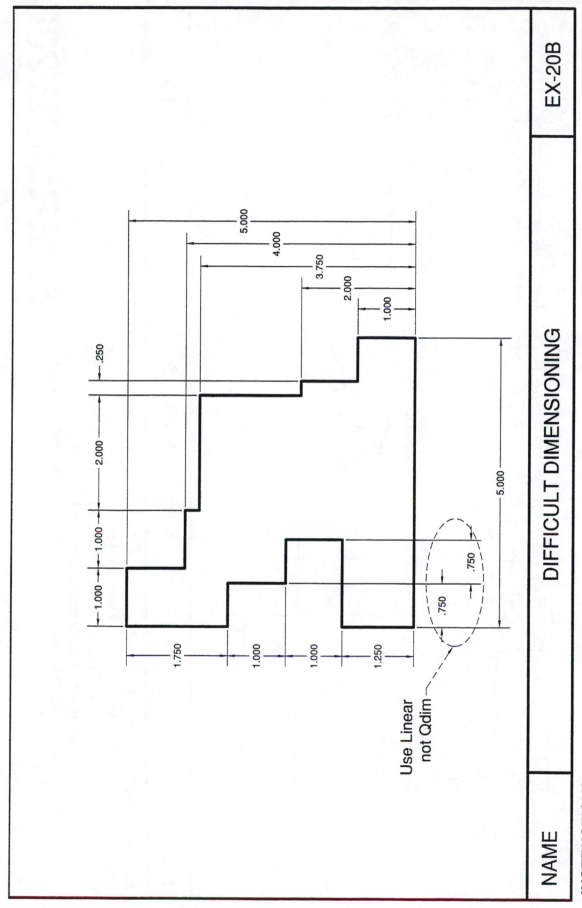

Use Linear
not Qdim

EXERCISE 20B

DIFFICULT DIMENSIONING

EX-20B

NAME

INSTRUCTIONS:
1. Open EX-16B.
2. Erase all of the Dimensions.
3. Dimension again using QDIM.
4. Save as: **EX-20B**

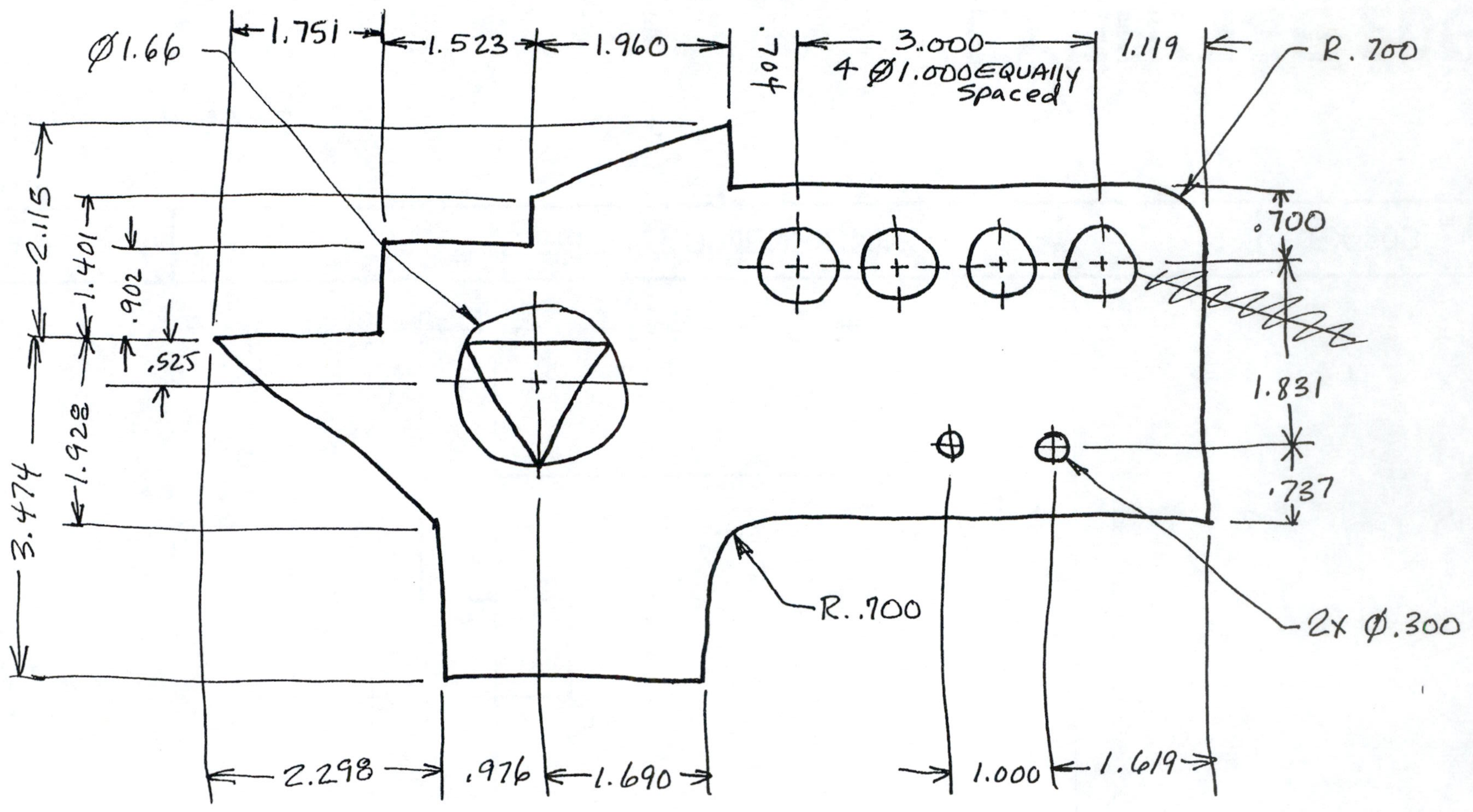

EX-20C

EXERCISE 20C

NAME

Clean up this sketch

INSTRUCTIONS:
Many times, on the job, you will be handed a sketch like the one shown above. You will be expected to create a clean and accurate drawing from this sketch. After drawing the objects accurately, try out the new Quick dimension command. You will find that you can use Quick dimension for some but you must use Linear, Continue and Baseline for others. You decide which is best.
Save as: **EX-20C**

After completing this lesson, you will be able to:

1. Change an object's properties to match the properties of another object.

LESSON 21

MATCH PROPERTIES

Match Properties is used to "paint" the properties of one object to another. This is a simple and useful command. You first select the object that has the desired properties (the source object) and then select the object you want to "paint" the properties to (destination object).

Only one "source object" can be selected but its properties can be painted to any number of "destination objects".

1. Select the Match Properties command using one of the following:

> **TYPE = MATCHPROP or PAINT or MA**
> **PULLDOWN = MODIFY / MATCH PROPERTIES**
> **TOOLBAR = STANDARD**

Command: matchprop
2. Select source object: ***select the object with the desired properties***
3. Select destination object(s) or [Settings]: ***select the object(s) you want to change***
4. Select destination object(s) or [Settings]: ***select more objects or <enter> to stop.***

PRACTICE

The following drawings (21A, B and C) should give you some practice with drawing and dimensioning commands. The more you practice, the more comfortable you will become with AutoCAD.

Check back on the previous lessons for instructions on commands you have forgotten.

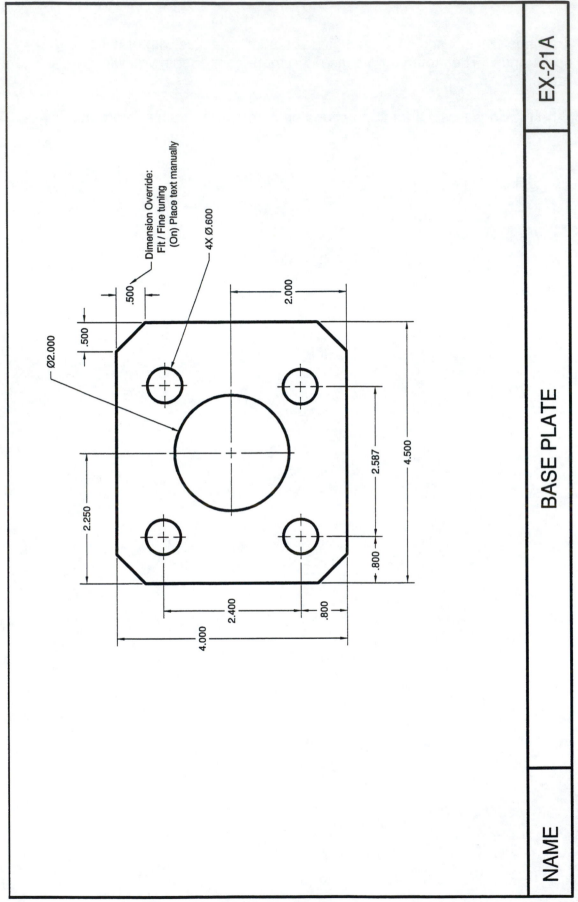

Dimension Override:
Fit / Fine tuning
(On) Place text manually

4X Ø.600

Ø2.000

.500

.500

2.000

2.250

2.587

4.500

.800

.800

2.400

4.000

EXERCISE 21A

EX-21A

BASE PLATE

NAME

INSTRUCTIONS:

1. Draw and dimension the Base Plate above.
2. Remember when drawing a RECTANGLE you may chamfer the corners.
   (Refer to Lesson 3)
3. Save as: **EX-21A**

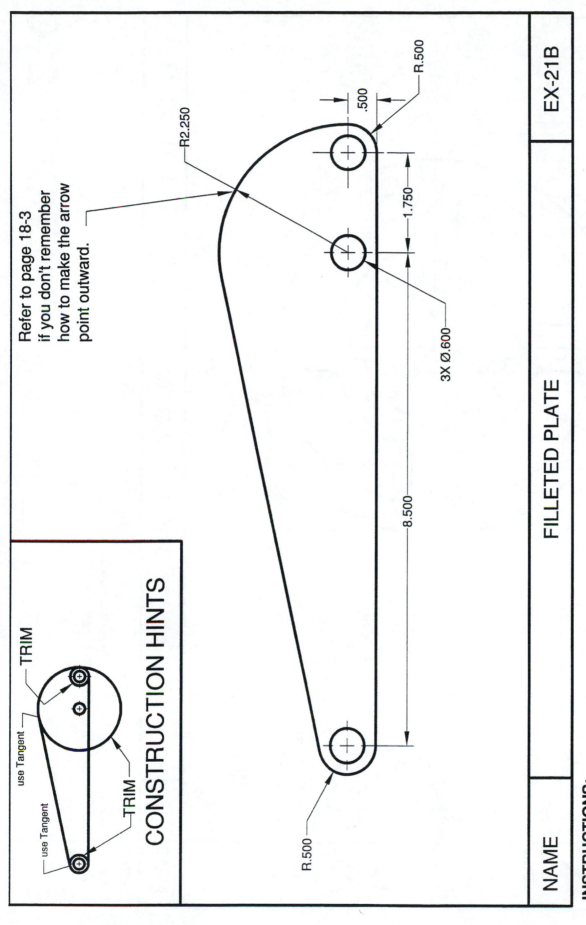

Refer to page 18-3
if you don't remember
how to make the arrow
point outward.

R2.250

R.500

.500

1.750

3X Ø.600

8.500

R.500

TRIM

use Tangent

use Tangent

TRIM

CONSTRUCTION HINTS

EX-21B

FILLETED PLATE

NAME

INSTRUCTIONS:

1. Draw and dimension the FILLETED PLATE above using:
   Lines, Offset, Copy, and Trim.

2. Dimension as shown.

3. Save as: **EX-21B**

EXERCISE 21B

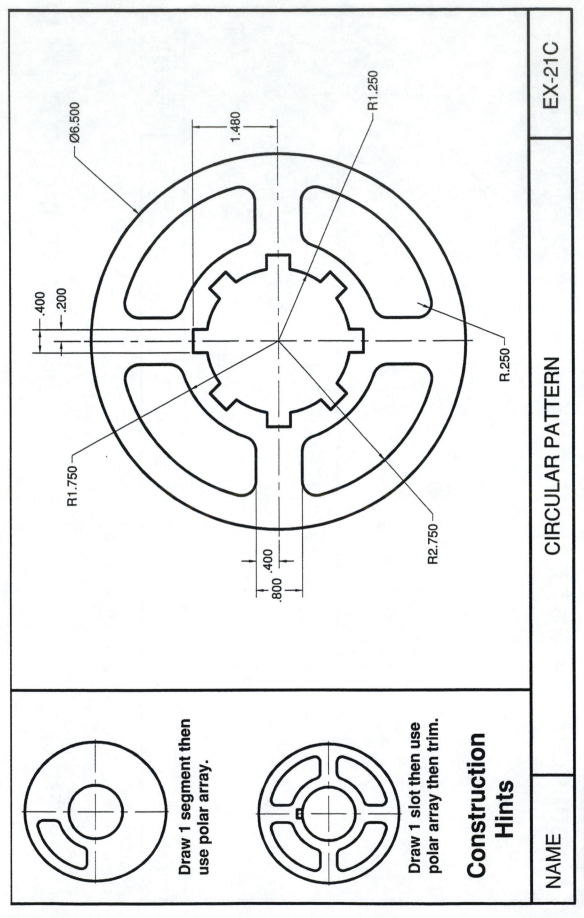

Ø6.500

1.480

R1.250

.400
.200

R1.750

.400
.800

R2.750

R.250

CIRCULAR PATTERN

EX-21C

EXERCISE 21C

Draw 1 segment then use polar array.

Draw 1 slot then use polar array then trim.

Construction Hints

NAME

INSTRUCTIONS:

1. Draw and dimension the FILLETED PLATE above using:
   Lines, Circles, Offset, Array, Fillet and Trim.
2. Dimension as shown.
3. Save as: **EX-21C**

LEARNING OBJECTIVES

After completing this lesson, you will be able to:

1. Draw an Arc using 10 different methods.

LESSON 22

ARC

TYPING = A
PULLDOWNS = DRAW / ARC
TOOLBARS =DRAW

There are 10 ways to draw an ARC in AutoCAD.   Not all of the ARCS options are easy to create so you may find it is often easier to **trim a Circle** or use the **Fillet** command.

An **ARC** is a segment of a circle and must be less than 360 degrees.

Most ARCS are drawn counter-clockwise but you will notice, in the examples on the following pages, that some may be drawn clockwise by entering a negative input.

Examples of each of the ARC options are shown in EXERCISES 22A through 22C.

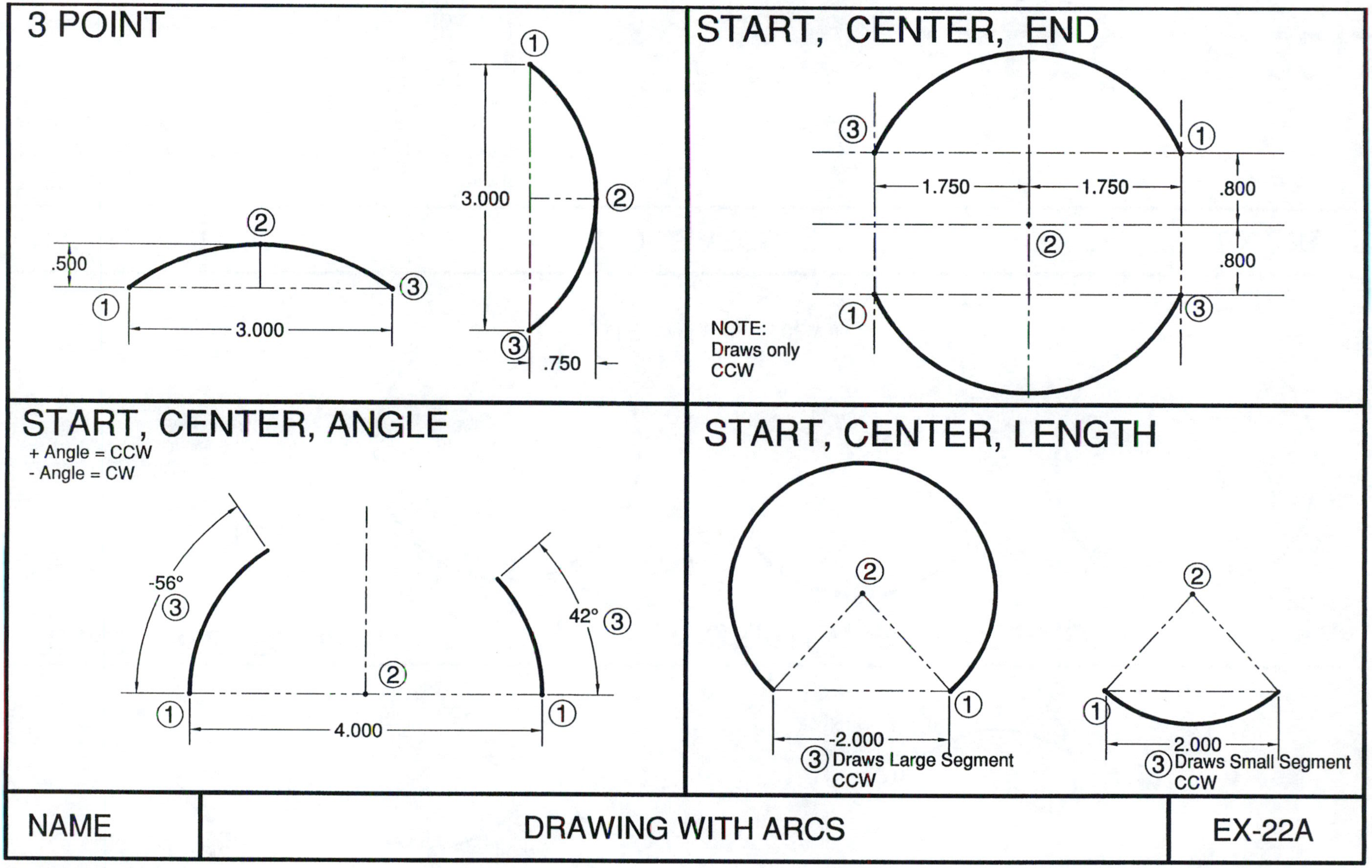

EXERCISE 22A

3 POINT

3.000

.750

3.000

.500

START, CENTER, END

.800

.800

1.750

1.750

NOTE:
Draws only
CCW

START, CENTER, ANGLE

+ Angle = CCW
- Angle = CW

42°

4.000

-56°

START, CENTER, LENGTH

2.000
Draws Small Segment
CCW

EX-22A

-2.000
Draws Large Segment
CCW

DRAWING WITH ARCS

NAME	

INSTRUCTIONS:

1. Draw the ARCS above. Select the method shown.
2. Save as: **EX-22A.**

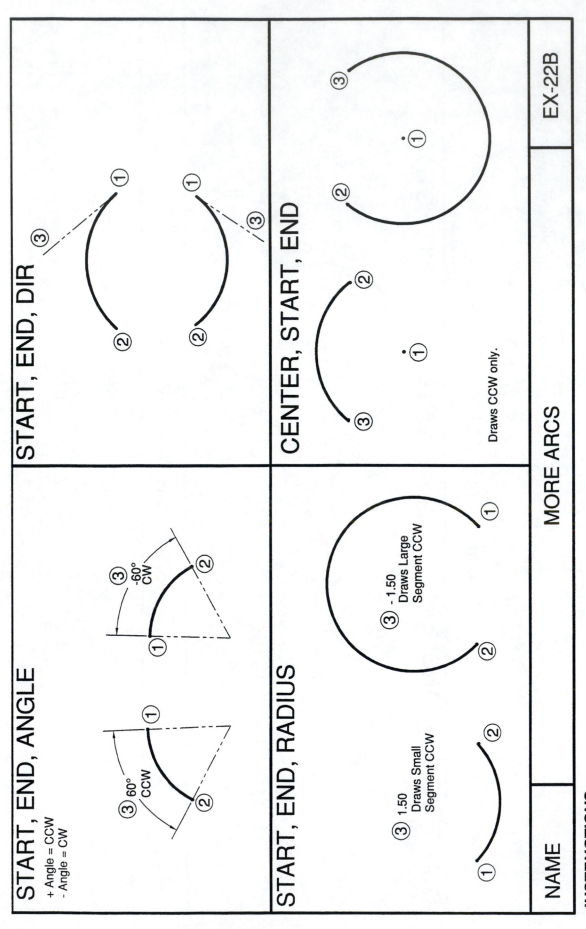

EXERCISE 22B

START, END, DIR

+ Angle = CCW
- Angle = CW

CENTER, START, END

Draws CCW only.

START, END, ANGLE

③ 60° CCW

③ -60° CW

START, END, RADIUS

③ 1.50
Draws Small
Segment CCW

③ -1.50
Draws Large
Segment CCW

MORE ARCS

EX-22B

NAME

INSTRUCTIONS:

1. Draw the ARCS above. Select the method shown.
2. Save as: **EX-22B.**

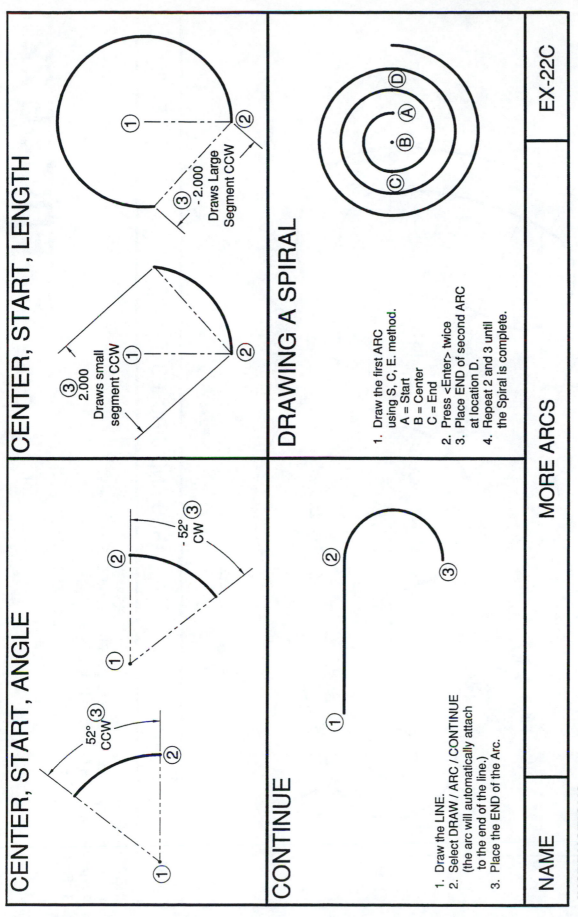

CENTER, START, ANGLE

52° CCW ③
②
①

② -52° CW ③
①

CENTER, START, LENGTH

① ②
③ -2.000
Draws Large Segment CCW

③ 2.000
Draws small segment CCW
① ②

CONTINUE

① ② ③

1. Draw the LINE.
2. Select DRAW / ARC / CONTINUE (the arc will automatically attach to the end of the line.)
3. Place the END of the Arc.

DRAWING A SPIRAL

Ⓓ
Ⓐ
Ⓑ
Ⓒ

1. Draw the first ARC using S, C, E. method.
   A = Start
   B = Center
   C = End
2. Press <Enter> twice
3. Place END of second ARC at location D.
4. Repeat 2 and 3 until the Spiral is complete.

NAME		MORE ARCS	EX-22C

INSTRUCTIONS:
1. Draw the ARCS above. Select the method shown.
2. Save as: **EX-22C.**

EXERCISE 22C

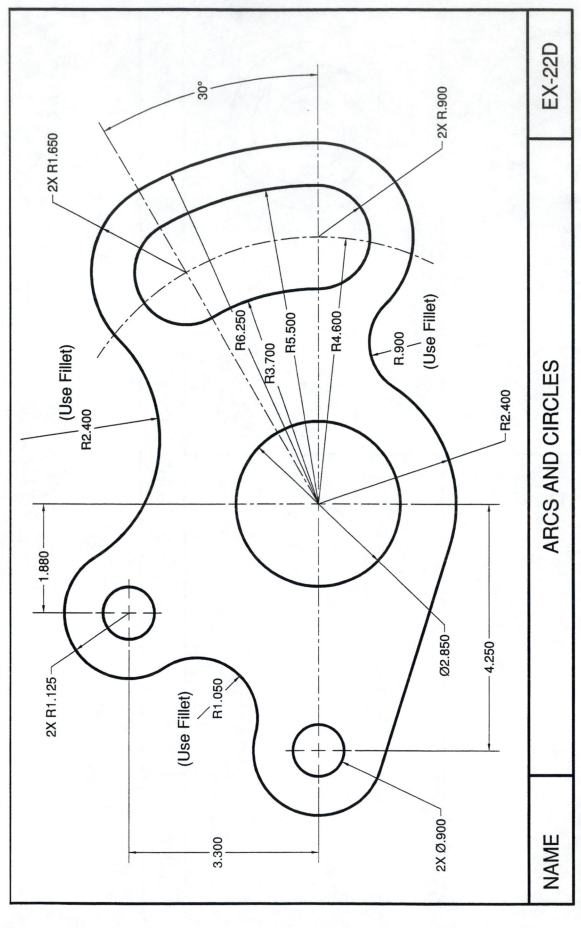

EXERCISE 22D

EX-22D
ARCS AND CIRCLES
NAME

INSTRUCTIONS:

1. Draw the Object above using ARCS, FILLET, CIRCLE and LINES.
2. Refer to lesson 18 for help with Dim Style settings
3. Save as: **EX-22D.**

LEARNING OBJECTIVES

After completing this lesson, you will be able to:

1. Understand what is a Polyline.
2. Draw a Polyline and Polyarc.
3. Assign widths to polylines.
4. Set the Fill mode to On or Off.

LESSON 23

POLYLINES

A **POLYLINE** is very similar to a LINE. It is created in the same way a line is drawn. It requires first and second endpoints. But a POLYLINE has additional features, as follows:

1. A **POLYLINE** is ONE object, even though it may have many segments.
2. You may specify a specific width to each segment.
3. You may specify a different width to the start and end of a polyline segment.

THE FOLLOWING ARE EXAMPLES OF POLYLINES WITH WIDTHS ASSIGNED.

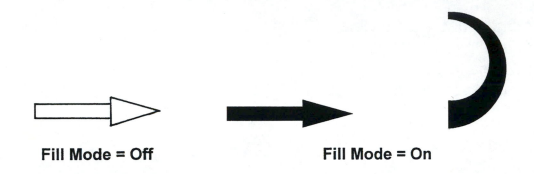

Fill Mode = Off   **Fill Mode = On**

To turn FILL MODE on or off.

1. Command: *type* **FILL** *<enter>*
2. Enter mode [On / Off] <ON>: *type ON or Off <enter>*
3. Command: *type REGEN <enter> or select: View / Regen*

NOTE: If you explode a POLYLINE it loses its width and turns into a regular line.

THE FOLLOWING IS AN EXAMPLE OF DRAWING A POLYLINE WITH "WIDTH"

1. Select the POLYLINE command using one of the following:

   TYPE = PL
   PULLDOWN = DRAW / POLYLINE
   TOOLBAR = DRAW

   Command: _pline
2. Specify start point: *place the first endpoint of the line*
   Current line-width is 0.000
3. Specify next point or [Arc/Close/Halfwidth/Length/Undo/Width]: *type w* <enter>
4. Specify starting width <0.000>: *type the desired width* <enter>
5. Specify ending width <0.000>: *type the desired width* <enter>
6. Specify next point or [Arc/Close/Halfwidth/Length/Undo/Width]: *place the next endpoint*
7. Specify next point or [Arc/Close/Halfwidth/Length/Undo/Width]: *place the next endpoint*
8. Specify next point or [Arc/Close/Halfwidth/Length/Undo/Width]: *place the next endpoint*
9. Specify next point or [Arc/Close/Halfwidth/Length/Undo/Width]: *type C <enter>*

OPTIONS:

WIDTH
Specify the starting and ending width.

You can create a tapered polyline by specifying different starting and ending widths.

HALFWIDTH
The same as Width except the starting and ending halfwidth specifies half the width rather than the entire width.

ARC
This option allows you to create a circular polyline less than 360 degrees.

CLOSE
The close option is the same as in the Line command. Close attaches the last segment to the first segment.

LENGTH
This option allows you to draw a polyline at the same angle as the last polyline drawn. This option is very similar to the OFFSET command. You specify the first endpoint and the length. The new polyline will automatically be drawn at the same angle as the previous polyline.

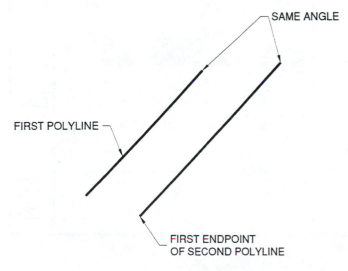

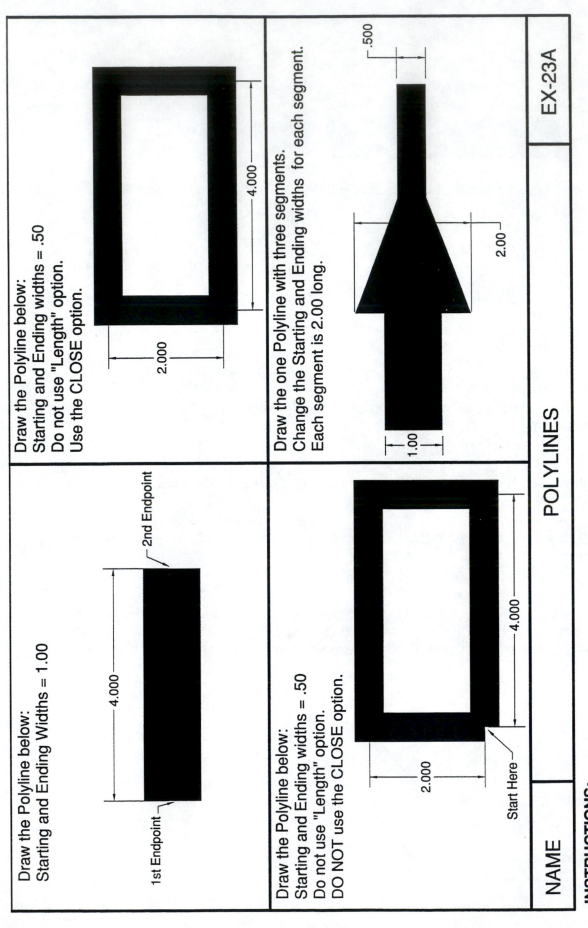

Draw the Polyline below:
Starting and Ending widths = .50
Do not use "Length" option.
Use the CLOSE option.

4.000

2.000

Draw the one Polyline with three segments.
Change the Starting and Ending widths for each segment.
Each segment is 2.00 long.

.500

2.00

1.00

Draw the Polyline below:
Starting and Ending Widths = 1.00

2nd Endpoint

4.000

1st Endpoint

Draw the Polyline below:
Starting and Ending widths = .50
Do not use "Length" option.
DO NOT use the CLOSE option.

4.000

2.000

Start Here

EX-23A

POLYLINES

NAME

EXERCISE 23A

INSTRUCTIONS:

1. Draw the POLYLINES above. Follow the directions in each section.

2. Save as: **EX-23A.**

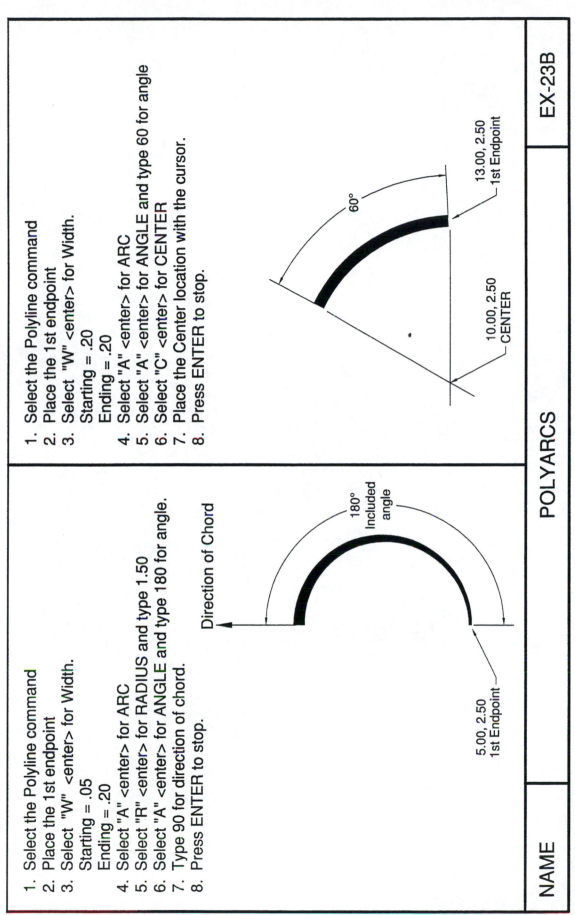

EXERCISE 23B

POLYARCS

1. Select the Polyline command
2. Place the 1st endpoint
3. Select "W" <enter> for Width.
   Starting = .20
   Ending = .20
4. Select "A" <enter> for ARC
5. Select "A" <enter> for ANGLE and type 60 for angle
6. Select "C" <enter> for CENTER
7. Place the Center location with the cursor.
8. Press ENTER to stop.

60°

13.00, 2.50
1st Endpoint

10.00, 2.50
CENTER

1. Select the Polyline command
2. Place the 1st endpoint
3. Select "W" <enter> for Width.
   Starting = .05
   Ending = .20
4. Select "A" <enter> for ARC
5. Select "R" <enter> for RADIUS and type 1.50
6. Select "A" <enter> for ANGLE and type 180 for angle.
7. Type 90 for direction of chord.
8. Press ENTER to stop.

Direction of Chord

180°
Included angle

5.00, 2.50
1st Endpoint

NAME

INSTRUCTIONS:
1. Draw the POLYLINES above. Follow the direction in each section.
2. Save as: **EX-23B.**

NOTES:

LEARNING OBJECTIVES

After completing this lesson, you will be able to:

1. Edit the width of a Polyline.
2. Join Polylines.
3. Convert a Polyline to a spline.
4. Convert a basic Line into a Polyline.

LESSON 24

EDITING POLYLINES

The **POLYEDIT** command allows you to make changes to a polyline's option, such as the width. You can also change a regular line into a polyline and JOIN the segments.

1. Select the **POLYEDIT** command using one of the following:

> **TYPE = PE**
> **PULLDOWN = MODIFY / OBJECT/ POLYLINE**
> **TOOLBAR =MODIFY II**

Note: AutoCAD 2002 allows you to modify "Multiple" polylines simultaneously.

2. PEDIT Select polyline or [Multiple]: *select the polyline to be edited or "M"*
3. Enter an option [Close/Join/Width/Edit vertex/Fit/Spline/Decurve/Ltypegen/Undo]: *select an Option (descriptions of each are listed below.)*

Note: If you select a line that is **NOT a POLYLINE**, the prompt will ask if you would like to turn it into a POLYLINE.

OPTIONS: (Step by step instructions in the following exercises)

CLOSE (Refer to Exercise 24A)
CLOSE connects the last segment with the first segment of an Open polyline. AutoCAD considers a polyline open unless you use the "Close" option to connect the segments originally.

OPEN (Refer to Exercise 24A)
OPEN removes the closing segment, but only if the CLOSE option was used to close the polyline originally.

JOIN (Refer to Exercise 24D)
The JOIN option allows you to join individual polyline segments into one polyline. The segments must have matching endpoints.

WIDTH (Refer to Exercise 24B)
The WIDTH option allows you to change the width of the polyline. But the entire polyline will have the same width.

EDIT VERTEX (Refer to Exercise 24C)
This option allows you to change the starting and ending width of each segment individually.

SPLINE (Refer to Exercise 24D)
This option allows you to change straight polylines to curves.

DECURVE
This option removes the SPLINE curves and returns the polyline to its original straight line segments.

EXERCISE 24A

1. Draw the Polyline below.
2. Select the POLY EDIT command.
3. Select the Polyline to be edited.
4. Select CLOSE from the options.
   (the polyline should be closed now)
5. Now Select the OPEN option.
   (the polyline should be open again)

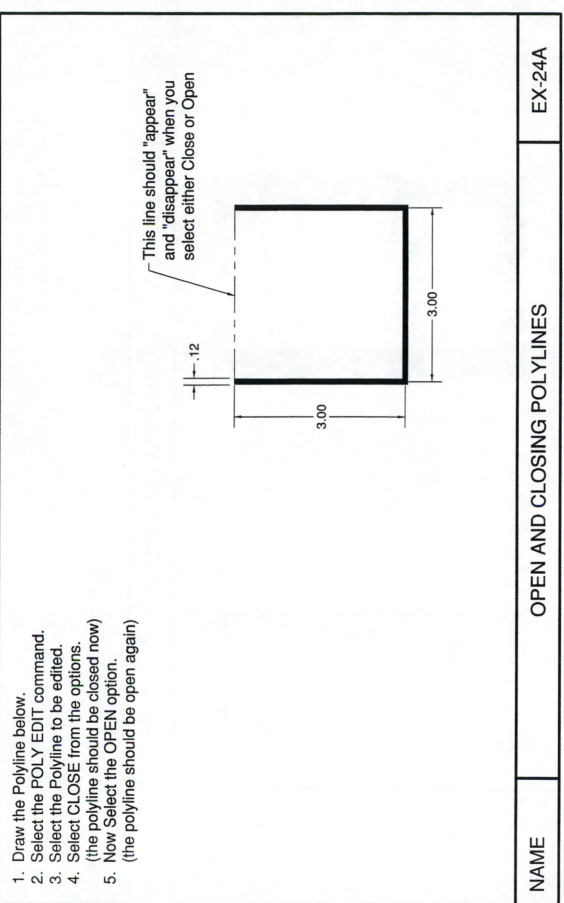

This line should "appear" and "disappear" when you select either Close or Open

.12

3.00

3.00

NAME	OPEN AND CLOSING POLYLINES	EX-24A

INSTRUCTIONS:

1. Draw the POLYLINES above. Follow the directions above.
2. Save as: **EX-24A.**

EXERCISE 24B

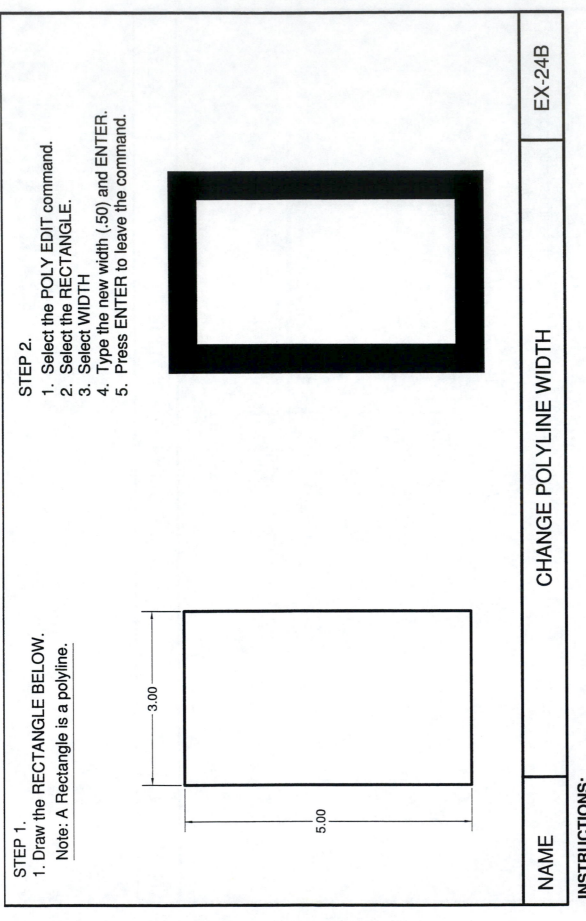

STEP 1.
1. Draw the RECTANGLE BELOW.
Note: A Rectangle is a polyline.

3.00

5.00

STEP 2.
1. Select the POLY EDIT command.
2. Select the RECTANGLE.
3. Select WIDTH
4. Type the new width (.50) and ENTER.
5. Press ENTER to leave the command.

EX-24B

CHANGE POLYLINE WIDTH

NAME

INSTRUCTIONS:
1. Draw the RECTANGLE above. Follow the directions above.
2. Save as: **EX-24B.**

STEP 1. Draw 1 polyline made of 3
        connecting (joined) segments, each
        2 inches long

STEP 2.
1. Select the POLY EDIT command.
2. Select the first segment.
3. Select the EDIT VERTEX option.

(Notice the "X" marking the starting point.)

4. Select the WIDTH option
5. Type the STARTING (1.00) and ENDING (.50) widths.
6. Select NEXT.

(Notice the "X" moved to the "next" segment starting point)

7. Select the WIDTH option.
8. Type the STARTING (.50) and ENDING (.50) widths.
9. Select NEXT. ("X" moved again)
10. Select the WIDTH option.
11. Type the STARTING (2.00) and ENDING (0)widths.
12. Press <enter> to stop.

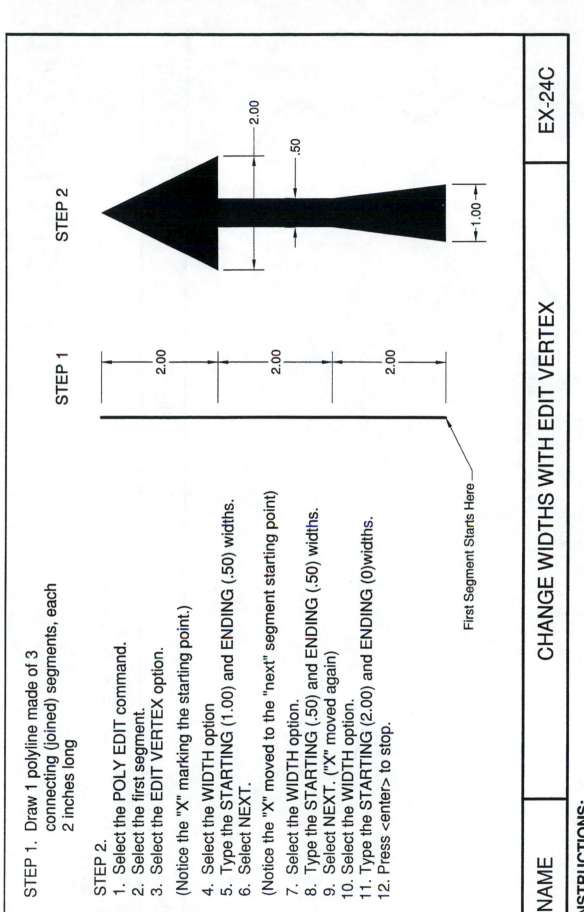

STEP 1

STEP 2

2.00

.50

2.00

2.00

2.00

2.00

1.00

First Segment Starts Here

EXERCISE 24C

NAME		CHANGE WIDTHS WITH EDIT VERTEX

INSTRUCTIONS:

1. Draw the POLYLINE above. Follow the directions above.

2. Save as: **EX-24C.**

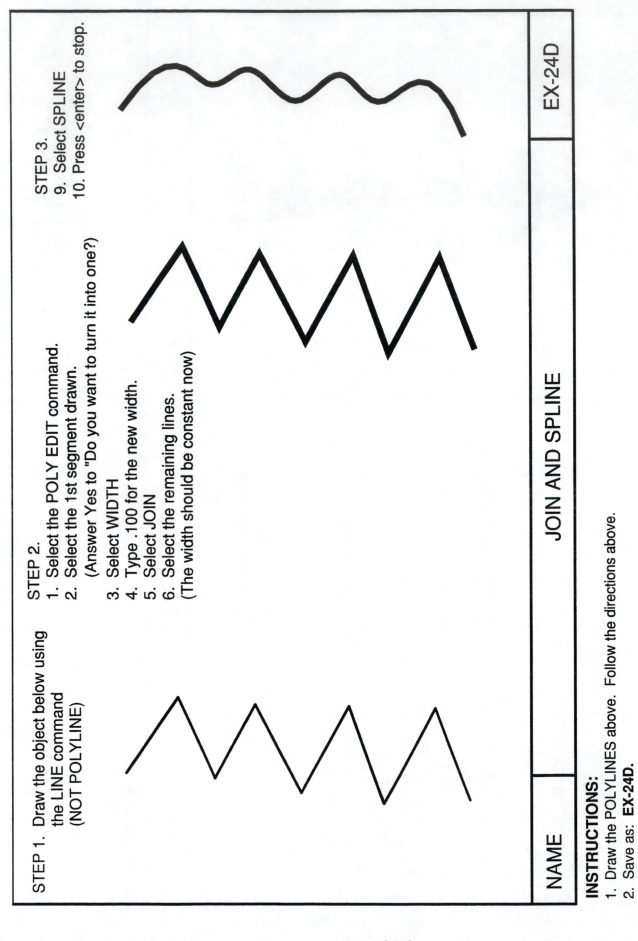

STEP 1. Draw the object below using the LINE command. (NOT POLYLINE)

STEP 2.
1. Select the POLY EDIT command.
2. Select the 1st segment drawn.
   (Answer Yes to "Do you want to turn it into one?)
3. Select WIDTH
4. Type .100 for the new width.
5. Select JOIN
6. Select the remaining lines.
   (The width should be constant now)

STEP 3.
9. Select SPLINE
10. Press <enter> to stop.

JOIN AND SPLINE

EX-24D

EXERCISE 24D

NAME

INSTRUCTIONS:
1. Draw the POLYLINES above. Follow the directions above.
2. Save as: **EX-24D.**

LEARNING OBJECTIVES

After completing this lesson, you will be able to:

1. Create a new Text Style.
2. Change and Existing Text Style.
3. Change the Point Style.
4. Place a Point at designated intervals on an object.

LESSON 25

CREATING NEW TEXT STYLES

AutoCAD provides you with only one Text Style named "Standard". You may want to create a new text style with a different font and effects. Steps 1 through 8 below will guide you through the process.

1. Select the TEXT STYLE command using one of the following:
   TYPE = STYLE or ST
   PULLDOWN = FORMAT / TEXT STYLE
   TOOLBAR = FORMAT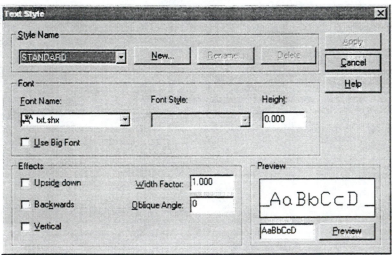

   The TEXT STYLE dialog box below should appear.

The information in this dialog box is a description of the Text Style highlighted in the Style Name box.

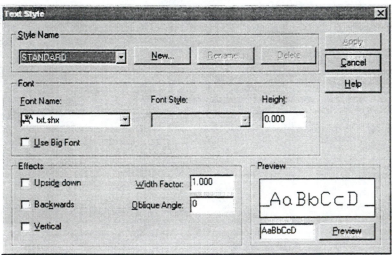

2. Select the **NEW** button.

4. Select the **FONT**.

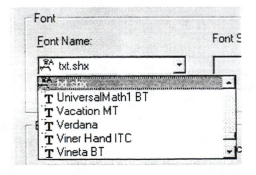

3. Type the new style name in **STYLE NAME** box. Then select the **OK** button.

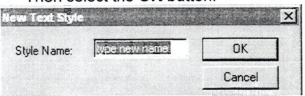

Text Styles can have a maximum of 31 characters, including letters, numbers, dashes, underlines and dollar signs. You can use Upper or Lower case.

5. Enter the value of the Height.
   (If the value is 0, AutoCAD will always prompt you for a height. If you enter a number the new text style will have a fixed height and AutoCAD will not prompt you for the height)

6. Assign **EFFECTS.**

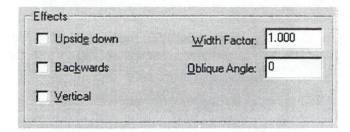

UPSIDE-DOWN
Each letter will be created upside-down in the order in which it was typed.
(Note: this is different from rotating text 180 degrees.)

BACKWARDS
The letters will be created backwards as typed.

VERTICAL
Each letter will be inserted directly under the other. Only **.shx** fonts can be used.
VERTICAL text will not display in the **PREVIEW** box.

OBLIQUING ANGLE
Creates letter with a slant, like italic. An angle of 0 creates a vertical letter. A positive angle will slant the letter forward. A negative angle will slant the letter backward.

WIDTH FACTOR
This effect compresses or extends the width of each character. A value less than 1 compresses. A value greater than 1 extends each character.

7. **PREVIEW** your settings.

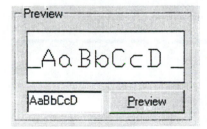

8. Select the **APPLY** button and then the **CLOSE** button.

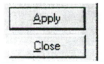

CREATING YOUR NEW TEXT STYLE IS NOW COMPLETE.

CHANGING TEXT STYLES

RENAMING

1. Select the **TEXT STYLE** command.
   The Text Style Dialog box appears.

2. Select the style
   you want to rename.

3. Click on
   RENAME button.

4. Type the New name then click on the
   OK button.

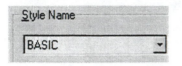

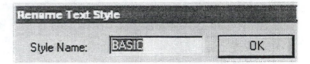

5. Click on the **CLOSE** button.

DELETING

1. Select the **TEXT STYLE** command.
   The Text Style Dialog box appears.

2. Select the style
   you want to DELETE.

3. Click on the
   DELETE button.

4. Warning appears, select
   Yes or No.

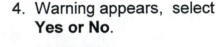

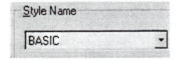

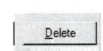

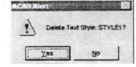

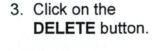

5. Click on the **CLOSE** button.

CHANGING EFFECTS

1. Select the **TEXT STYLE** command.
   The Text Style Dialog box appears.

2. Make the changes.

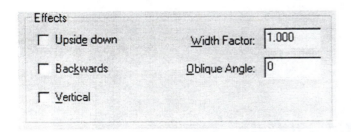

3. Click on the **APPLY** button and then **CLOSE.**

DIVIDE

The DIVIDE command divides an object mathematically by the NUMBER of segments you designate. It then places a POINT (object) at each interval on the object.

Note: the object selected is **NOT** broken into segments. The POINTS are simply drawn **ON** the object.

First select the **POINT STYLE** to be placed on the object. *Refer to lesson 5*

Next select the **DIVIDE** command using one of the following:

    TYPE = DIV
    PULL DOWN = DRAW / POINT / DIVIDE
    TOOLBAR = DRAW

Select object to divide: *select the object to divide.*
Enter the number of segments or [Block]: *type the number of segments* *<enter>*

EXAMPLE:

This LINE has been DIVIDED into 4 EQUAL segments.

MEASURE

The **MEASURE** command is very similar to the **DIVIDE** command because point objects are drawn at intervals on an object. However, the **MEASURE** command allows you to designate the **LENGTH** of the segments rather than the number of segments.

Note: the object selected is **NOT** broken into segments. The **POINTS** are simply drawn **ON** the object.

First select the **POINT STYLE** to be placed on the object. *Refer to lesson 5*

Next select the **MEASURE** command using one of the following:

> **TYPE = ME**
> **PULL DOWN = DRAW / POINT / MEASURE**
> **TOOLBAR = DRAW**

Command: _measure
Select object to measure: *select the object to measure.*
(Note: this selection point is also where the MEASUREment will start.)
Specify length of segment or [Block]: *type the length of one segment <enter>*

EXAMPLE:

Select Object here to start the measurement from the left.

The MEASUREment was started at the left endpoint, and ended just short of the right end of the line.   The remainder is less than the measurement length designated.

EXERCISE 25A

INSTRUCTIONS:

1. Open your **"BSIZE"** drawing.
2. Create the 3 text styles listed below.
3. Save as EX-25A (The text is not visible, but it will be after completing EX-25B)

Follow the instruction **"CREATING NEW TEXT STYLES"** on page 25-2.

Name:	Style1
Font:	Romand.shx
Height:	.50
Upside down:	No
Backwards:	No
Vertical:	Yes
Width factor:	1
Obliquing angle:	30

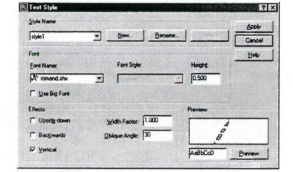

Name:	Style2
Font:	gothice.shx
Height:	1.00
Upside down:	No
Backwards:	Yes
Vertical:	No
Width factor:	.75
Obliquing angle:	0

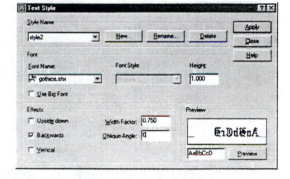

Name:	Style3
Font:	Italict.shx
Height:	2.00
Upside down:	Yes
Backwards:	No
Vertical:	No
Width factor:	.75
Obliquing angle:	0

START POINT 5, 8

START POINT 4, 5

START POINT 7, 1.5

| NAME | DRAWING WITH NEW TEXT STYLES | EX-25B |

EXERCISE 25B

INSTRUCTIONS:

1. Open drawing 25A.
2. Draw the text styles above using the text style you created.
3. Select the appropriate text style before typing.
4. Notice "Start Point" locations.
5. Save as: **EX-25B.**

STYLE1

STYLE3

STYLE2

Text

Alphabetic | Categorized

⊟ General
Color   ■ ByLayer
Layer   OBJECT
Linetype   ———— ByLayer
Linetype scale 1.000
Plot style
Lineweight   ———— ByLayer
Hyperlink
Thickness   .000
⊟ Text
Contents   STYLE3
Style   STANDARD
Justify   STANDARD
Height   style1
Rotation   style2
Width factor   style3
Obliquing   SSBOLD
Text alignment X 0
Text alignment Y

| NAME | CHANGING THE TEXT STYLE | EX-25C |

INSTRUCTIONS:

1. Open drawing 25B.
2. Using MODIFY / PROPERTIES change the 3 text styles to Text Style "Standard".
3. Note: you must change one at a time and "deselect" between style changes.
   If you do not deselect between style changes, you will not acheive the same results.
4. Save as: **EX-25C.**

EXERCISE 25C

EXERCISE 25D

INSTRUCTIONS:

1. Open File **25C**.
2. Delete text styles **1,2 and 3**.

There are 2 methods. Try both.

METHOD 1.

1. Select **FORMAT / TEXT STYLE**
2. Select the "Standard" text style.
3. Select the CLOSE button. (This makes Standard the current text style)
4. Now return to **FORMAT / TEXT STYLE**
5. Select the style you want to **delete**.
6. Click on the **DELETE** button.

AutoCAD will not allow you to delete an active or current text style. That is why number 2, above, said to select Standard and close.

METHOD 2.

1. Select **File / Drawing Utilities / Purge**

2. Select the **+ sign** beside Text Styles

3. Select the Style 1, 2 and 3

4. Select **Purge All** button.

5. Select **Close**.

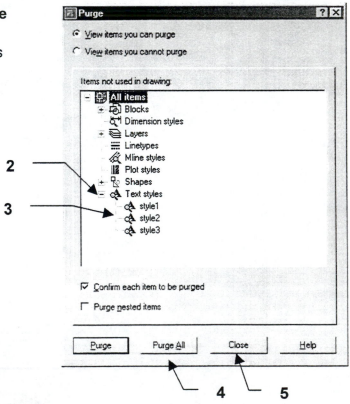

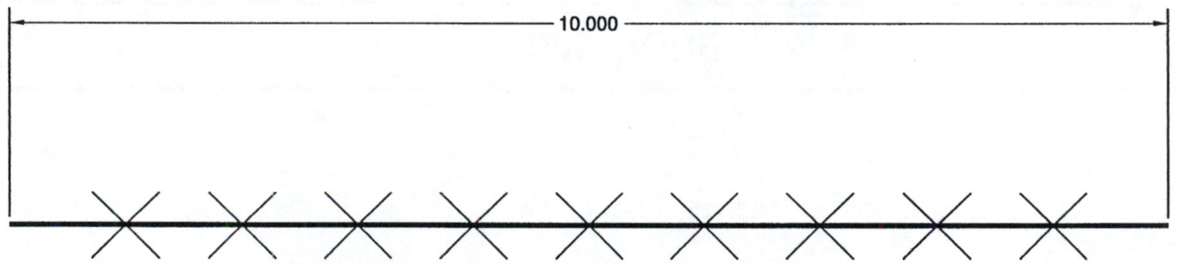

EXERCISE 25E

10.000

NAME	DIVIDE	EX-25E

INSTRUCTIONS:

1. Draw a LINE 10 inches long.
2. Set the POINT STYLE to **X** using: FORMAT / POINT STYLE.
3. DIVIDE the line into 10 equal divisions using: **a.** DRAW / POINT / DIVIDE.
   b. *Select the object to divide.*   **c.** *Type 10 for number of segments.*
4. Save as: **EX-25E.**

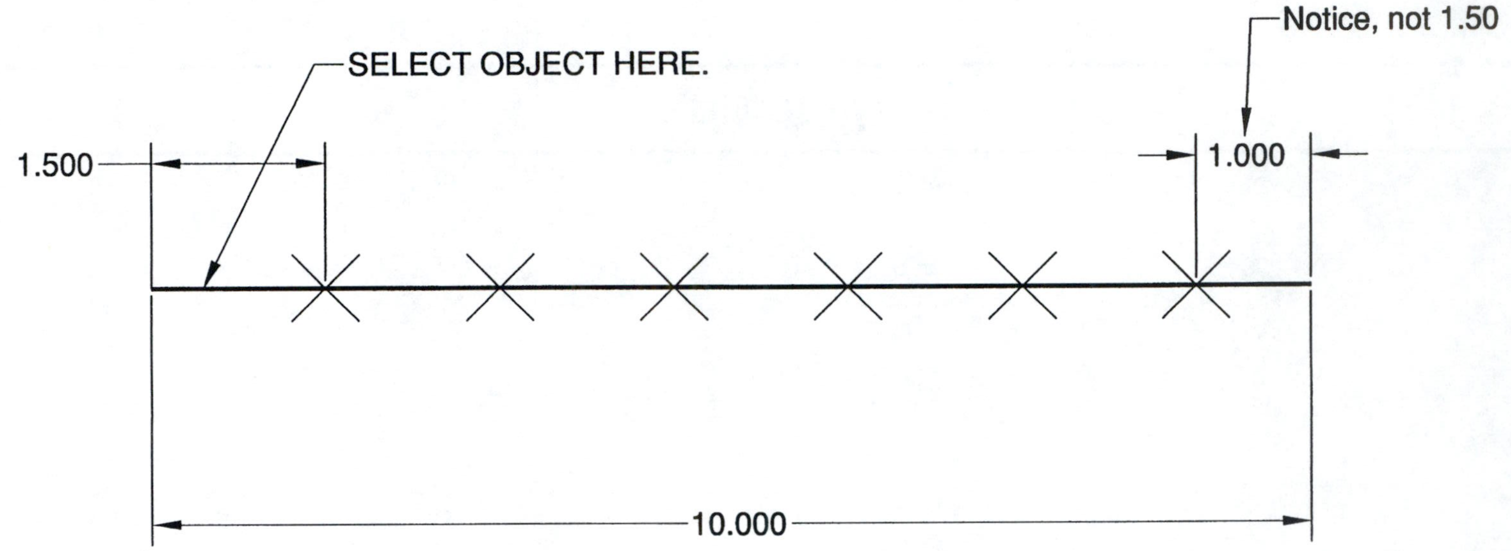

EXERCISE 25F

Notice, not 1.50

1.000

10.000

SELECT OBJECT HERE.

1.500

MEASURE

NAME

INSTRUCTIONS:

1. Draw a LINE 10 inches long.
2. Set the POINT STYLE to **X** using: FORMAT / POINT STYLE.
3. Place POINTS at a measurement of 1.50 using: **a.** DRAW / POINT / MEASURE.
     b. *Select the location to start the measurement from .* **c.** *Type 1.50 for the measurement.*
4. Save as: **EX-25F.**

3X Ø1.00 EQUALLY SPACED

4.000

6.750

1.500

1.500

1.500

1.500

1.500

4X Ø.75

8X Ø.50
EQUALLY SPACED

MORE DIVIDE and MEASURE

EXERCISE 25G

NAME

INSTRUCTIONS:

1. Draw the RECTANGLE and the DIAGONAL LINE.
2. EXPLODE the Rectangle and set the POINT STYLE.
3. Place POINTS as shown using: DIVIDE or MEASURE.
4. Draw the Circles using NODE snap to locate the center locations.
5. Dimension and Save as: **EX-25G.**

NOTES:

LEARNING OBJECTIVES

After completing this lesson, you will be able to:

1. Adjust the size of the "Pick" box.
2. Create your own Layers.
3. Load Linetypes into your drawing.
4. Understand the difference between Model and Layout tabs.
5. Create Floating Viewports
6. Create a Page Setup for plotting your drawings.
7. Create a Mechanical "Setup" master file for future use.
8. Create a new Mechanical Border to use when plotting.

LESSON 26

SETTING THE PICK BOX SIZE

When AutoCAD prompts you to *select objects,* such as when you are erasing objects, the cursor (crosshairs) turns into a square. This square is called a **Pick box.** The size of the **Pick box** can be changed. Some AutoCAD users prefer large boxes, some like small boxes. The size of the box is your personal preference, however, the smaller the Pick box the more **accurate** you must be when placing the pick box on an object to select it. If the Pick box is too large it could overlap objects that you didn't want to select.

1. Select **TOOLS / OPTIONS**
2. Select the **SELECTION** tab.

The following dialog box will appear.

Notice: You may also make changes to Grips. (Refer to 16-4)

4. Select **OK** when size adjustment is complete.

3. Adjust the size by sliding the tab (click and drag) to the right (max) or to the Left (Min.). A preview of the new size is displayed.

CREATING NEW LAYERS

1. Select the Layer command using one of the following:

       TYPE = LA
       PULLDOWN = FORMAT / LAYER
       TOOLBAR = OBJECT PROPERTIES

The Layer & Linetype Properties dialog box shown below will appear.

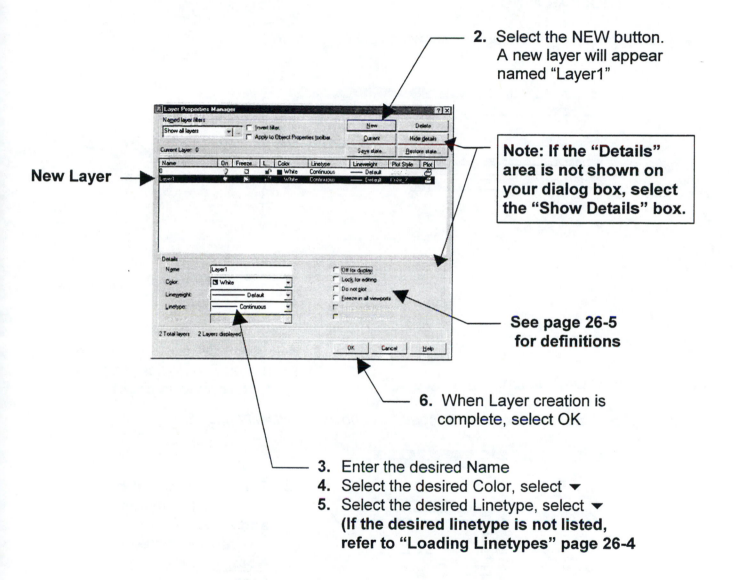

2. Select the NEW button. A new layer will appear named "Layer1"

New Layer →

Note: If the "Details" area is not shown on your dialog box, select the "Show Details" box.

See page 26-5 for definitions

6. When Layer creation is complete, select OK

3. Enter the desired Name
4. Select the desired Color, select ▼
5. Select the desired Linetype, select ▼
    (If the desired linetype is not listed, refer to "Loading Linetypes" page 26-4

LOADING A LINETYPE

If the **Linetype** you desire is not listed in the **Layer & Linetype Properties** dialog box, you must **LOAD** it as follows.

1. Select the LINETYPE command using one of the following:

> **TYPE = LT**
> **PULLDOWN = FORMAT / LINETYPE**
> **TOOLBAR = NONE**

The Linetype Manager dialog box shown below will appear.

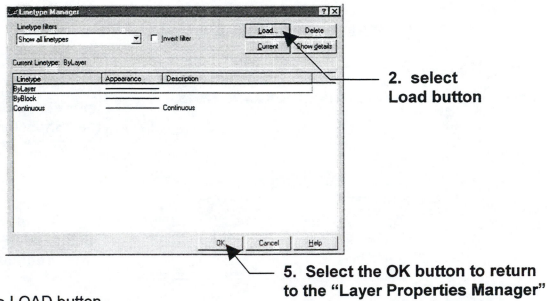

2. select Load button

5. Select the OK button to return to the "Layer Properties Manager" dialog box. (previous page)

2. Select the LOAD button.

*The **Load or Reload Linetypes** dialogue box shown below will appear.*

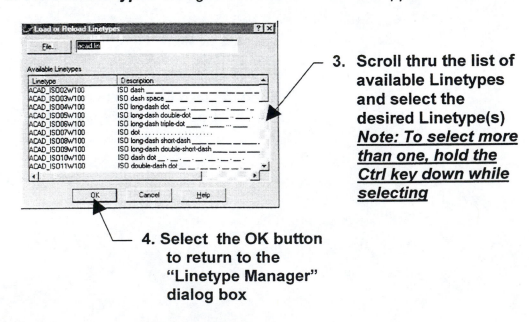

3. Scroll thru the list of available Linetypes and select the desired Linetype(s) *Note: To select more than one, hold the Ctrl key down while selecting*

4. Select the OK button to return to the "Linetype Manager" dialog box

LAYER CONTROL DEFINITIONS

OFF FOR DISPLAY

If a layer is **ON** it is **visible**. If a layer is **OFF** it is **not visible**.
Only layers that are **ON** can be **edited** or **plotted**.
(Warning: Objects on a Layer that is OFF can be <u>accidentally erased</u> by typing **ALL** when using the ERASE command.)

LOCK FOR EDITING

LOCKED layers are visible but can not be edited. They are visible so they **will** be plotted. (Locked layers cannot be selected by typing ALL.)

DO NOT PLOT

This option prevents a layer from plotting even though it is visible.

FREEZE IN ALL VIEWPORTS

Freeze and **Thaw** are very similar to On and Off. A Frozen layer is <u>not visible</u>.
Thawed layers <u>are visible</u>. Only thawed layers can be edited or plotted.
Additionally:
a. Objects on a Frozen layer **can not** be accidentally erased by typing All.
b. Freezing saves time, when working with large and complex drawings, because frozen layers are not **regenerated** when you zoom in and out.

FREEZE IN CURRENT VIEWPORT
FREEZE IN NEW VIEWPORTS

These options are only available when creating multiple viewports.
These settings are discussed in "**Exercise Workbook for Advanced AutoCAD**".

MODEL and LAYOUT tabs

Read this information carefully. It is very important that you understand this concept.

AutoCAD 2002 provides two drawing spaces; **MODEL** and **LAYOUT**. You move into one or the other by selecting either the MODEL or LAYOUT tabs, located at the bottom left of the drawing area.

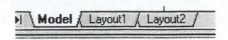

Model Tab (Also called *Model Space*)
When you select the Model tab you enter <u>MODEL SPACE</u>. (This is where you have been for the last 25 lessons)
Model Space is where you **create** and **modify** your drawings.

Layout1 and Layout2 Tab (Also called Paper Space)

When you select one of the Layout tabs you enter <u>PAPER SPACE</u>.
The primary function of Paper Space is to prepare the drawing for plotting.

When you select the Layout tab, for the first time, the "Page Set up" Dialog box will appear. Using this dialog box, you will tell AutoCAD which plotting device and paper size to plot on. For now, select the OK button to go on. *(More information on this in "How to create a Page Setup" page 26-10)*

Model space disappears and a <u>blank sheet of paper</u> appears on the screen. This sheet of paper is basically laying on top of the Model Space. (See illustration below) To see your drawing (Model Space), while still in paper space, you must <u>cut a hole</u> in this sheet. This hole is called a **"Viewport"** *(Refer to "Viewports" page 26-7.)*

<u>Try to think of this as a picture frame (paper space) laying on top of a photograph.</u>
<u>(model space)</u>

Generally, the only drawing that should be in paper space is the "Title Block, Border, Dimensions and Notes.

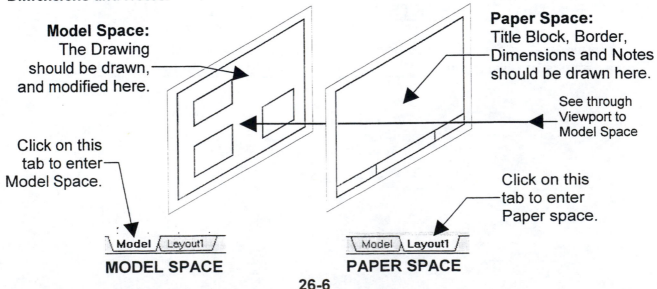

Model Space:
The Drawing should be drawn, and modified here.

Click on this tab to enter Model Space.

Paper Space:
Title Block, Border, Dimensions and Notes should be drawn here.

See through Viewport to Model Space

Click on this tab to enter Paper space.

MODEL SPACE   **PAPER SPACE**

VIEWPORTS

Viewports are only used in Paper Space (Layout tab).
Viewports are holes cut into the sheet of paper displayed on the screen.
Viewports are separate objects, similar to a picture frame, and they can be moved, stretched, scaled, copied and erased.
You can have multiple Viewports and their size and shape can vary. *But we will only be working with **single** viewports in this workbook. Multiple viewports will be explained in the "Exercise Workbook for Advanced AutoCAD 2000".*

Note: It is considered good drawing management to create a layer for the Viewport "frames" to reside on. This will allow you to control them separately. Such as setting the viewport layer to "No plot".

CREATING A VIEWPORT

1. Create your drawing in Model Space.
2. Select a "Layout" tab (If the "Page setup" dialog box appears, select the **OK** button or refer to "How to create a Page setup" on page 26-10.)
3. You are now in Paper Space where your Border, notes and dimensions will be placed.
4. Select layer "Viewport" (You may need to create one, refer to 26-3)
5. Activate the Viewport toolbar (View / toolbars / viewports)
6. Select "Single Viewport" icon. (See page 26-9 for tool bar icons)
7. Draw the Viewport "frame" by specifying the location for the "first corner" and then the opposite corner. (Similar to drawing a Rectangle but **do not** use the Rectangel command)

You should now be able to look through the sheet to Model Space.
(Make sure your grids are ON in Model Space and OFF in paperspace)

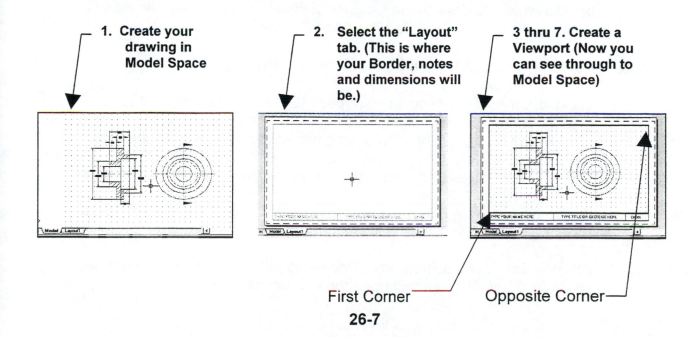

1. Create your drawing in Model Space

2. Select the "Layout" tab. (This is where your Border, notes and dimensions will be.)

3 thru 7. Create a Viewport (Now you can see through to Model Space)

First Corner   Opposite Corner

TO REACH THROUGH TO MODEL SPACE WHILE IN PAPER SPACE

If you double click <u>inside</u> the viewport frame, it will activate the model space and you can reach through the sheet of Paper to Model space. *Double click in the gray area to return to Paper Space.*

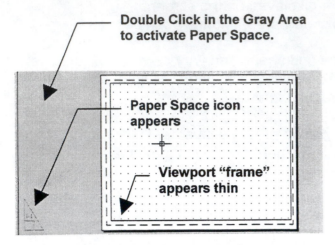

Double Click in the Gray Area to activate Paper Space.

Double Click inside the Viewport to activate Model Space

Paper Space icon appears

Viewport "frame" appears thin

Viewport "frame" appears thick

UCS Icon appears

Paper Space Active   **Model Space Active**

You can draw or make changes to the drawing within this Viewport whenever the UCS icon is displayed. *(UCS icon appearance may be different than the one shown)*
To return to Paperspace, double click in the gray area on the screen.

OPTIONS

I prefer to use the Viewports toolbar shown on page 26-9, but you may type "MV <enter>" at the command line, the following options will appear:

ON / OFF   Turns On or Off the Model Space display within the viewport. (The same as double clicking in the Viewport or gray area as mentioned above)

FIT   a. (default) If you press <enter> this option automatically creates a single rectangular viewport that fills the entire printable area on the sheet
b. Allows you to draw the rectangular viewport by specifying the location of the first corner and then the opposite corner.

HIDEPLOT   Prevents hidden lines in a 3D model from being plotted.

LOCK   Locks the model space and paperspace together. They move and zoom in and out together. The model space scale cannot be changed until you unlock the viewport. (For short cut menu method see page 26-24H)

RESTORE   Converts saved viewport configurations into individual floating viewports.

OBJECT   Converts an object, drawn in paperspace, into a viewport. Objects must be closed, such as: circles, polygons and closed polylines.

POLYGONAL Allows you to draw a viewport outline using polylines. If you do not use CLOSE, AutoCAD 2000 will close them automatically.

To activate the "VIEWPORTS" Toolbar:
1. Select VIEW / TOOLBARS
2. Select the VIEWPORTS toolbar from the list.

TOOLBAR FOR <u>2002</u> SHOWN BELOW:

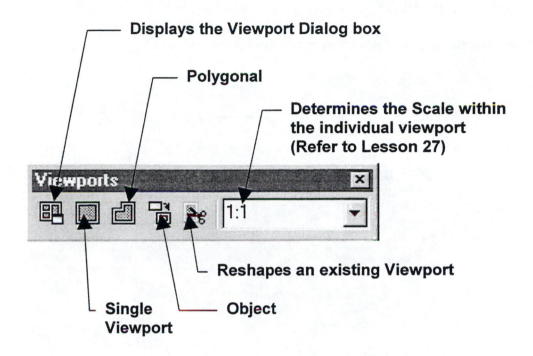

Displays the Viewport Dialog box

Polygonal

Determines the Scale within the individual viewport (Refer to Lesson 27)

Reshapes an existing Viewport

Single Viewport

Object

TOOLBAR FOR <u>LT</u> SHOWN BELOW:

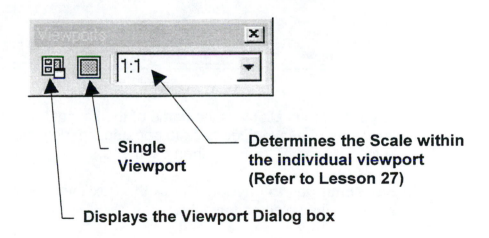

Single Viewport

Determines the Scale within the individual viewport (Refer to Lesson 27)

Displays the Viewport Dialog box

HOW TO CREATE A PAGE SET UP

NOTE: This is not an exercise. This is an overview. Refer to Exercise 26D.

A. Begin by Opening a drawing onto the screen.

B. Select **FILE / PLOT**

(The Plot dialog box shown below should appear)

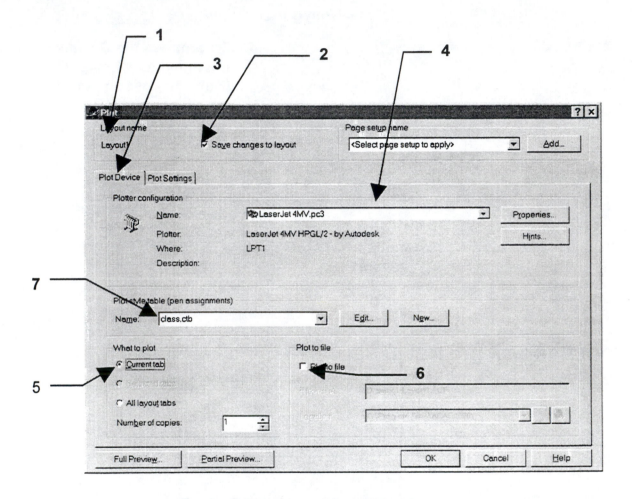

1. **Layout Name**: Displays the name of the Layout tab you selected. (To change the name of a layout, go back to paperspace, right click on the layout tab and select "Rename" from the short cut menu.)

2. **Save changes to Layout:** Check this box if you want your settings to be saved to the selected Layout tab.

3. Select the **"Plot Device"** tab.

4. Select the **"Plotter Name"** from the list. All previously configured devices are listed. (If your printer / plotter is not listed refer to "Add a Printer / Plotter" Appendix A.

5. **What to Plot:** defines what you want to plot.
   Current tab = plots current Model or Layout tab
   Selected tabs = plots multiple preselected tabs. This option is not available if
   only one tab is selected.
   All Layouts tabs = plots all layout tabs, selected or not.
   Number of copies = specify number of copies to be plotted.

6. **Plot to File:** Creates a plot file instead of plotting the drawing. If this option is
   selected, enter the **filename** and specify saving **location**. This is an advanced option,
   refer to the AutoCAD 2000 User's Guide for more information.

7. Select a **"Plot Style Table"** form the list.
   You can also **Create a New** plot style table (see page 26-14)

C. Select the **"Plot Settings"** tab.

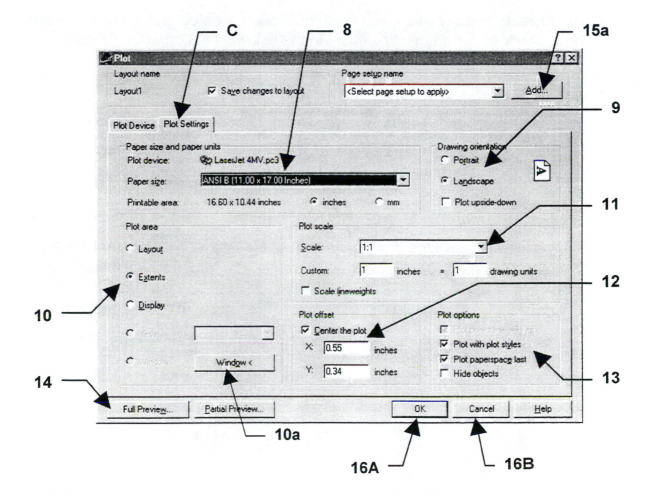

8. Select the desired **Paper Size** from the drop down list. The list should contain all
   available paper sizes for the plotter device you selected. (Remember, you must
   select the plot device first)

9. Select the desired **Drawing Orientation**. (page 26-11)
   Landscape = the long edge of the paper represents the top of the page.
   Portrait = the short edge of the paper represents the top of the page.
   (Landscape is the most common selection.)

10. Select the **Plot Area**. (page 26-11)
    Limits = plots the area inside the drawing limits. (Plotting from Model)
    Layout = plots the paper size (Plotting from Layout)
    Extents = plots all objects in the drawing file even if out of view.
    Display = plots the active viewport.
    View = plots a previously saved view.
    Window = plots objects inside a window. To specify the window, choose the
    Window button (10a) and designate the first and opposite (diagonal) corner of the
    window. (Similar to the Zoom Window command)

11. Select a **scale** (page 26-11) from the drop down list or enter a custom scale or
    select "plot to scale". *(If you are plotting from a "LAYOUT" tab, you should
    always use plot scale 1:1. Scaling will be discussed in Lesson 27)*

12. **Plot Offset:** Specify where you want the drawing located on the sheet of paper.
    The **X** and **Y** boxes defines the offset from the lower left corner of the paper.
    The "**Center the Plot**" box automatically centers the drawing on the paper.

13. **Plot Options:** (page 26-11)
    Plot Object Lineweights = plots objects with assigned lineweights.
    Plot with Plot Styles = plots using the selected Plot Style Table.
    Plot paperspace last = plots model space objects before plotting paper
        space objects. Not available when plotting from model space.
    Hide Objects = used for 3D only. Plots with hidden lines removed.

14. Select **Plot Preview** button. (page 26-11)
    Plot preview displays the drawing as it will plot on the sheet of paper. (Note: If
    you can not see through to Model space, you have not cut your viewport yet)

    a. If the drawing is centered on the sheet, press the **Esc** key and go on to
       step 15.
    b. If the drawing does not look correct, press the **Esc** key and check all
       your settings, then preview again.

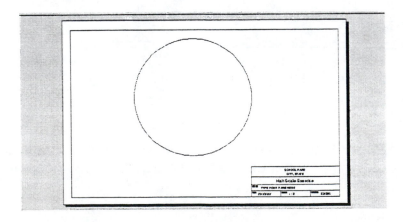

15. Page Set up Name
a. Select the **"Add"** button (15a on page 26-11)
b. Type the new page set up name
c. Select the **OK** button

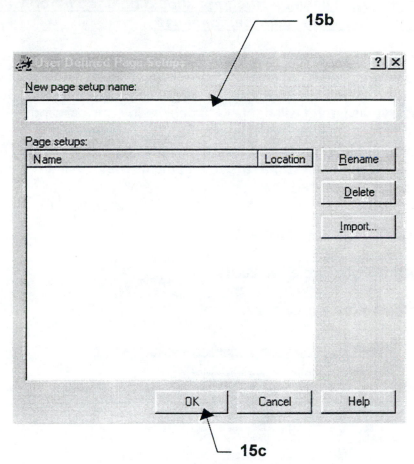

15b

15c

16. *If your computer is connected to the plotter / printer*, select the **OK** button (16A on page 26-11) to plot, then proceed to step 17.
   If your computer is not connected to the plotter / printer, select the **Cancel** button (16B on page 26-11) and proceed to step 17.

17. **Save this drawing again** using **File / Save as**. This will guarantee that the Page Setup you just created will be saved to this drawing for future use.

HOW TO CREATE A NEW "*PLOT STYLE TABLE*"

NOTE: This is not an exercise. The Plot Style Table we are using in this workbook is "Class.ctb". These instructions should be used if you want to create a different "Plot Style Table" for your personal use.

A Plot Style Table is a list of colors. Each color can be assigned different properties. Properties are line weight, line type, line end style, joint style, fill pattern, gray scale, screen percentage etc. When you plot your drawing using a specific Plot Style Table, the properties you have assigned will apply to the colors in your drawing.

For example: I could create a Plot Style Table called "XYZ" with the line weight of color red to be .7mm. When I plot the drawing I will select the "XYZ" Plot Style Table (Refer to 7 on page 26-10). All the objects that are red, in the drawing, will have a line weight of .7mm on the paper when plotted.

A. Select **FILE / PLOT STYLE MANAGER**

B. Select "**Add-A-Plot Style Table**" Wizard

Add-A-Plot
Style Tab...

The following dialog boxes will appear.

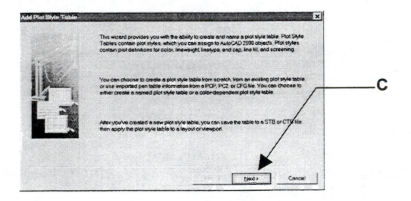

C

C. Select the **Next** button.

D. Select "**Start from Scratch**" then the **Next** button.

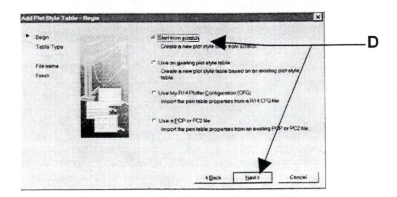

D

E. Select **"Color-Dependent Plot Style Table"** then the **Next** button.

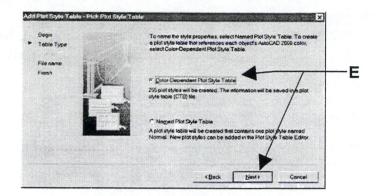

F. Type the new Plot Style Table **name** then select the **Next** button.

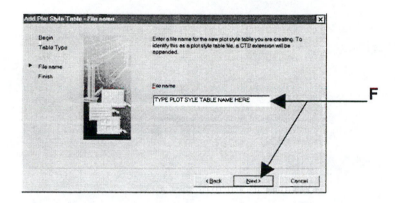

G. Select the **"Plot Style Table Editor"** button.

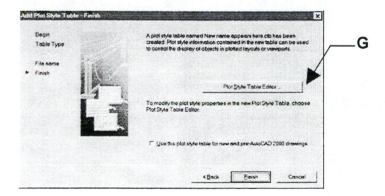

H. Make changes to the **"PROPERTIES"** then select the **Save & Close** button.

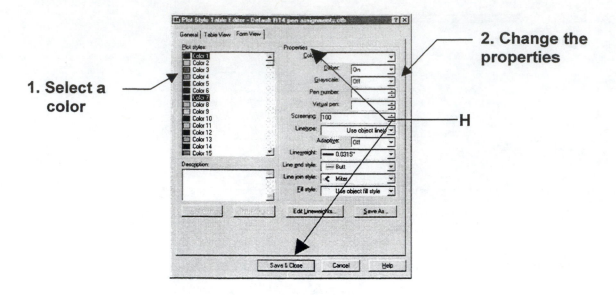

1. Select a color

2. Change the properties

H

I. Select the **FINISH** button.

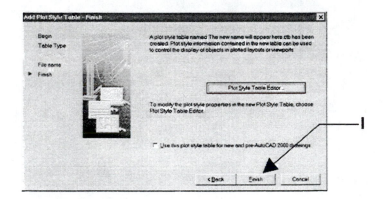

I

Now select File / Plot.
Check the list of Plot Style tables to see if your new style is listed.

HOW TO *DELETE* OR *RENAME* A PLOT STYLE TABLE

1. Select **FILE / PLOT STYLE MANAGER**

2. Right Click on the PLOT STYLE TABLE "icon" you want to Delete or Rename.

3. Select DELETE or RENAME from the short cut menu.

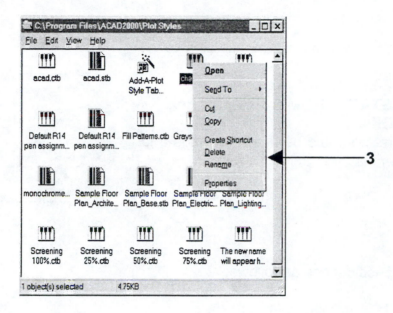

EXERCISE 26A
CREATE A MECHANICAL SETUP DRAWING

The following instructions will guide you through creating a "setup" drawing. A setup drawing is basically a master. (The "1Class template.dwt" is an example of a setup drawing) Even though the screen is blank, the actual file is full of information, such as; Units, Drawing Limits, Snap and Grid settings, Layers, Text styles and Dimension Styles. Once you have created this "setup" drawing, you just open it and draw. No more repetitive inputting of settings.

NEW SETTINGS

A. Begin your drawing without a template as follows:

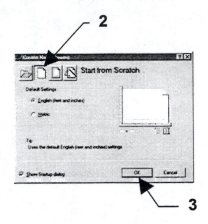

1. Select **"FILE / NEW"**
2. Select **"START FROM SCRATCH"** Box.
3. Select "**OK**".
4. Your screen should be blank, no grids and the current layer is 0

B. Set drawing specifications as follows:

1. Set **"UNITS"** of measurement
   Use "**FORMAT / UNITS** and change the settings as shown then select **OK.**

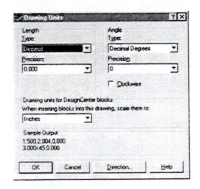

2. Set **"DRAWING LIMITS"** (Size of drawing area)
   USE "**FORMAT / DRAWING LIMITS**
   a. Lower left corner = 0.000,0.000
   b. Upper right corner = 17 , 11
   c. Use **"VIEW / ZOOM / ALL"** to generate the new limits
   d. Set your **Grids** to **ON** to display the paper size.

3. Set **"SNAP AND GRID"**
Use **"TOOLS / DRAFTING SETTINGS**

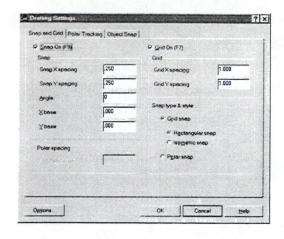

4. Set **"PICK BOX"** size (your preference)
See page 26-2 for instructions.

NEW LAYERS

C. Create new layers

1. **Load** linetypes (See page 26-4 for instructions)
   CENTER2
   HIDDEN
   PHANTOM2

2. Assign names, colors, linetypes and plotability. (See page 26-3 for instructions)

NAME	COLOR	LINETYPE	PLOT
BORDER	RED	CONTINUOUS	YES
CENTER	CYAN	CENTER2	YES
CONSTRUCTION	WHITE	CONTINUOUS	NO
DIMENSION	BLUE	CONTINUOUS	YES
HATCH	GREEN	CONTINUOUS	YES
HIDDEN	MAGENTA	HIDDEN	YES
OBJECT	RED	CONTINUOUS	YES
PHANTOM	MAGENTA	PHANTOM2	YES
SECTION	WHITE	PHANTOM2	YES
TEXT HEAVY	WHITE	CONTINUOUS	YES
TEXT LIGHT	BLUE	CONTINUOUS	YES
THREADS	GREEN	CONTINUOUS	YES
VIEWPORT	GREEN	CONTINUOUS	NO

NEW TEXT STYLE

D. Create a text style

    1. Select **"FORMAT / TEXT STYLE"**
    2. Make the changes shown in the dialog box.

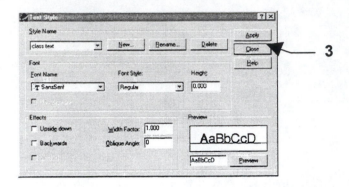

    3. When complete, select APPLY then CLOSE.

NEW DIMENSION STYLE

E. Create a new Dimension Style named **Class Style**
   (Refer to Page 16-8 for step by step instructions)

NEW DIMENSION SUB-STYLE

F. Create a new Dimension Sub-Style for **Radius**
   (Refer to Page 18-6 for step by step instructions)

THIS NEXT STEP IS VERY IMPORTANT..

G. SAVE ALL THE SETTINGS YOU JUST CREATED
    1. Select File / Save as
    2. Save as: **My Mechanical Setup**

EXERCISE 26B
CREATE A MECHANICAL BORDER FOR PLOTTING

The following instructions will guide you through creating a Border drawing that will be used in combination with "My Mechanical Setup" when plotting. You will create a Layout and draw a border with a title block. All of this information will be saved and you will not have to do this again.

A. Open **My Mechanical Setup**

B. Select a **LAYOUT** tab.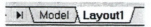

Note: If the Page Setup dialog box shown below does not appear automatically, right click on the Layout tab, then select Page Setup.

1. Type the new name:
17-11-FULL

2. Select the "*Plot Device*" tab.

3. Select the Plotter.

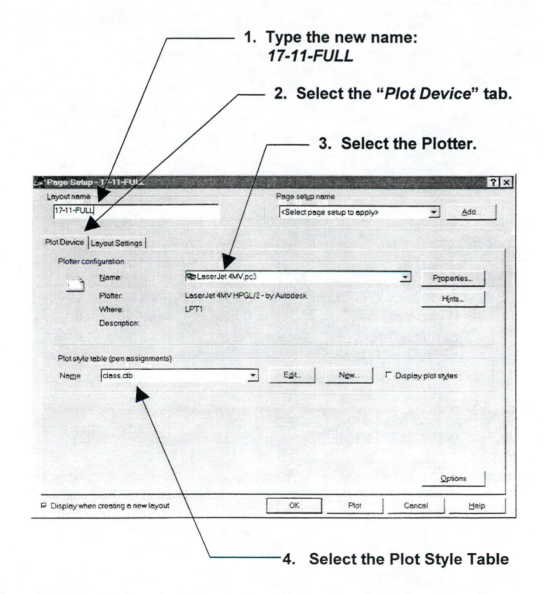

4.   Select the Plot Style Table

5. Select the "*Layout Settings*" tab.

6. Select the "*Paper Size*".

7. Select scale "1:1"

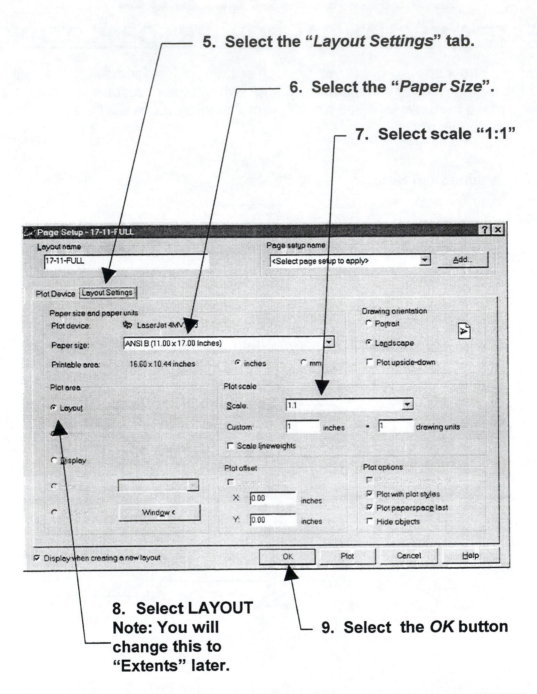

**8. Select LAYOUT
Note: You will
change this to
"Extents" later.**

9. Select the *OK* button

You should now have a sheet of paper displayed on the screen and the Layout tab should now be displayed as "17-11-FULL". This sheet is in front of "Model". In Exercise 26C, you will cut a hole (viewport) in this sheet so you can see through to Model.

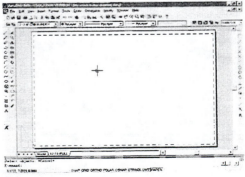

C. Draw the Border with title block, shown below, on the sheet of paper shown on the screen.

D. When you have completed the Border, shown below:
1. Select File / Save as
2. Save as: **My Mechanical Setup** (Again)

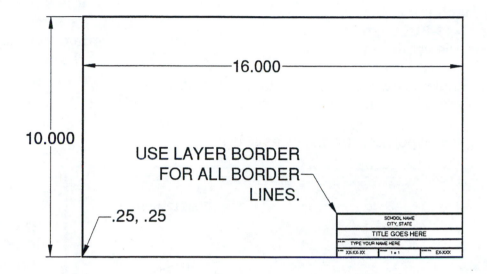

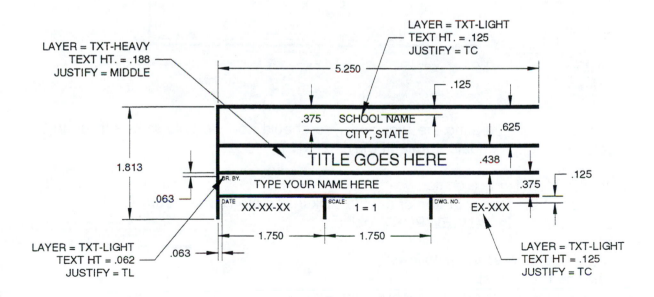

Don't forget to save, refer to "D" above.

EXERCISE 26C
CREATE A VIEWPORT

The following instructions will guide you through creating a VIEWPORT in the Mechanical Border Layout sheet. Creating a viewport has the same effect as cutting a hole in the sheet of paper. You will be able to see through the hole to Model.

A. Open **My Mechanical Setup**
B. Select the **17-11-FULL** tab.
C. Select layer "Viewport"

Single Viewport icon (LT's toolbar looks a little different but it works the same)

D. Select the Single Viewport icon from the Viewports Toolbar or Type MV <enter>.

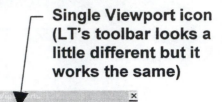

E. Draw a Single viewport approximately as shown.

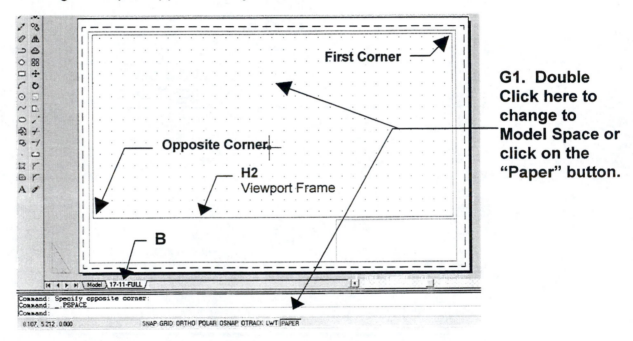

First Corner

G1. Double Click here to change to Model Space or click on the "Paper" button.

Opposite Corner

H2
Viewport Frame

B

F. After successfully creating the Viewport, you should now be able to see through to Model. (Your grids should appear if they are ON.)

G. Adjust the Model space scale.
  1. Select the **Paper** button or double click inside the Border Area.
  2. Select 1:1 in the **VIEWPORT** toolbar.

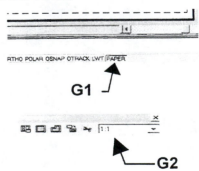

G1

G2

H. Lock the Viewport scale as follows:
  1. Change to Paperspace
  2. Click on the Viewport frame. (See above)
  3. Right click (the shortcut menu will appear)
  4. Select "Display Locked" and select "Yes"

J. File / Save as: **My Mechanical Setup**

EXERCISE 26D
CREATE A PAGE SETUP

The following instructions will guide you through creating a **PAGE SETUP** named "Full Size" for **My Mechanical Setup** file. You need a Page Setup to plot the drawing. The Page Setup remembers which plotter to use, paper size, scale, and lineweights. This Page Setup will stay with **My Mechanical Setup** and you will be able to use it over and over again. But you only have to create this page setup once. (Refer to Page 26-10 **How to create a Page Setup** for more detailed explanations of each area.

A. Open **My Mechanical Setup**

B. Select the **17-11-FULL** layout tab. (You should be looking at your Mechanical Border and Title Block)

C. Select **File / Plot** or Place the cursor on the **17-11-FULL** tab, press the right mouse button then select **Plot** from the Short cut menu.

The Plot dialog box should appear

D. Select the **Plot Device** tab and select the options 1 thru 3 below:

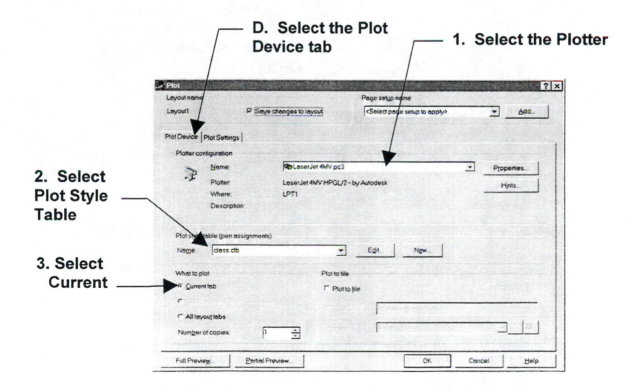

D. Select the Plot Device tab

1. Select the Plotter

2. Select Plot Style Table

3. Select Current

E. Select the **Plot Settings** tab then select options 1 thru 7 below:

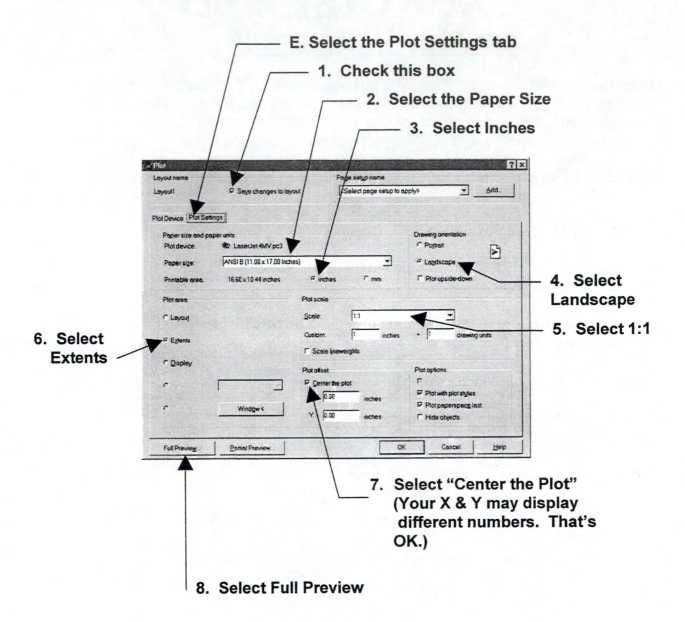

E. **Select the Plot Settings tab**

1. **Check this box**

2. **Select the Paper Size**

3. **Select Inches**

4. **Select Landscape**

5. **Select 1:1**

6. **Select Extents**

7. **Select "Center the Plot" (Your X & Y may display different numbers. That's OK.)**

8. **Select Full Preview**

F. Preview the Layout

    1. If the drawing is centered on the sheet, press the Esc key and go to **G**.

    2. If the drawing does not look correct, press the Esc key and check all your settings, then preview again.

G. Select the **ADD** button.

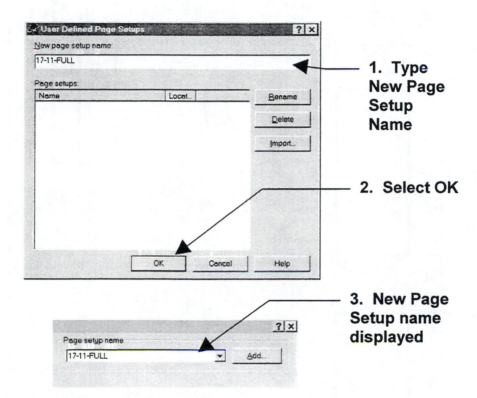

1. **Type New Page Setup Name**

2. **Select OK**

3. **New Page Setup name displayed**

H. If your computer **is** connected to the Plotter / Printer, select the **OK** button to plot.

I. If your computer **is not** connected to the Plotter / Printer, select the **CANCEL** button. (Your settings **will not** be lost)

J. **Save** this file one more time:
    1. Select **File / Save** as
    2. Save as: **My Mechanical Setup**

You have now created a **Page Setup** for the *My Mechanical Setup*. This page setup can also be used on other layouts. Now you are ready to use this setup file to create many drawings in the future.

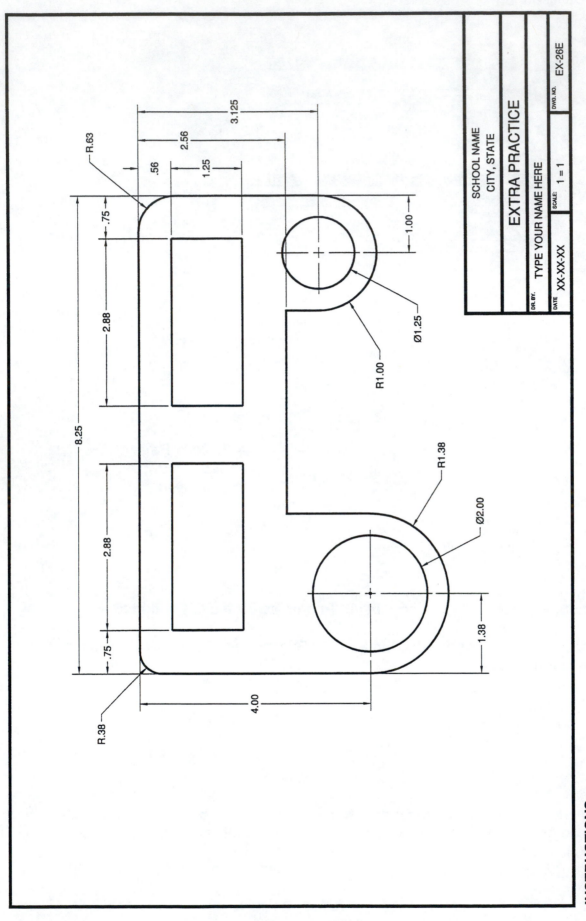

EXERCISE 26E

SCHOOL NAME
CITY, STATE

EXTRA PRACTICE

DR. BY. TYPE YOUR NAME HERE

DWG. NO. EX-26E

SCALE: 1 = 1

DATE XX-XX-XX

INSTRUCTIONS:

1. Open MY MECHANICAL SETUP
2. Draw the drawing above inside the viewport frame (Model Space).
3. Check to make sure the viewport's scale is 1:1 and locked. (Refer to 26-24)
4. Dimension as shown. Use Dim. Style, Class style.
5. Save as: EX-26E
6. Plot using "17-11-FULL" Page Setup.

LEARNING OBJECTIVES

After completing this lesson, you will be able to:

1. Understand scaled drawings.
2. Adjust the scale within a viewport.
3. Dimension a scaled drawing.
4. Understand how scale affects Linetypes and Hatch.
5. Import previously created Page Setups.
6. Create an Architectural "Setup" file for future use.
7. Create a new Architectural Border to use when plotting.

LESSON 27

CREATING and PLOTTING SCALED DRAWINGS

In the lessons, previous to lesson 26, you worked only in Model space. Then in lesson 26 you learned that AutoCAD actually has another environment called Paper space or Layout. In this lesson we need to learn more about why we need 2 environments and how they make plotting drawings easier.

<u>**A very important rule in CAD you must understand and agree to is, all objects are drawn full size.**</u> In other words, if you want to draw a line 20 feet long, you actually draw it 20 feet long. If the line is 1/8" long, you actually draw it 1/8" long.

Drawing a house or a paper clip
In the previous lessons you created basically medium sized drawings. Not too big, not too small. But what if you wanted to draw a house? Could you print it, to scale, on a 17 X 11 piece of paper? How about a small paper clip. Could you make it big enough to dimension? Let's start with the house.

Drawing a house.
1. Set the units for the drawing to Architectural.
2. Set the drawing limits, in model space, big enough for the entire house to be drawn <u>full size</u>. In other words set the drawing area on your screen, in model space, big enough to draw a house. For example, if the house was 30 ft. long and 20 ft. tall, your drawing limits would be approximately 0, 0 for the lower left corner and 45', 35' for the upper right corner. Your drawing area would be 45 ft wide by 35 ft. high.
3. Draw the house, in model space, <u>full size</u>.

Plotting the house drawing
Now you want to plot this house drawing on a 17 x 11 piece of paper. This is where paper space makes it easy.

1. Open the drawing of the house.
2. Change to paper space. This is where you would draw your border and title block.
3. Specify the plotter and the paper size.
4. Open the "Viewport" tool bar and cut a viewport so you can see through to the house drawing in model space. (26-7)
5. Change to model space.
6. Select View / Zoom / Extents so the entire house is visible within the viewport frame.

Now here is where the magic happens.

7. Adjust the scale of model space. Scroll down the scales and select ¼" = 1'. If that doesn't look good, try one of the other scales. (Refer to 27-4)

Do you understand what happened? Remember the photo and picture frame example I suggested in lesson 26? (Refer to 26-6) This time think of standing in front of your house with that picture frame in your hands. You will look through the picture frame and you see your house. But the house is way too big to fit in the frame. So you walk across the street and look through the picture frame again. Does the house appear smaller? If you could walk far enough away from the house, it would eventually appear small enough to fit in the picture frame. But....the house did not actually change size did it? It only appears smaller because you are farther away from it.

That is the concept that you need to understand. When you adjust the scale of model space, it does not actually change size, it just gets farther away and appears smaller. When you dimension the house, the dimension values will be the actual size of the drawing. In other words, the 20 ft. line will have a dimension of 20'-0".

8. Lock the viewport when you have adjusted the model space scale to your satisfaction. (Refer to 27-19)

9. Plot the paper space / model space combination using File / Plot.
   The Plot scale should be 1 = 1 (Remember you have already adjusted the model space scale, you do not need to scale the combination, it is just fine.

10. Preview and plot.

Now what about that Paper Clip.
When plotting something smaller you have to move the picture frame closer to model space rather than farther away. So in that case, you would adjust the model space scale to 2 : 1 or 4 : 1 or more until the object in model space appeared large enough to see easily and dimension. Remember, even though the object appears larger, when you dimension it the dimension values will be the correct information.

Note: it is very important that you LOCK the viewport after adjusting the scale. This will prevent the scale from changing when you zoom in and out. If you need to adjust the scale again, you must UNLOCK the viewport, adjust the scale and then LOCK the viewport again. (27-19)

You will understand this concept better after you have completed the exercises in this lesson.

ADJUSTING THE SCALE INSIDE A VIEWPORT

It is important that you understand the concept of adjusting the scale of a viewport. Read page 27-2 before going on.

The following will walk you through the process of adjusting the scale within a viewport.

1. **Open** a drawing.

2. Select a **Layout** tab. (paper space)

3. Specify a plotter and paper size. (If you haven't already)

4. Create a Viewport.

5. Open the Viewport toolbar

6. Double click inside of the Viewport _(It is very important that you be inside the Viewport. You want to scale the Model geometry not the Layout)_

7. _Adjust the scale_ of the Model geometry by selecting a scale from the "Viewports" toolbar.

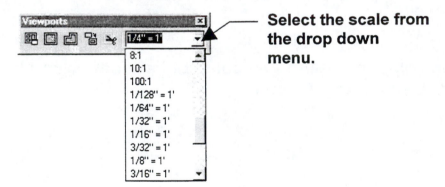

Select the scale from the drop down menu.

The Model geometry should have changed. If you don't like the way it looks, select a different scale. It's that easy.

TRANS-SPATIAL DIMENSIONING

This is another very important concept to understand, so read this carefully.

In Lesson 26 you learned about a new environment called paper space and how it works with model space. Right now, I am sure you do not understand the value of these two environments but hopefully you will after completing exercise 27G.

In Lesson 16 you learned about True Associative dimensioning. (Refer to 16-2) Remember, the dimension is actually attached to the object. If the object changes, the dimension changes. True Associative dimensioning is a very important and powerful tool within AutoCAD.

In AutoCAD 2002, True Associative dimensioning gets even better because it can also be trans-spatial. Trans-spatial means that you have the ability to place the dimensions in paper space while the object you are dimensioning is in model space. And the dimensions, in paper space, are actually attached to that object, in model space.

For example,
1. You draw a house in model space.
2. Now go to paper space.
3. Cut a viewport so you can see the drawing of the house.
4. Go to model space and adjust the scale of the viewport (model space) and lock it.
5. Now go to paper space and dimension the house.

Why is Trans-spatial dimensioning so great?
Model Space can be any scale but paper space should always stay 1:1. As a result, the dimension settings can be full scale, they do not have to be adjusted to the scale of model space. If the dimensions were in model space, the scale of the dimensions would have to be changed.

Try this example after completing Ex-27E, it will help you visualize the concept:
1. Open **My Architectural Setup**
2. Set True Associative dimensioning to **2** (On)   (Dimassoc <enter>   2 <enter>)
3. Select the **Qtr equals foot** tab.
4. Draw a 20 ft. long line, in model space.
   (If the line seems huge, you are still in paper space.)
5. Now stay in model space and dimension the line using linear.
   (Can you see the text or arrows?)
6. Now go to paper space and dimension the line.
   (That should look better)

The dimensions are actually the same size but model space is far away but paper space has not moved. Paper space is 1:1, so an 1/8" dimension text height appears 1/8". But the model space is far away, so the 1/8" dimension text height appears smaller. But they are both set to 1/8".

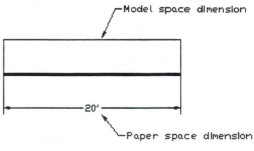

Note: If the viewport scale is 1:1, you can dimension in model or paper space.

LINETYPE SCALE

It is important that you understand the concept of adjusting the scale of a viewport. Read page 27-2 before going on.

AutoCAD has many Linetypes, as you learned in Lesson 26. (26-4) A Linetypes is a series of dashes, lines and spaces. Each linetype has specific dimensions for the lines, dashes and spaces. When you are in paper space and you adjust the scale of the model space, AutoCAD automatically adjusts the scale of the linetype dashes, lines and spaces. So you do not have to do any modifications unless you desire.

If you want to change the scale of the dashes, lines and spaces, you can accomplish this with Properties.

For example, if the linetype used for layer hidden originally was designed to have 1/2" lines with 1/4" spaces and you wanted them larger, you would do the following.

1. Select the line that you wish to change.
2. Right click and select Properties from the short cut menu.
3. Find the "Linetype Scale" and change it to 2.
4. Press enter.

The lines should now be 1" and the spaces 1/2", twice a big as they were.

If you wanted the lines to be half the original size, you would change them to .5.

Note:
1. Linetypes may not appear the same if you are in the model tab rather than the Layout tab.

2. Linetype scaling is a visual preference. There is not a rule for spacing in cad.

HATCH

The **Hatch** command was previously discussed in Lesson 15. But we need to think about what happens to the hatch patterns when using Predefined or the line spacing when using User defined, if you adjust the scale of the model space.

Think about this....
When the model space appears smaller the hatch pattern will also appear smaller. This means the hatch lines could be so close together that they appear as a blob. So you must adjust the scale of the hatch pattern or increase the spacing.
When the model space appears larger the hatch pattern will also appear larger. Now the pattern could be too far apart. So you must adjust the scale of the hatch pattern or decrease the spacing.

To adjust the scale of the hatch patterns or line spacing you must change its scale or size.
1. Select the hatch to change. (Click on it)
2. Right click and select Properties from the short cut menu.
3. Find "Scale" if the hatch is Predefined, Find "Spacing" if the hatch is "User defined".
4. If the hatch is too small, increase the scale or spacing. If the hatch is too large, decrease the scale or spacing.

To determine how much to increase or decrease you need to calculate the drawing scale factor. The drawing scale factor (DSF) means "How many times smaller or larger did the drawing get when you adjusted the scale".

Here are a few of the most commonly used scales and their drawing scale factors:

Scale	DSF	Scale	DSF
1" = 1'	12	1 = 2	2
1/4" = 1'	48	2 = 1	1/2
1/8" = 1'	96	4 = 1	1/4

How to calculate Drawing Scale Factor (DSF):
1. ¼" = 1' (This is the scale)
2. 1/4 = 12 (change feet to inches)
3. Divide 12 by ¼
4. DSF = 48

For Example:
If you adjusted the scale of model space to 1/4" = 1'.

If the hatch was "Predefined" change the scale of the hatch pattern to 48.

If the hatch was "User defined" change the size of the spacing to 48.

HOW TO IMPORT A PAGE SETUP

NOTE: This is not an exercise. This is an overview. Refer to Exercise 27F.

A. **Open** the drawing.

B. Select **File / Plot.**

C. Select the "Page Set up Name" **Add** box.

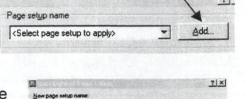

1. Select the **Import** box.
2. Find and select the drawing that contains the Page Setup you
   desire and select the **Open** box.
   (Just like opening a drawing)

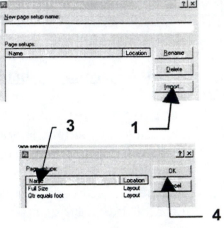

3. Select the **Setup Name** from the list.
4. Select the **OK** button

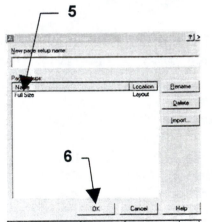

5. Select the Page set up you just imported
6. Select the **OK** button.

7. Select the imported Page
   setup name from the list.

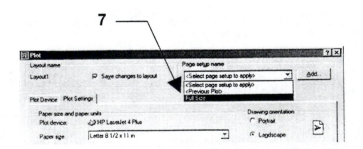

27-8

EXERCISE 27A
CREATE AN ARCHITECTURAL SETUP DRAWING

The following instructions will guide you through creating a "setup" drawing. A setup drawing is basically a master. (The "1Class template.dwt" is an example of a setup drawing) Even though the screen is blank, the actual file is full of information, such as; Units, Drawing Limits, Snap and Grid settings, Layers, Text styles and Dimension Styles. Once you have created this "setup" drawing, you just open it and draw. No more repetitive inputting of settings.

NEW SETTINGS

A. Begin your drawing without a template as follows:

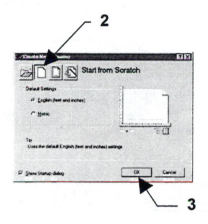

1. Select **"FILE / NEW"**
2. Select **"START FROM SCRATCH"** Box.
3. Select **"OK"**.
4. Your screen should be blank, no grids and the current layer is 0

B. Set drawing specifications as follows:

1. Set **"UNITS"** of measurement
   Use "**FORMAT / UNITS** and change the settings as shown below, then select **OK.**

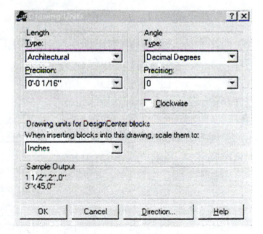

2. Set **"DRAWING LIMITS"** (Size of drawing area)
   USE "**FORMAT / DRAWING LIMITS**
   a. Lower left corner = 0'-0", 0'-0"
   b. Upper right corner = 68', 44'
   c. Use **"VIEW / ZOOM / ALL"** to generate the new limits

3. Set **"SNAP AND GRID"**
   Use **"TOOLS / DRAFTING SETTINGS**

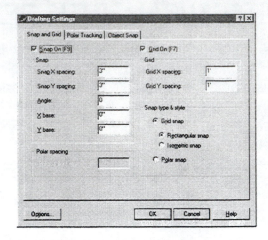

4. Set **"PICK BOX"** size (your preference)
   See page 26-2 for instructions.

NEW LAYERS

C. Create new layers

1. **Load** linetype (See page 26-4 for instructions)
    DASHED

2. Assign names, colors, linetypes and plotability. (See page 26-3 for instructions)

NAME	COLOR	LINETYPE	PLOT
BORDER	RED	CONTINUOUS	YES
CABINETS	CYAN	CONTINUOUS	YES
CONSTRUCTION	WHITE	CONTINUOUS	NO
DIMENSION	BLUE	CONTINUOUS	YES
DOORS	GREEN	CONTINUOUS	YES
ELECTRICAL	CYAN	CONTINUOUS	YES
FURNITURE	MAGENTA	CONTINUOUS	YES
PLUMBING	9	CONTINUOUS	YES
TEXT HEAVY	WHITE	CONTINUOUS	YES
TEXT LIGHT	BLUE	CONTINUOUS	YES
VIEWPORT	GREEN	CONTINUOUS	NO
WALLS	RED	CONTINUOUS	YES
WINDOWS	GREEN	CONTINUOUS	YES
WIRING	CYAN	DASHED	YES

NEW TEXT STYLE

D. Create a text style named *ARCH TEXT*

    1. Select **"FORMAT / TEXT STYLE"**
    2. Make the changes shown in the dialog box.

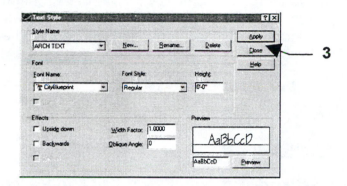

    3. When complete, select **APPLY** then **CLOSE**.

NEW DIMENSION STYLE

E. A new dimension style should also be created but that will be discussed separately in Exercise 27C, page 27-15.

THIS NEXT STEP IS VERY IMPORTANT..

F. SAVE ALL THE SETTINGS YOU JUST CREATED
    1. Select File / Save as
    2. Save as: **My Architectural Setup**

EXERCISE 27B
CREATE AN ARCHITECTURAL BORDER FOR PLOTTING

The following instructions will guide you through creating a Border drawing that will be used in combination with your "My Architectural Setup" when plotting. You will create a Layout and draw a border with title block. All of this information will be saved and you will not have to do this again.

A. Open **My Architectural Setup**

B. Select the **LAYOUT1** tab.   ▶ \ Model / Layout1

> *Note: If the Page Setup dialog box shown below does not appear automatically, right click on the Layout tab, then select Page Setup from the short cut menu.*

1. **Type the new name:**
    Qtr equals foot

2. **Select the "*Plot Device*" tab.**

3. **Select the Plotter.**

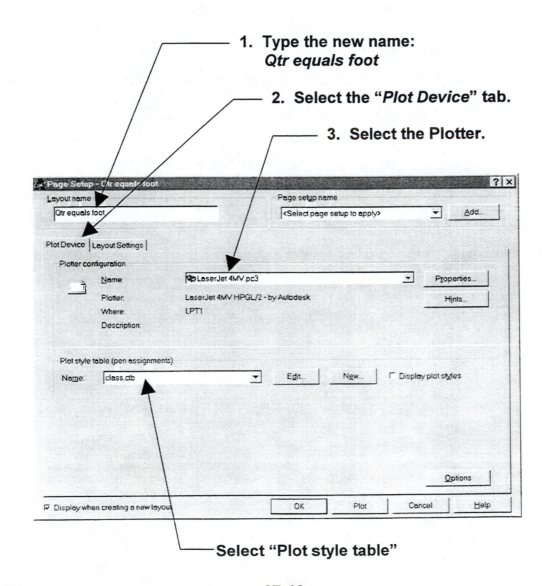

Select "Plot style table"

5. Select the "*Layout Settings*" tab.

6. Select the "*Paper Size*".

7. Select scale "1:1"

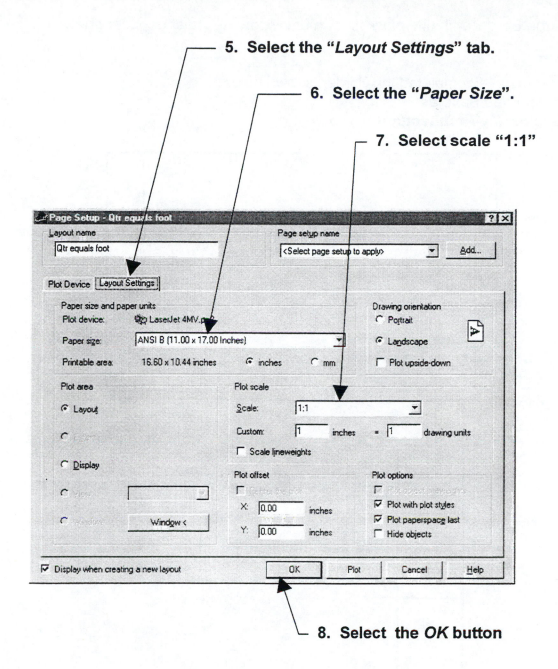

8. Select the *OK* button

You should now have a sheet of paper displayed on the screen and the Layout tab should now be displayed as **"Qtr equals foot"**. This sheet is in front of "Model". In Exercise 27D, you will cut a hole in this sheet so you can see through to Model.

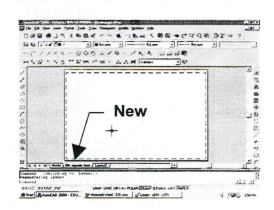

27-13

C. Draw the Border with title block, shown below, on the sheet of paper shown on the screen.

D. When you have completed the Border, shown below:
1. Select File / Save as
2. Save as: **My Architectural Setup** (Again)

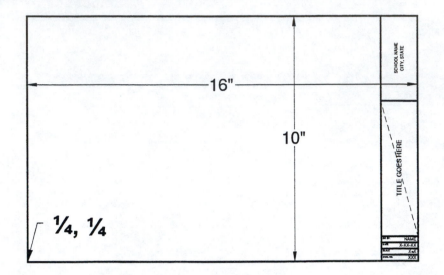

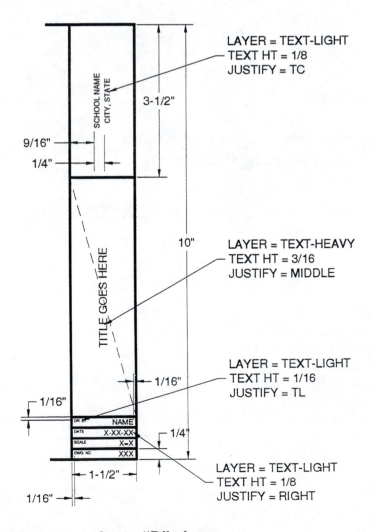

LAYER = TEXT-LIGHT
TEXT HT = 1/8
JUSTIFY = TC

LAYER = TEXT-HEAVY
TEXT HT = 3/16
JUSTIFY = MIDDLE

LAYER = TEXT-LIGHT
TEXT HT = 1/16
JUSTIFY = TL

LAYER = TEXT-LIGHT
TEXT HT = 1/8
JUSTIFY = RIGHT

Don't forget to save, refer to "D" above.

EXERCISE 27C
CREATE A NEW ARCHITECTURAL DIMENSION STYLE

1. Open **My Architectural Setup.**

2. Set **DIMASSOC** to **2**

3. Select **FORMAT / DIMENSION STYLE**

4. Select the **NEW** button.

5. New Style Name: **ARCH DIM**

6. Start With: **Standard**

7. Use For: **All dimensions**

8. Select the **CONTINUE** box.

9. Select the **"Primary Units"** tab and make the following changes.

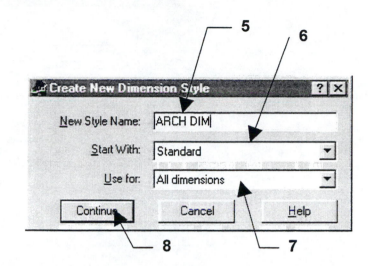

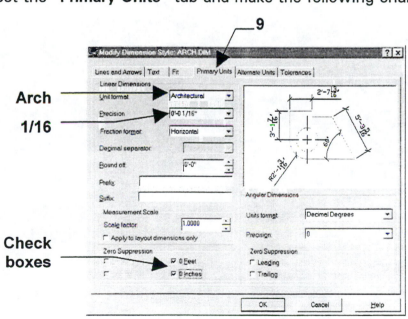

DO NOT SELECT THE OK BUTTON YET

10. Select the *"Lines and Arrows"* tab and make the following changes.

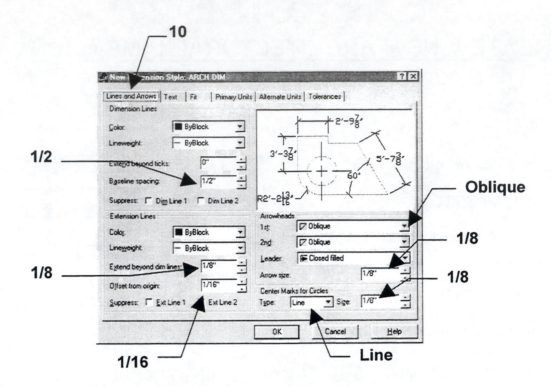

DO NOT SELECT THE OK BUTTON.

11. Select the **"Text"** tab and make the following changes .

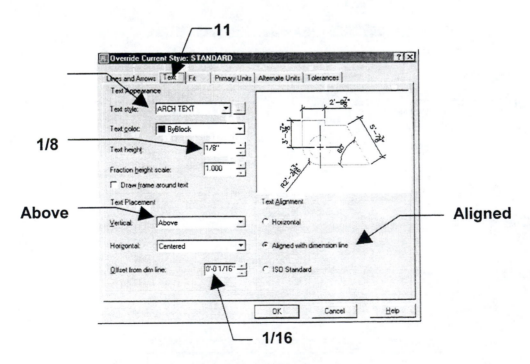

DO NOT SELECT THE OK BUTTON

12. Select the **"Fit"** tab and make the following change.

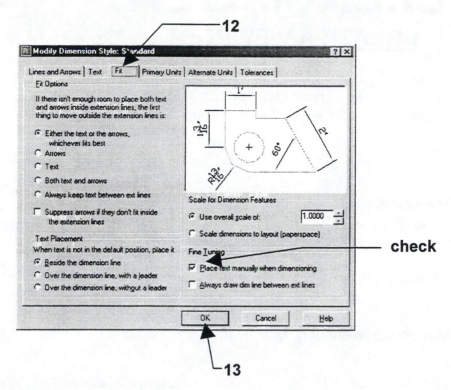

13. **NOW** select the **OK** button.

14. *Your new style "ARCH DIM" should be listed.*

15. Select the **"Set Current"** button to make your new style "**ARCH DIM**" the style that you will use.

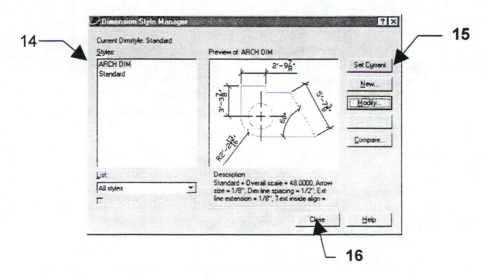

16. Select the **Close** button to **exit**.
17. Save your drawing as **My Architectural Setup**

EXERCISE 27D
CREATE A VIEWPORT

The following instructions will guide you through creating a VIEWPORT in the Architectural Border Layout sheet. Creating a viewport has the same effect as cutting a hole in the sheet of paper. You will be able to see through the viewport frame to Model.

A. Open **My Architectural Setup**
B. Select the **Qtr equals foot** tab.
C. Select layer "Viewport"

D. Select the Single Viewport icon from the Viewports Toolbar

Single Viewport icon (LT's toolbar looks a little different.)

E. Draw a Single viewport approximately as shown.

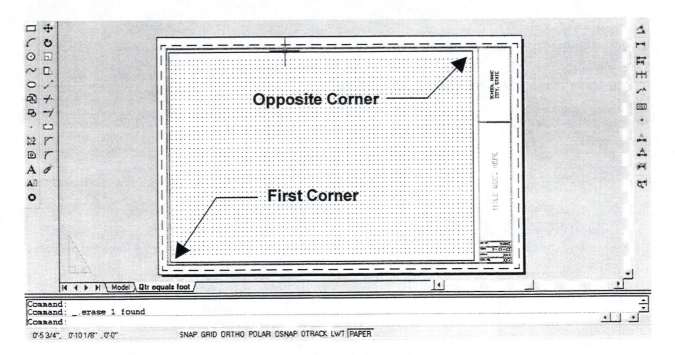

F. After successfully creating the Viewport, you should now be able to see through to Model. (Note: Grids can be on in both model and paper space.)

G. File / Save as: **My Architectural Setup**

EXERCISE 27E
ADJUSTING THE SCALE INSIDE THE VIEWPORT

1. **Open** My Architectural Setup.

2. Move to the **Qtr equals foot** tab.

3. Double click inside of the Viewport *(It is very important that you be inside the Viewport. You want to scale the Model geometry not the Layout)*

4. Select View / Zoom / All (This puts your drawing limits in the correct location)

5. *Adjust the scale* of the Model geometry as follows:

   a. Select ¼″ = 1′ from the **"Viewports"** toolbar.

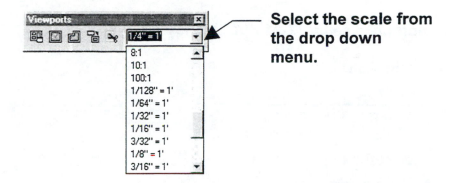

Select the scale from the drop down menu.

The Model geometry should have changed. You will not notice too much of a change other than your grid spacing should appear smaller. Now your "Qtr equals foot" layout is ready to accept a very large drawing. You will understand better after you complete Exercise 27G.

6. **Lock the Viewport scale**
   a. Change to Paperspace
   b. Click on the Viewport frame.
   c. Right click (the shortcut menu will appear)
   d. Select "Display Locked" and select "Yes"

EXERCISE 27F
CREATE A PAGE SETUP USING "IMPORT"

The following instructions will guide you through **IMPORTING** a previously created page setup into your new layout. This process will not be difficult and it will save you time. Importing page setups with similar settings, is more efficient than starting from scratch each time. (Refer to Page 26-14) **How to Import a Page Setup** for more detailed explanations of each area.

A. Open **My Architectural Setup**

B. Select the **Qtr equals foot** tab. (You should be looking at your Architectural Border)

C. Select **File / Plot** or Place the cursor on the **Qtr equals foot** tab, press the right mouse button then select **Plot** from the Short cut menu.

The Plot dialog box should appear

D. **Import** page setup *17-11-FULL* as follows:

1. Select the ADD button.

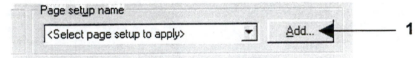

2. Select the Import button.

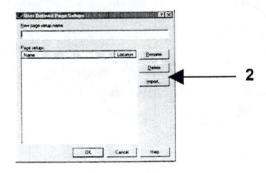

3. Find *My Mechanical Setup* in your files and select **OPEN**.

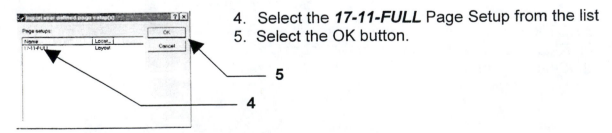

4. Select the *17-11-FULL* Page Setup from the list
5. Select the OK button.

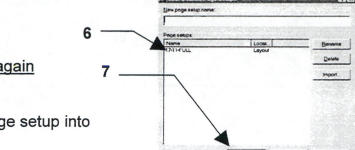

6 **7**

6. Select **17-11-FULL** <u>again</u>

7. Select **OK** button.
(You just imported a page setup into this drawing.)

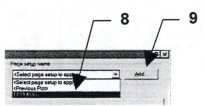

8 **9**

8. Select **17-11-FULL** from the Page Setup Name drop down menu to activate it.

9. Select the **ADD** button <u>again</u> to change it's name.

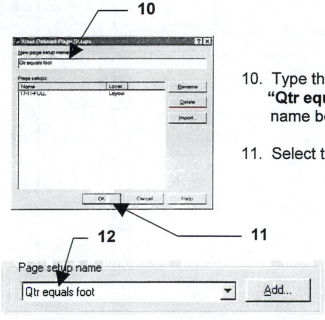

10

12 **11**

10. Type the new page setup name **"Qtr equals foot"** in the New page setup name box.

11. Select the **OK** box.

12. The new page setup **"Qtr equals foot"** should now be displayed in the Page Setup Name box.

E. If your computer **is** connected to the Plotter / Printer, select the **OK** button to plot. If your computer **is not** connected to the Plotter / Printer, select the **CANCEL** button.

F. Save this file:
   1. Select **File / Save** as
   2. Save as: **My Architectural Setup**

You have now successfully imported a previously created page setup. You didn't have to selected the device, paper size, scale or color properties. They were all set in the page setup you imported. You just rename the page setup and start plotting.

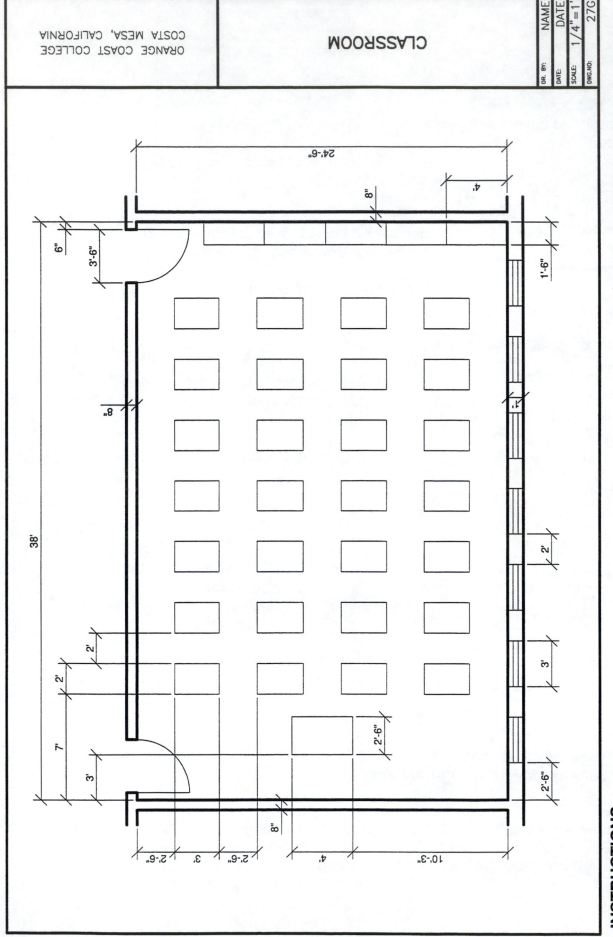

EXERCISE 27G

CLASSROOM

DR. BY:	NAME
DATE:	DATE
SCALE:	1/4" = 1'
DWG.NO:	27G

INSTRUCTIONS:

1. Open **My Architectural Setup.**
2. Move to the **Qtr equals foot** tab
3. Draw the classroom, shown above, in the viewport (model space) .
4. Dimension in Paper space (Use Dimension Style = Arch Dim)
5. Save as **EX-27G** and plot using **Qtr equals foot** Page Setup

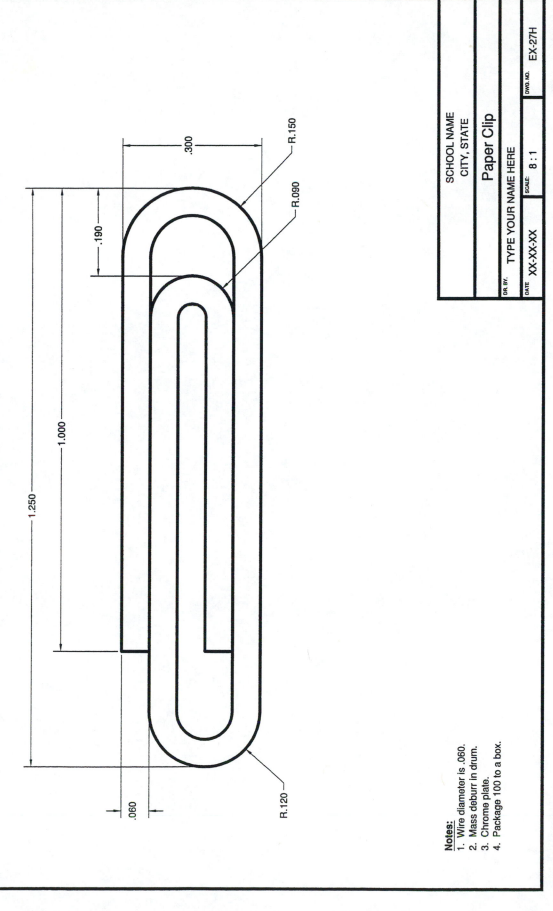

.300

.190

R.150

R.090

1.000

1.250

.060

R.120

EXERCISE 27H

Notes:
1. Wire diameter is .060.
2. Mass deburr in drum.
3. Chrome plate.
4. Package 100 to a box.

INSTRUCTIONS:

Now let's try drawing that Paper Clip that needs to be larger.

1. Open MY MECHANICAL SETUP
2. Unlock the viewport.
3. Adjust the scale of the viewport to 8 : 1 and Lock.
4. Draw the drawing above in the viewport (Model Space).
5. Dimension and Notes (1/8 ht.) In Paper space (Use Dim. style: **Class style**)
6. Save as: EX-27H
7. Plot using "17-11-FULL" Page Setup.

NOTES:

LEARNING OBJECTIVES

After completing this lesson, you will be able to:

1. Understand what are Blocks.
2. Create a Block.
3. Insert a Block into your drawing.
4. Understand the rules governing color and linetype.

LESSON 28

BLOCKS

A BLOCK is a group of objects that have been converted into ONE object. A Symbol is a typical application for the block command. First a BLOCK must be created. Then it can be INSERTED into the drawing. An inserted Block uses less file space than a set of objects copied.

CREATING A BLOCK

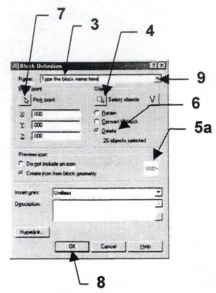

1. First draw the objects that will be converted into a Block.
   (Refer to page 28-3   **Color and Linetype.**)

2. Select the **BMAKE** command using one of the following:

   TYPE = BLOCK
   PULLDOWN = DRAW / BLOCK / MAKE
   TOOLBAR =DRAW

   (the dialog box, on the right, will appear)

3. Enter the New Block name in the **Name** box.

4. Select the **SELECT OBJECTS** button.

   The Block Definition box will disappear and you will return temporarily to the drawing.

5. Select the objects you want in the block, then press <enter>
   a. The Block Definition box will reappear and the objects you selected should be
      illustrated in the Preview Icon area.

6. Select **Delete** (Refer to 28-3 for definitions)

7. Select the **Pick Point** button. (Or you may type the X and Y coordinates)
   The Block Definition box will disappear again and you will return temporarily to the drawing.

   Select the location you would like to be the insertion point of the Block. Later when you insert this block, it will appear on the screen attached to the cursor at this point. Usually this point is the CENTER, MIDPOINT or ENDPOINT of an object.

8. Select the **OK** button.
   The objects will disappear but the new block is now stored in the drawing's block definition table.

9. To verify the creation of this Block, select the Name (▾). A list of all the blocks, in this drawing, will appear.

ADDITIONAL DEFINITIONS OF OPTIONS.

Retain
If this option is selected, the original objects will stay visible on the screen after the block has been created.

Convert to block
If this option is selected, the original objects will disappear after the block has been created, but will immediately reappear as a block. It happens so fast, you won't even notice the original objects disappeared.

Delete
If this option is selected, the original objects will disappear from the screen, after the block has been created.

Do not include an icon or Create icon from block geometry
These options determine whether a " preview thumbnail" sketch is created. This option is used with the "Design Center" to drag and drop the blocks into a drawing. The Design Center is an advanced option and is not discussed in this book.

Insert Units
You may define the units of measurement for the block. This option is used with the "Design Center" to drag and drop with Autoscaling. The Design Center is an advanced option and is not discussed in this book.

COLOR and LINETYPE

If a block is created on Layer 0:

When the block is inserted, it will assume the color and linetype of the layer that is current at the time of insertion.
The block will also reside on the layer that was current at the time of insertion.
If the Block is then **Exploded**, the objects included in the block, will go back to their original color, linetype and layer.

If a block is created on Specific layers:

When the block is inserted, it will retain its own color and linetype. It **will not assume** the color and linetype of the layer that is current.
But the block **will reside** on the current layer at the time of insertion.
If the Block is then **Exploded**, the objects included in the block, will go back to their original layer. The color and linetype remain the same.

INSERTING BLOCKS

A **BLOCK** can be inserted at any location on the drawing. When inserting a Block you can **SCALE** or **ROTATE** it.

1. Select the INSERT command using one of the following:
   TYPE = DDINSERT
   PULLDOWN = INSERT / BLOCK
   TOOLBAR =DRAW

   The INSERT dialog box will appears.

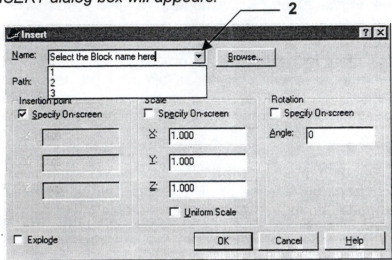

2. Select the BLOCK name then select the OK button.
   a. If the block is in the drawing that is open on the screen:
      select the block from the drop down list shown above
   b. The Browse button can be used to find an entire drawing or a WBlock.
      Wblocks will be discussed in the Advanced workbook.

   This returns you to the drawing and the selected block should be attached to the cursor.

3. Select the location for the block by pressing the left mouse button or typing coordinates.

NOTE: If you want to scale or rotate the block before you actually place the block, press the right hand mouse button, and you may select an option from the short cut menu or select an option from the command line menu shown below.

   Command: _insert
   Specify insertion point or **[Scale/X/Y/Z/Rotate/PScale/PX/PY/PZ/PRotate]:**

You may also "preset" the insertion point, scale or rotation. This is discussed on Page 28-5.

PRESETTING THE "INSERTION POINT", "SCALE" OR "ROTATION"

You may want to specify the **Insertion point, Scale or Rotation** in the **"INSERT"** box instead of at the command line.

1. Remove the check mark from the **"SPECIFY ON-SCREEN"** box.
2. Fill in the appropriate information describe below:

Insertion point
Type the X and Y coordinates from the Origin. The Z is for 3D only.
The example below indicates the blocks insertion point will be 5 inches in the X direction and 3 inches in the Y direction, from the Origin.

Scale
You may scale the block proportionately by typing the scale factor in the X box and then check the Uniform Scale box.
If the block will be scaled non-proportionately, type the different scale factors in both X and Y boxes.
The example below indicates that the block will be scale proportionate at a factor of 2.

Rotation
Type the desired rotation angle relative to its current rotation angle.
The example below indicates the block will be rotated 45 degrees from it's originally created angle orientation.

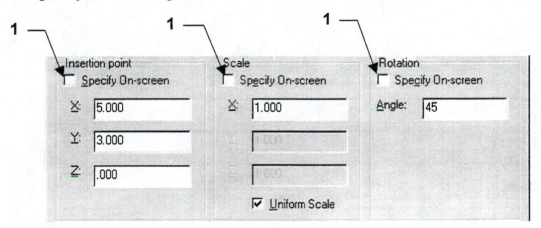

Blocks have many uses and will be discussed further in the "Exercise Workbook for Advanced AutoCAD 2002" along with the new "DesignCenter".

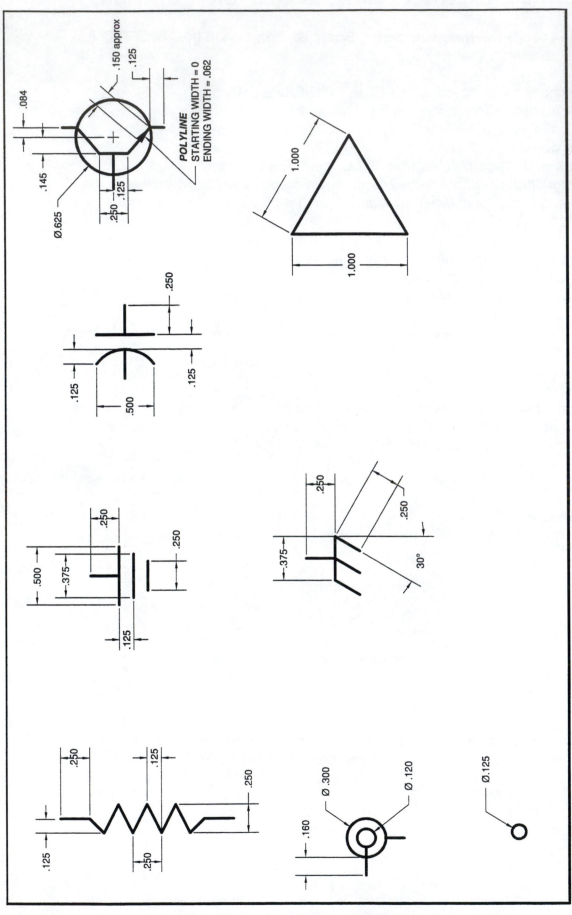

EXERCISE 28
STEP 1

INSTRUCTIONS:

1. Open **My Mechanical Setup.**
2. Draw the Objects above in the viewport (Model space) Use Layer = Object.
3. Now change each one into a Block. (They should disappear as they are made)
4. Name them 1, 2, 3, etc.
5. Save as **EX-28 Step 1.**
6. Now follow the instructions for Step 2 on the next page. (Do not start a new drawing)

28-6

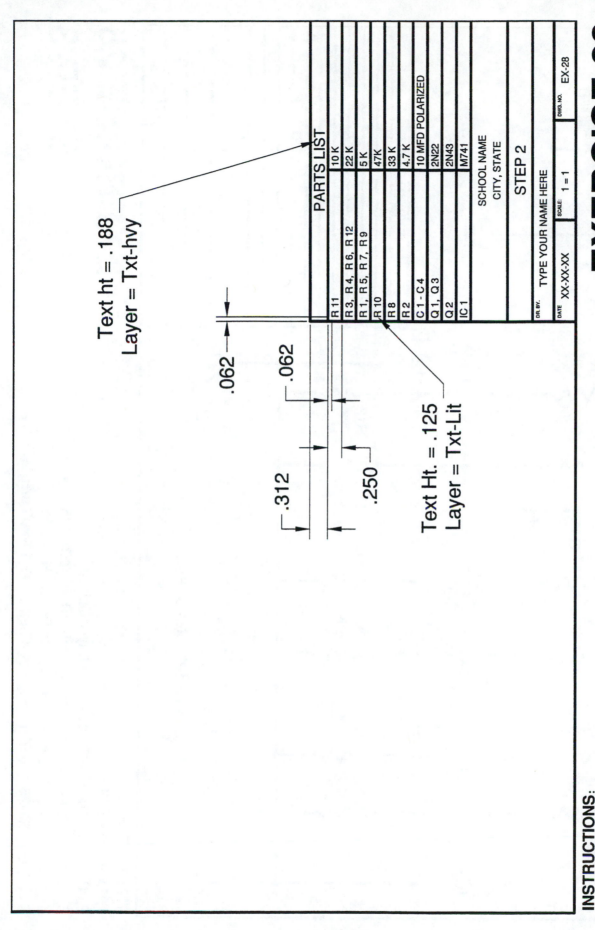

Text ht = .188
Layer = Txt-hvy

PARTS LIST	
R 11	10 K
R3, R4, R 6, R 12	22 K
R1, R5, R7, R9	5 K
R 10	47K
R 8	33 K
R 2	4.7 K
C 1 - C 4	10 MFD POLARIZED
Q 1, Q 3	2N22
Q 2	2N43
IC 1	M741

SCHOOL NAME
CITY, STATE

STEP 2

DR. BY.	TYPE YOUR NAME HERE		
DATE	XX-XX-XX	SCALE: 1 = 1	DWG. NO. EX-28

Text Ht. = .125
Layer = Txt-Lit

.062
.062
.312
.250

EXERCISE 28
STEP 2

INSTRUCTIONS:

1. Open **EX-28 Step 1**
2. Create the Parts List above the title block in paper space (17-11-Full tab)
3. Use Layer **Border** for the lines and Layer **Text-Lit** for the text.
4. Save as **EX-28 Step 2.**
5. Now follow the instructions for Step 3 on the next page. (Do not start a new drawing)

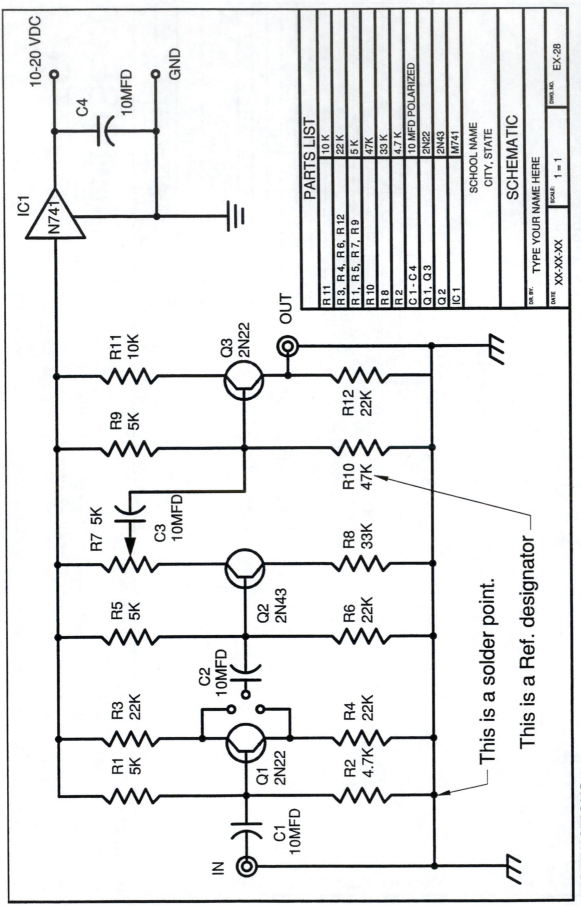

EXERCISE 28
STEP 3

PARTS LIST

R 11	10 K
R3, R4, R6, R12	22 K
R1, R5, R7, R9	5 K
R 10	47 K
R 8	33 K
R 2	4.7 K
C1 - C4	10 MFD POLARIZED
Q1, Q3	2N22
Q 2	2N43
IC 1	M741

SCHOOL NAME
CITY, STATE

SCHEMATIC

DR. BY. TYPE YOUR NAME HERE

SCALE: 1 = 1

DATE XX-XX-XX

DWG. NO. EX-28

This is a solder point.

This is a Ref. designator

INSTRUCTIONS:

1. Open EX-28 Step 2.
2. Draw the schematic above. Use Layer Object.
3. Use Donuts to make the Solder points, ID=0   OD=.125.
4. Add Reference Designators on Layer Txt-Lit. Ht = .125
5. Save as **EX-28** and Plot using Page Setup **"17-11-Full size"** .

LEARNING OBJECTIVES

After completing this lesson, you will be able to:

1. Use the Spacetrans command to adjust text to the scale of Paper space.

We will also review:

1. "Tools / Inquiry" commands. (Lesson 9)
2. "Object snap" settings. (Lesson 4)
3. "Ltscale" command. (Lesson 27)

LESSON 29

'SPACETRANS

In the previous lessons you learned the difference between model space and paper space. You learned that paper space is always 1 : 1 and model space can be adjusted to any scale.

Now we need to discuss what do you do if you need to add text to a model space that has had its scale adjusted. How do you determine what text height to specify?

For example, in Exercise 27G, the model space has been adjusted to 1/4 " = 1". That means that model space is 48 times smaller than actual size. Remember, model space is far away from viewport frame, so it appears smaller. Now, what if you wanted to put text in the classroom to name the objects, such as "desks". What text height would you use?

Try this: I would like the text height to be 1/4.
1. Open EX-27G
2. Go to model space.
3. Select Draw / Text / Single line Text
4. Select a location beside one of the desks for the start point.
5. Enter text ht. 1/4 and rotation 0
6. Type: DESK <enter>
Can you see the text?? Pretty teeny huh?? That's because it is 48 times smaller.

The following will explain the 3 methods you should use to get the correct height.

Method 1. (Most difficult)
 When entering the text height, multiply the height times the drawing scale factor. If model space was 1/4" = 1' the drawing scale factor would be 48. So the Text height should be = 1/4 times 48 = 12" (Refer to page 27-7)

Method 2. (Probably the easiest)
Place the text in Paper space not model space. Just like dimensions. 1/4 text ht would be 1/4 because paper space has not been scaled, it is 1:1.

Method 3. (New command in AutoCAD 2002)
Use the command 'Spacetrans. 'Spacetrans will calculate what height the text should be in model space. (Note: this only works with Single Line Text not Multiline text.)
1. Get into model space
2. Select Draw / Text / Single Line Text
3. Select a location for start point or justify
4. When prompted for the text ht., type **'spacetrans <enter> (Note: the apostrophe is necessary)**
5. Type the height of the text, such as 1/4"
6. Enter rotation angle <enter>
7. Type the text.
The apostrophe designates transparency. Transparent means you can use this command in the middle of another command. Thus we interrupted the Text command to run the spacetrans command and then you returned to the Text command.

EXERCISE 29

INSTRUCTIONS:

A. Open drawing **My Architectural Setup.**

B. **STEP 1:** **Create the Blocks**
Draw the objects shown on page 29-4. Draw in **Model Space.**
Use the layers indicated.

Change each one into a **BLOCK.** They should disappear as you create the
Blocks. (Refer to Lesson 28 for assistance)

Do not start a new drawing, continue on to Step 2.

C. **STEP 2:** **Drawing the Cabin**
Select the **"Qtr equals foot"** tab. (You should see your title block)
Next double click in the viewport to activate the Model space. (Do not draw in
Paper space)
Draw the **CABIN** shown on page 29-4.
Design your own Kitchen. Use appropriate layers.

Walls = 6" thick   **Space behind doors = 2"**

Room Names = Text Height = 3/16" (Refer to 29-2 for instructions)

Window sizes: In the Kitchen = 3 ft. In the Sleeping and Living rooms = 6 ft.

D. **How to draw the dashed Electrical Lines.**
A. Use Layer **Wiring.**
B. Draw the lines using **Arc** (Start, End, Direction)
C. Change the **Ltscale** to **.5** as follows:
Globally:
Type at the command line: **Ltscale <enter>**
Enter new linetype scale factor <1.0000>:**type .5 <enter>**
Individually: Use Properties
(Refer to page 27-2 for information on Linetype scales)

E. Dimension the drawing as shown in paper space. Use dimension style: Arch

F. **Save** as **EX-29** and **Plot** using Page Setup: **Qtr equals foot**

DR. BY.	NAME
DATE	X-XX-XX
SCALE	1/4"=1'
DWG. NO.	29

LIBRARY SYMBOLS STEP 1

SCHOOL NAME
CITY, STATE

USE LAYER = PLUMB

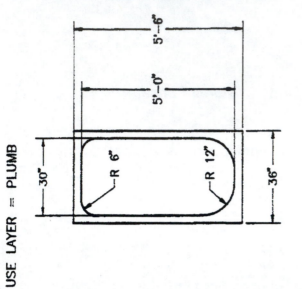

5'-6"

5'-0"

30"

R 6"

R 12"

36"

USE LAYER = DOORS

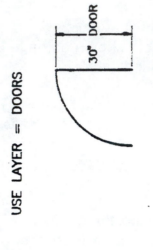

30" DOOR

30"

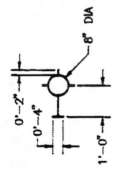

8" DIA

0'-2"

0'-4"

1'-0"

TEXT HT.= 8"

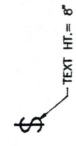

0'-8"

4" HT

8" DIA

1'-4"

8" DIA

8" DIA

1'-0"

0'-2"

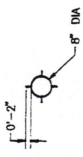

8" DIA

0'-2"

USE LAYER = ELECT

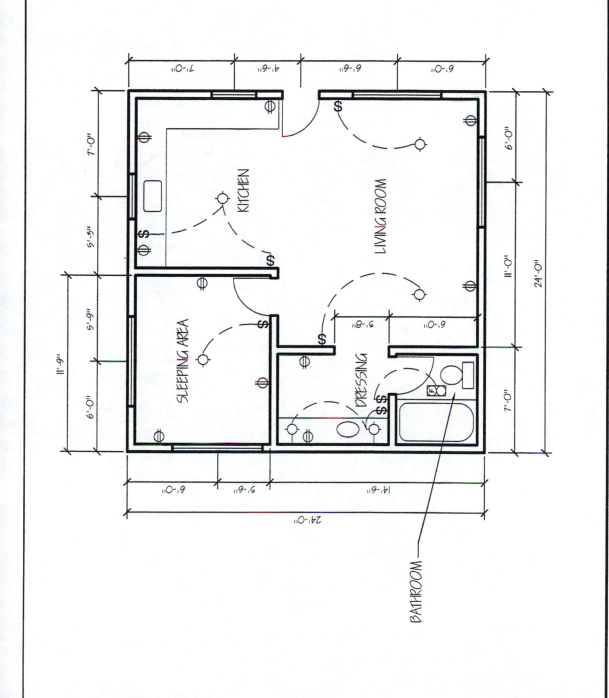

SIERRA CABIN FLOOR PLAN

SCHOOL NAME
CITY, STATE

NAME
DR. BY.
DATE X-XX-XX
SCALE 1/4"=1'
DWG. NO. 29

EXERCISE 29
STEP 2

29-5

NOTES:

LEARNING OBJECTIVES

In this lesson we will review and practice:

1. "Polyline / Spline" commands. (Lesson 23)

LESSON 30

EXERCISE 30

INSTRUCTIONS:

A. Open drawing **My Mechanical Setup**
Select the Full size tab. (You should see your title block)
Double click in the viewport area to get into model space.

B. **STEP 1.**
Draw the details shown on page 30-3. Do not dimension.
Draw the break line as follows:
    a. Draw the break line using **POLYLINE**.
    b. Change it to a curved line using:
        MODIFY / OBJECT / POLYLINE
           Select the Polyline
           Select **S**pline
    c. Draw the Hatch
        Use Hatch pattern ANSI 31,   Layer = Hatch
    d. Thread dimensions below. Use Layer Threads.

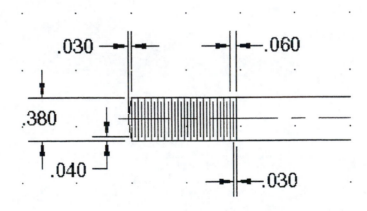

C. **STEP 2.**
Double click in the gray area to return to paperspace.
Draw the **PARTS LIST** (in paperspace) shown on page 30-4, STEP 2.
Make the changes to the title block.

D. **STEP 3.**
Move the parts into the proper locations to form the assembly shown.
The distance between the jaws is 1".
Draw the Balloons:
    a. Use Leader
    b. Use a .50 dia circle.
    c. Text ht. = .187

E. Save as **EX-30** and **PLOT** using Page setup "17-11 Full Size".

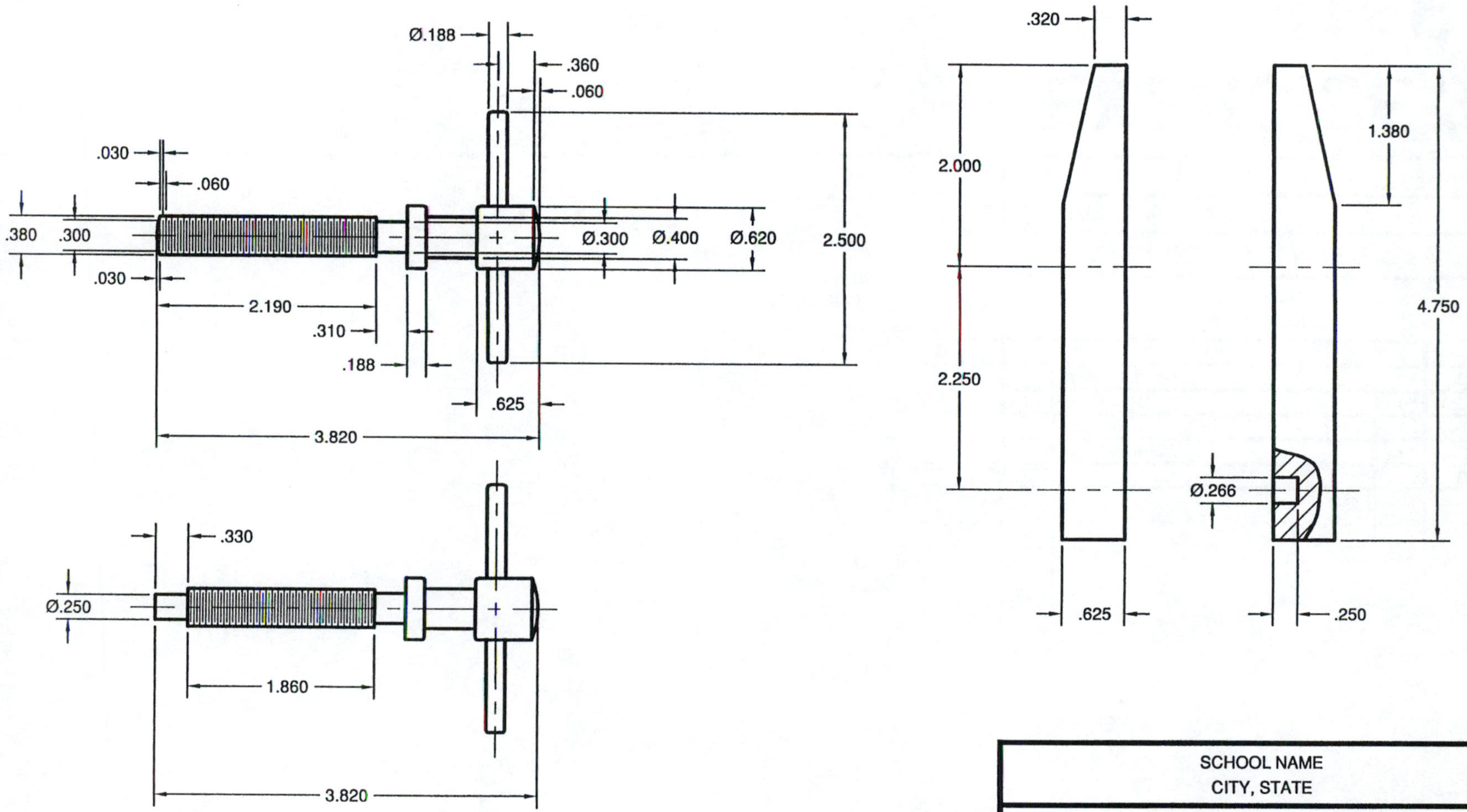

MACHINIST'S CLAMP STEP 1

SCHOOL NAME
CITY, STATE

DR. BY.
TYPE YOUR NAME HERE

DATE XX-XX-XX

DWG. NO. EX-30

SCALE: 1 = 1

NOTE:
1. All Fillets to be R.030

EXERCISE 30
STEP 1

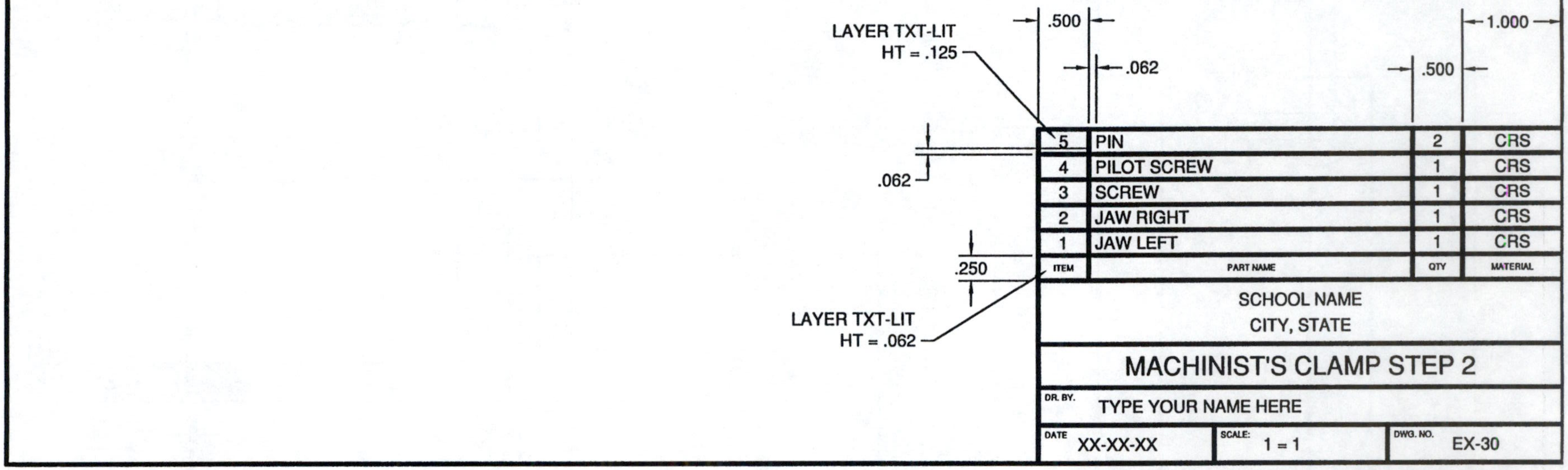

EXERCISE 30
STEP 2

ITEM	PART NAME	QTY	MATERIAL
5	PIN	2	CRS
4	PILOT SCREW	1	CRS
3	SCREW	1	CRS
2	JAW RIGHT	1	CRS
1	JAW LEFT	1	CRS

SCHOOL NAME
CITY, STATE

MACHINIST'S CLAMP STEP 2

DR. BY. TYPE YOUR NAME HERE

| DATE | XX-XX-XX | SCALE: 1 = 1 | DWG. NO. EX-30 |

— 1.000 —

— .500 —

— .062 —

— .500 —

.062

.250

LAYER TXT-LIT
HT = .125

LAYER TXT-LIT
HT = .062

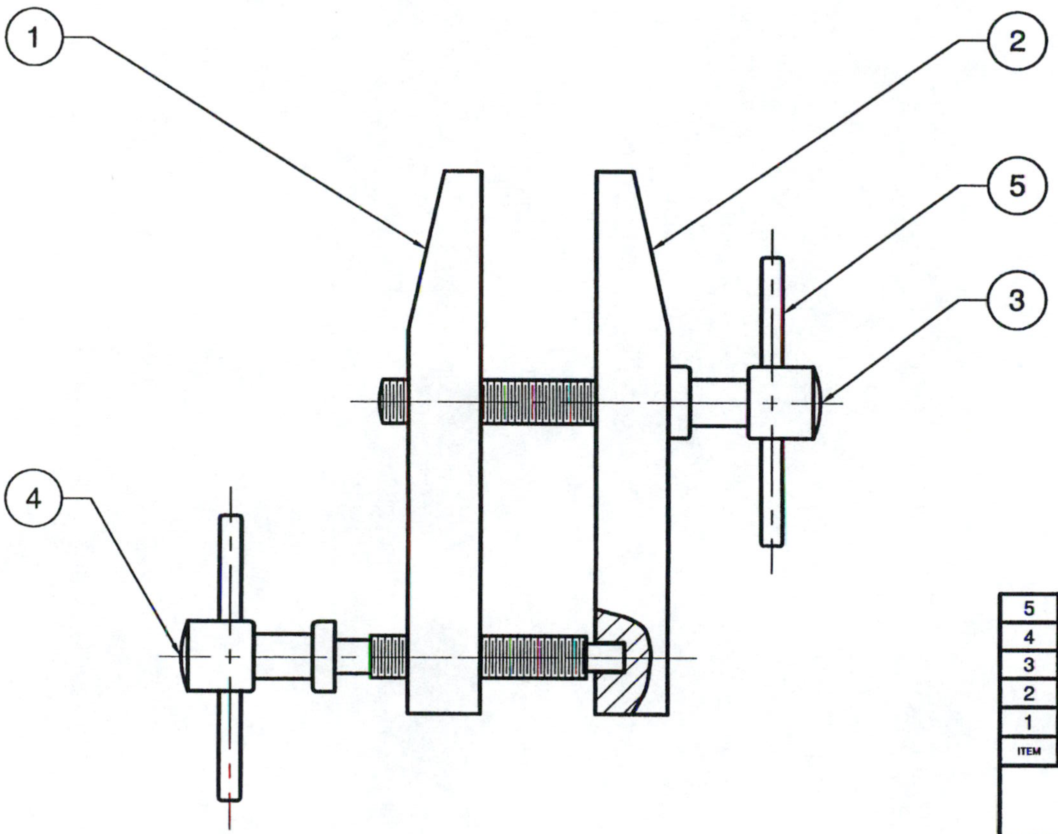

ITEM	PART NAME	QTY	MATERIAL
5	PIN	2	CRS
4	PILOT SCREW	1	CRS
3	SCREW	1	CRS
2	JAW RIGHT	1	CRS
1	JAW LEFT	1	CRS

SCHOOL NAME
CITY, STATE

MACHINIST'S CLAMP

DR. BY. TYPE YOUR NAME HERE

DWG. NO. EX-30

DATE XX-XX-XX

SCALE: 1 = 1

EXERCISE 30
STEP 3

NOTES:

APPENDIX A
Add a Printer / Plotter

The following are step by step instructions on how to configure AutoCAD for your printer or plotter. These instructions assume you are a single system user. If you are networked or need more detailed information, please refer to your AutoCAD users guide.

Note: You can configure AutoCAD for multiple printers. I suggest that you configure the plotter shown below to match the exercises in this workbook.

A. Select **File / Plotter Manager**
B. Select "Add-a-Plotter" Wizard

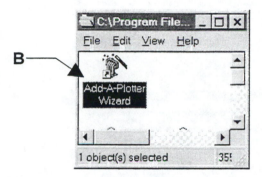

C. Select the **"Next"** button.

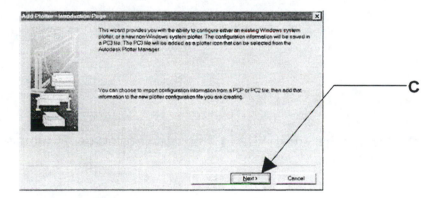

D. Select "**My Computer**" then **Next**.

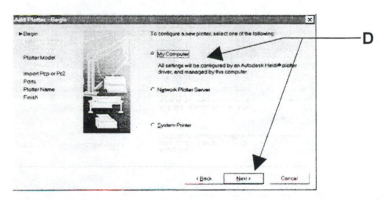

E. Select the **Manufacturer** and the specific **Model** desired then **Next**.

(If you have a disk with the specific driver information, put the disk in the disk drive and select "Have disk" button then follow instructions.)

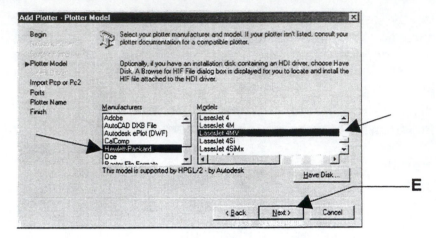

F. Select the **"Next"** box.

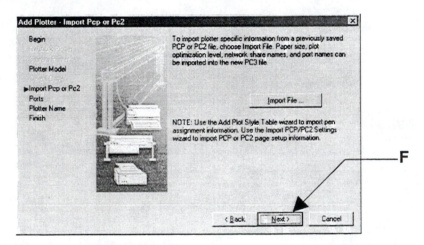

G. Select **"Plot to a port"** and **"LPT1"** unless your printer is attached to a Com port. Then Select **"Next"**.

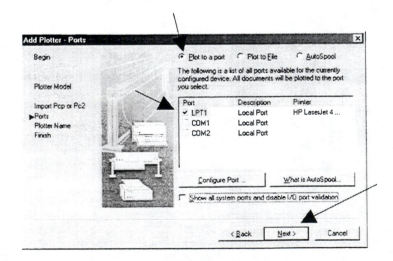

H. Type the **plotter name** then **"next"**. (This name should be descriptive so you will recognize it for selection later)

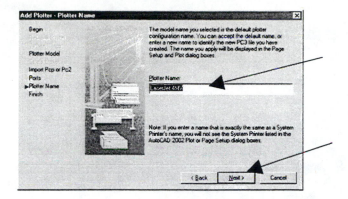

I. Select the **"Edit Plotter Configuration..."** box.

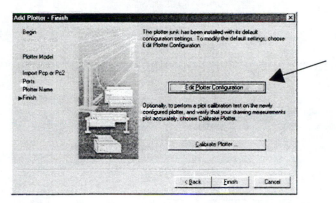

J. Select:
1. Device and Document Settings tab.
2. Media: Source and Size
3. Size: Ansi B (11 X 17 inches)
4. OK box.

K. Select **"Finish"**.

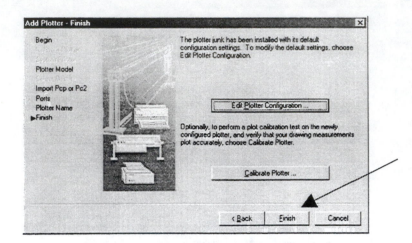

L. Now check the **File / Plotter Manager.** Is your printer / plotter there?

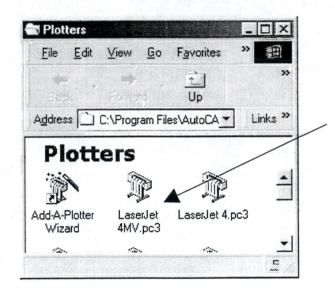

APPENDIX B
Today Window

The default startup window in AutoCAD 2002 is the **AutoCAD Today** window shown below. The AutoCAD Today window appears when you first open AutoCAD and each time you select File / New. You may also produce the Today startup window anytime by typing **Today** at the command line or selecting the **Today icon** 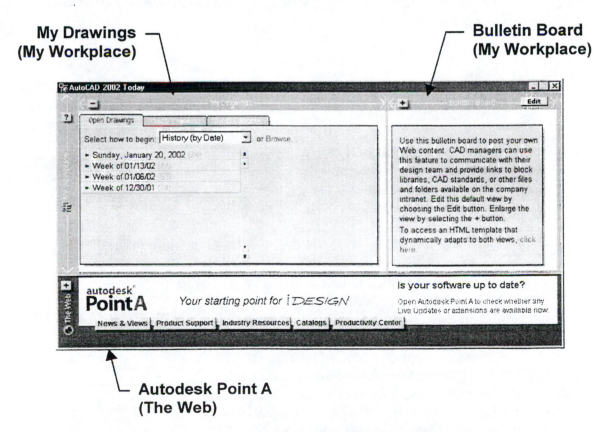 from the Standard toolbar.

The AutoCAD Today window is actually a separate Windows application. If you minimize it, it continues to run in the background while you draw. If you select the "close" button (X), the AutoCAD Today window closes completely until you select it again or start a new drawing.

The AutoCAD Today window not only allows you to Open existing drawings and Create New drawings, but it allows you to connect to the Autodesk Point A Web site.

I prefer to not use the Today window as my default start up window. I prefer to use the "Traditional Startup Window" and select the "Today icon" when I need the Today Window. (That is how this workbook is setup) To designate a startup window as your default startup window use the **"Options / System"** dialog box as shown on page Intro-4-G.

My Drawings
(My Workplace)

Bulletin Board
(My Workplace)

Autodesk Point A
(The Web)

On the following page, the three sections of the AutoCAD Today window are briefly described.

My Drawings

This area has 3 tabs to 1. Open and existing drawing, 2. Create a new drawing or 3. access a symbol library.

1. Open drawings tab
Use this tab to open an existing drawing. First you must "<u>Select how to begin</u>" or "<u>Browse</u>".

    A. "<u>Select how to begin</u>" <u>drop down list</u>:

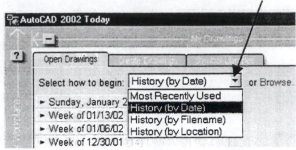

    <u>**Most Recently Used**</u>: The files are listed in the order of last used first.

    <u>**History (by Date)**</u>: Files are arranged according to the day or week in which they were opened.

    <u>**History (by Filename)**</u>: Files are arranged alphabetically.

    <u>**History (by Location)**</u>: Files are arranged according to the folders in which they are stored.

Note: "History" is a list of "shortcuts" to the files. This list can get very long. To delete a shortcut go to: Windows / Applications Data / Autodesk / AutoCAD / Recent / Save Drawing As.

2. <u>Create drawings tab</u>
    Use this tab to create a new drawing using a template, Start from Scratch or Wizards.

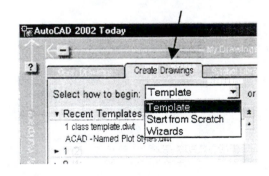

    <u>**Template**</u>: Use this option to create a new drawing using a previously created template. Recently used templates will be listed first, numerical second, and alphabetical last.

    <u>**Start from Scratch**</u>: Allows you to start a drawing with all default settings.

    <u>**Wizards**</u>: Allows you to select the "Quick or Advanced" Setup Wizard.

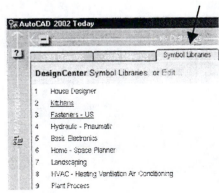

3. <u>Symbol Libraries</u>
This tab provides access to a list of AutoCAD provided symbol libraries. (The drawing files for these symbols are stored in the "AutoCAD \ Sample \ DesignCenter" folder.) When you select a Library from the list, the AutoCAD Today window minimizes and the DesignCenter appears. You may insert the symbols by "drag and drop" or "Right Click". (Note: the DesignCenter is discussed in the "Advanced" workbook)

Bulletin Board

This area is a source of communication to a team working on a specific project.

Items that might be displayed here are: Calendars, News, Instructions and Links to websites.
Any .htm, .gif, or .jpg file may be displayed.

Generally, the CAD manager controls this site.

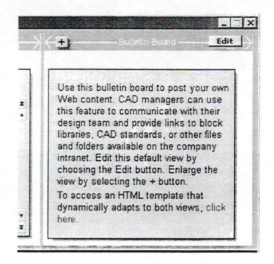

Autodesk Point A

This area provides a direct link to the Autodesk Point A website.

APPENDIX C
Active Assistance

The Active Assistance window provides information about the AutoCAD commands as you work. The information you get from Active Assistance is just enough to get you started. Blue text links will link you to additional information and topics.

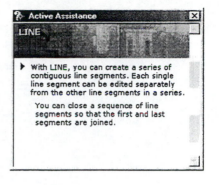

You may "close" or "open" Active Assistance.
Temporarily close: select the Close button (X).

Turn Off: See "On Demand" below.

Open it: select the Active Assistance **icon** 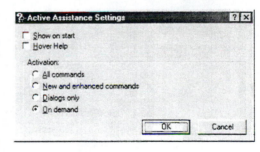 on the Standard toolbar or type **ASSIST** at the Command Line.

You may select "when" and "how" the Active Assistant displays.
How and when Active Assistance is displayed is a personal preference. When you are first learning AutoCAD you may want it to display often. After you are more experience, you may want it displayed less frequently.   The settings below allow you to select your preference.

Place the cursor on the Active Assistance and press the right mouse button then select "Settings".

Show on start: Starts Active Assistance when AutoCAD starts. If this is off, you must open Active Assistance when you need it. See "Open it" above.

Hover Help: If you select the Hover Help option, the Active Assistance will display information about a specific option in any dialog box when you pass the cursor over that option.

All Commands: Automatically opens the Active Assistance window when any command is activated

New and enhanced commands: Automatically opens the Active Assistance window when any new or enhanced commands are activated.

Dialogs only: Automatically opens the Active Assistance window when a dialog box is displayed. You cannot close the Active Assistance window while a dialog box is displayed.

On Demand: Turns Active Assistance OFF. You must open the Active Assistance when you need it. See "Open it" above.

APPENDIX D
Dimension Style Definitions

When you select **Dimension / Style / Modify** the following dialog box will appear.

The following are descriptions for each setting within each section tab.

Lines and Arrows tab

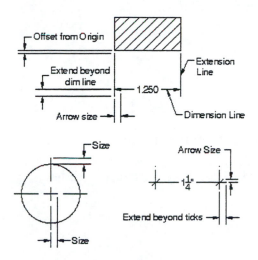

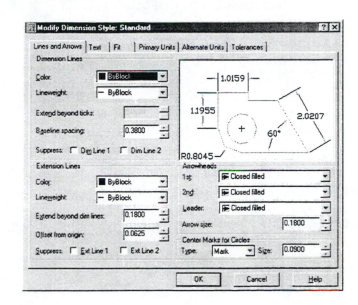

Dimension Lines
Color: Color of the dimension line.
Lineweight: Sets the width of the dimension lines.
Extend beyond ticks: Distance to extend <u>dimension</u> line beyond the <u>extension</u> line. Example above.
Baseline spacing: Spacing between baseline dimensions.
Suppress: Suppress means disappear. You may suppress individually or both.

Extension Lines
Color: Color of the extension lines
Lineweight: Sets the width of the extension lines.
Extend beyond dim. line: Distance to extend <u>extension</u> line beyond the <u>dimension</u> line. Example above.
Offset from origin: The distance between the object and the extension line. Example above.
Supress: You may suppress individually or both.

Arrowheads
1st : Sets the style for the symbol inserted for the first extension point
2nd: Sets the style for the symbol inserted for the second extension point and for <u>Diameter</u> and <u>Radius</u>.
Leader: Sets the style for the symbol inserted for Leaders.
Arrow Size: Sets the Size of Arrowheads. Example above.

Center Marks for Circles
Type: Select None, Mark or Line   **Size:** Specify Size. Example above.

TEXT tab

Text Appearance

Text Style: Select which text style to use for the dimension text. To create or change a style, select the [...] button.

Text Color: Sets the color of the dimension text.

Text height: Sets the height.

Fraction Height Scale: Sets the size of fractions relative to the dimension text height. This is a factor not and actual height. Example: A setting of .50 would be half of the dimension text height.

Draw Frame Around Text: If this box is checked, a box will be drawn around the text.

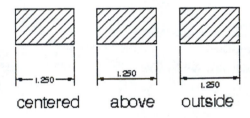

Text Placement

Vertical

Centered: Centers dimension text between extension lines.
Above: Places dimension text above the dimension line.
Outside: Places dimension text on the side of the dimension line farthest away from the object.

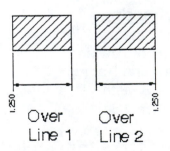

Horizontal

At Ext Line 1: Moves text near first extension line.

At Ext Line 2: Moves text near second extension line.

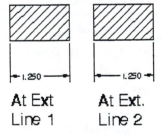

Over Ext Line 1: Places text over first extension line.

Over Ext Line 2: Places text over second extension Line

Offset from Dim Line: Sets the gap between the dimension text and the dimension line.

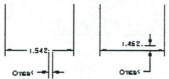

Text Alignment

Horzontal: Places dimension text horizontal.

Aligned: Aligns dimension text with the dimension line.

ISO Standard: Aligns text with the dimension line when text is inside the extension lines, but aligns it horizontally when text is outside extension lines.

FIT tab

Fit Options: Controls the placement of text and arrowheads based on the space available between the extension lines. If there is not enough room to place both text and arrows inside extension lines, you must choose what to move outside the extension lines.

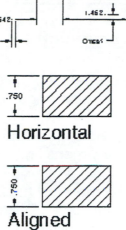

Text Placement: When dimension text is moved from its dim. style location, this setting controls the placement.

Scale for Dimension Features:

Use overall scale of: Set the factor for all dimension settings. Example: if this is set to 10 and the dimension text height is set to 1/8, the dimension text height would appear 1-1/4" ht. (10 x 1/8") The value does not change. *Note: this feature is left over from previous AutoCAD releases. It is not necessary now because of "Trans-spatial" dimensioning.*

Scale dimensions to layout (paper space): Calculates a scale factor based on the scaling of model space vs. paper space. *Note: this feature is left over from previous AutoCAD release. It is not necessary now because of "Trans-spatial" dimensioning.*

Fine Tuning

Place text manually when dimensioning: You control the placement of the text if this feature is ON. It is not automatic.

Always draw dim Line between Ext Lines: Draws the dimension line inside the extension lines even if the arrows are on the outside.

PRIMARY UNITS tab

Linear Dimensions

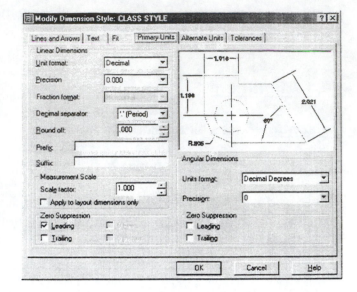

Unit Format: Sets the units format for all dimensions except Angular.

Precision: Sets the number of decimal places in the dimension.

Fraction Format: Set the format for fraction to Horizontal, Diagonal or not stacked. Only available if Unit Format (above) is set to "Fractional".

Decimal Separator: Sets the style for the decimal separator to period, comma or space. Not available if Unit Format is set to Fractional.

Round Off: Sets rounding limits for dimensioning, such as .000 or 1/8. Rounds **up** to the nearest 3 place decimal or nearest 1/8".

Prefix: Add text in front of the dimension text. (**Flat for** 2.00)

Suffix: Add text after the dimension text. (1'-0" **Max**)

Measurement scale:
Scale Factor: AutoCAD multiples the dimension measurement by the value entered here. Example: If you draw a 1/2 inch line. Set this feature to 2. When you dimension the line, the dimension text will display 1. (2 X 1/2) If you set this feature to .50, when you dimension the line, the dimension text will display 1/4. (.50 X 1/2)
Apply to Layout Dimensions Only: Unnecessary now that we have Trans-spatial dimensioning.

Zero Suppression

The following two only work with decimals:
Leading: Controls the display of zeros before the decimal point. 0.50 = Off   .50 = ON
Trailing: Controls the display of zeros at the end of the dimension. .500 = Off .5 = ON

The following tow only work with architectural:
Feet: Controls the display of zeros for feet. 0'-6" = OFF   6" = ON
Inches: Controls the display of zeros for inches. 6'-0" = OFF   6" = ON

Angular Dimensions
Units Format: Sets the units format for Angular. Does not affect Linear.
Precision: Sets the number of decimal places past the whole degree.
Zero suppression: Same as Linear.

Note: Alternate Units and Tolerance tabs are discussed in the "Advanced" workbook.

Appendix-D4

INDEX

NOTES: